THE DEFINITION OF PROGRAMMING LANGUAGES

Cambridge Computer Science Texts · 11

The Definition of Programming Languages

ANDREW D. McGETTRICK

Lecturer in Computer Science
University of Strathclyde
Glasgow, Scotland

CAMBRIDGE UNIVERSITY PRESS
CAMBRIDGE
LONDON   NEW YORK   NEW ROCHELLE
MELBOURNE   SYDNEY

Published by the Press Syndicate of the University of Cambridge
The Pitt Building, Trumpington Street, Cambridge CB2 1RP
32 East 57th Street, New York, NY 10022, USA
296 Beaconsfield Parade, Middle Park, Melbourne 3206, Australia

First published 1980

Printed in the United States of America
by Publishers Production, Inc., Bronx, New York
Bound by Arnold's Book Bindery, Reading, Pennsylvania

Library of Congress cataloguing in publication data

McGettrick, Andrew D. 1944-

The definition of programming languages

(Cambridge computer science texts)
Bibliography: p.
Includes index.
1. Programming languages (Electronic computers) I. Title.
QA76.7.M28   001.6'42   79-21635

ISBN 0 521 22631 7 hard covers
ISBN 0 521 29585 8 paperback

To my mother and father

CONTENTS

The subject matter of this book evolved from a desire which I had to learn and understand two of the relatively recent developments in computer science and what motivated them. The first relates to the definition of the programming language ALGOL 68, the second to the work of Dana Scott and the late Christopher Strachey in Oxford and their development of mathematical or denotational semantics. The common theme is, of course, the definition of programming languages.

The first programming language I learned was ALGOL 60. The Revised ALGOL 60 Report was attractive and relatively easy to read and to understand. With the more recent development of ALGOL 68 it seemed natural to look closely at this newer language. Initially, and for several months thereafter, I found the ALGOL 68 Report bordering on the incomprehensible. But what was more disturbing and more important to me was the fact that I could not begin to understand the reasons for the gulf which existed between those two documents.

Again my initial reaction to the topic of mathematical semantics was that it was extremely difficult to understand. It was not clear why such an approach was necessary or even desirable and it seemed a curious way of tackling the problem of describing the semantics of a programming language. The underlying mathematical theory was rather deep and the benefits were not obvious.

Given these interests and the difficulty I had in putting everything in perspective it seemed natural to write a book on the definition of programming languages. The topic has received very little serious attention in textbooks and it seemed to me that a text such as this might fill a gaping hole in the literature. It is curious that such an important topic as language definition has received so little attention. Programming languages themselves are, of course, extremely important. They are central to the whole topic of Computer Science. It is essential for all concerned with computing that every aspect of a language should be defined properly – clearly, accurately and unambiguously.

In the course of writing the book I was struck by the subtle inter-relationship between language definition and language design and implementation. I had not previously realised the extent to which these topics were connected. In the text I have tried to stress this.

This text is not intended for novice Computer Scientists. It is assumed that the reader has a basic grounding in Computer Science. It would be suitable for advanced undergraduate classes or early post-graduate classes in language definition or language design.

The original proposal for this book bore little resemblance to the final version. Dr Charles Lang, then of Cambridge University Press, solicited many invaluable views and criticism from anonymous referees. These resulted in alterations for the better and for them I am most grateful. Professor Colin Reeves, of Keele University, deserves special mention for his efforts as editor. Apart from his most useful criticisms he provided constant encouragement throughout the later stages of the writing. The latter I found to be most important; it was always appreciated and always effective in forcing me to greater efforts. Finally let me thank Dr Keith Burnett also of Keele University for his valuable comments on an earlier draft of the book. For providing typing and other forms of secretarial assistance, I wish to thank my mother Mrs Marion McGettrick, my sister-in-law Miss Patricia Girot, Mrs Margaret McDougall and Miss Agnes Wisley from the Computer Science Department, and Miss Morag Barron from the Computer Centre at Strathclyde University.

On a personal note I cannot end without recording my special thanks to my wife Sheila for her constant support, encouragement, help and understanding during the writing of this book.

I am greatly indebted to the Press Syndicate of the University of Cambridge for publishing this book.

June 1979   A. D. McGettrick

1

INTRODUCTION

Computer scientists of different persuasions might put forward different arguments in favour of having a precise and accurate definition of a given programming language. Their differing backgrounds, attitudes and needs will lead to differing sets of requirements and demands. But they will all be united in the view that a precise and accurate definition is desirable, even essential.

In any examination of the definition of programming languages it is important to distinguish between a language and its method of definition. Historically the two have been confused since new languages have often gone hand-in-hand with new methods of definition. It is also important to decide just what constitutes a method of definition. Given one method of definition it may be possible to apply it in different ways and thereby produce different results; one particular method of definition may be applied with differing amounts of rigour and differing levels of detail.

1.1 Reasons for having a definition

The language designer should seek to define his language in a clear and precise fashion. The various terms and concepts must all be clearly described and their meaning noted. All the details must be explained in one document which then acts as a kind of reference or standard for the language. Accuracy, precision and formality are all desirable; informal documents on programming languages tend to be notoriously bad at including fine detail. The basic problem is that programming languages (especially languages such as PL/I) are very complex objects and there are usually various interrelated and interlocking concepts. It is therefore no easy task to describe the meaning of any one of these or any aspect of the programming language in isolation.

A good language definition can also serve the needs of a sophisticated user. In that definition he should be able to find, with relative ease, answers to all his detailed questions about the language. Textbooks on programming languages and programming manuals are not normally written for sophisticated audiences who look for fine detail.

Such texts are usually written for novice programmers and typically discuss both programming and the programming language. The nature of their audience, marketing considerations, etc. tend to dictate against rigour and precision. A sophisticated user may also look to the language definition for guidance on matters of standardisation and of portability, i.e. program interchangeability – what characters should be used in his programs, what is the range and precision of numbers, and, in general, what aspects of the language are implementation-dependent?

For a manufacturer, or someone who commissions the writing of a compiler, a language definition can be used as part of the contract to provide answers to questions about the proper implementation of features of the language.

The compiler writer requires a document to act as his authority or reference. Given a particular program, different implementations should cause the equivalent object programs to produce identical results. For this to be likely, the compiler writer must be told in a clear and unambiguous manner the intended meaning of each particular construct so that he can produce code which will accurately reflect the intention of the high-level programmer. The compiler writer may also want to know the area of applicability of the language definition. Does he, the compiler writer, have a choice in deciding the acceptable range of integers, the range and precision of reals, the character set, the means of representing reserved words, and so on? The definition might also attempt to help the compiler writer by providing hints on how to implement. Yet he should be allowed the freedom to invent and to apply his skills.

The language theorist may seek to use a language definition in various ways. He may wish to use it to prove properties of programs, e.g. proofs of correctness, proofs that certain optimisations are permissible, proofs that certain program transformations such as replacing recursion by iteration are permissible, proofs about efficiency of programs. Proofs of correctness, for example, can only be given if the meaning of every aspect of the language is clearly understood.

Incidentally, almost, a language definition will usually provide a notation and vocabulary of terms for the various constructs and aspects of the programming language. Various sets of people may seek to use such a vocabulary and the definition to talk about the language and to argue about how its constructs encourage good programming and reliable programming, how they ease the tasks of programming or proving correctness, and so on.

Now it may not be possible to meet all these different requirements within the one formal definition. This has led to the remark that in defining a programming language there should perhaps be more than one definition of the language. In this way all the interested parties could be satisfied. On the other hand, of course, it raises the awkward question: do different definitions define the same language? This in turn leads to problems about proving such matters; two equivalent definitions are said to be *complementary*. We shall not pursue this matter any further here but we merely note the possibility.

1.2 Desirable qualities

The various users of a language definition will all look for certain basic qualities which include clarity, completeness and accuracy. All aspects of the definition should possess them in abundance.

A definition must be complete in the sense that all the fundamental aspects of the language are defined. It should be clear in the sense that answers to questions can be found with relative ease; in stating this it should be assumed that the person using the document is familiar with the method of definition (not necessarily the definition itself). One implication of this remark is that a language definition need not be used to provide an uneducated reader with a means of learning the programming language.

The method of definition should employ a natural and understandable notation and should preferably be concise. Of course, understandability and conciseness are interrelated but the former should not be sacrificed in favour of the latter. The method of definition should tend to encourage accuracy and precision, the discovery of unnecessary restrictions in the programming language, missing facilities, undesirable interrelationships between different constructions, and, in general, irregularities and complications of any kind. If a method of definition is itself unsuitable or awkward then any definition based on this method cannot realistically hope to succeed without the expenditure of enormous effort.

The definition itself should be natural and easy to read. Opaque and contorted descriptions (or indeed methods of description) lead to confusion and bewilderment on behalf of the reader. The application of the method of definition should make the programming language itself seem natural. There should be no lists of peculiar restrictions or exceptional cases for which there is no apparent explanation. Considerations of this nature tend to ensure that the language is consistent and understandable, they tend to ease the task of learning and remembering the language and they simplify the tasks of proving properties about programs expressed in that language, about compilers for the language, and so on.

Having stated that there are certain desirable features of a language definition it is worth noting that there are various grey areas. Should a language definition include such details as the range and precision of numbers, the method of rounding numbers, the maximum size and complexity of acceptable programs, hardware representation or character codes, the effects of errors? Should the language definition be oriented towards the language designer, the user, the implementor or the theorist? If so, to what extent? Compiler writers, for example, prefer to have a certain amount of freedom in deciding how best to implement, optimise and so on. Yet they like to be given some assistance. On the other hand, implementation details tend to be largely unnecessary from the point of view of a user who merely wishes to determine meaning, or from the point of view of a theorist who wishes to devise proofs.

A language definition should have an applicability or scope section stating clearly which aspects of the language are dealt with by the defining document. There should also be statements of the aim of the document. It should then be clear where, for example, the province of the language designer ends and the province of the compiler writer begins.

1.3 The scope of this book

In this book we look at the major developments in language definition over the years. The book is not primarily a book on programming languages, or even on programming language design, but it is intended as a text on language definition. As a result it is not intended primarily for novice computing scientists. It is assumed that the reader has attended a basic course on computing science and is aware of such matters as the existence and function of interpreters and compilers and the differences between these, and knows in a very general way their basic structure. It is also assumed that the reader knows FORTRAN and ALGOL 60 and has a nodding acquaintance with ALGOL-like programming languages.

It was earlier mentioned that it is important to distinguish between a language and its method of definition. Yet new programming languages and new methods of definition have historically gone hand-in-hand, at least to some extent. The method of definition has often had some influence on the language itself and this aspect of language design will be of some interest to us.

We shall look initially at the definitions of FORTRAN, ALGOL 60 and LISP. We shall criticise these, especially the FORTRAN and ALGOL 60 definitions, rather severely. In fact our criticisms could almost be described as savage or unfair but we justify them on the grounds that it was precisely such criticism that led to the later developments in programming language definition.

We then follow through the development in the methods of definition by looking at methods used in defining ALGOL W, COBOL, BASIC, PASCAL and later Revised ALGOL 68 and PL/I (the PL/I Standard and the Vienna Definition Language). In the penultimate chapter we look at the work of Scott and Strachey on mathematical semantics. A final chapter draws some conclusions and comparisons and indicates other areas of work. At each stage, we shall attempt to describe the reasons and motivations for the various developments, their inadequacies and their merits. But we begin with a brief introduction to the theory of grammars to provide some necessary background.

2

THEORETICAL FOUNDATIONS

In this chapter the theory of grammars is introduced, for grammars play a very central and fundamental role in certain language definitions. Grammar theory itself is a highly mathematical topic but we shall not stress this aspect of the subject since it is not the main concern of this book. Instead we shall be interested in the relationship of grammar theory to programming languages, especially their definition. We therefore include only those aspects of grammars which are important from this point of view, and state without proof any important theoretical results. Any reader interested in delving deeper into the subject should use the relevant references at the end of the book as initial sources for further reading.

To motivate the work in this chapter we shall be interested in discovering why certain kinds of grammars are used in language definition and why other kinds are not. We would also like to know what properties a grammar (used in defining a programming language) might be expected to possess, what properties are desirable, what properties are undesirable, and to what extent these properties can be checked automatically by a suitable program.

2.1 Introduction to grammar theory

2.1.1 Background
The motivation for the work on grammars has its origins in the linguistic study of natural languages such as English. It is common practice in studying English grammar to take a sentence such as

> The boy kicked the blue ball.

and parse it, thereby producing a subject phrase, verb and object phrase. Further decomposition of the subject phrase and object phrase can also take place. The result can be represented diagrammatically – see figure 2.1.

In what follows a clear distinction must be made between the words used in the sentence, 'the', 'ball', 'kicked', etc. and the terms used in the parsing process, 'subject phrase', 'verb', etc. The former we refer to as terminals, the latter as non-terminals.

The tree structure of figure 2.1, the *syntax* of the sentence, can be represented in a linear notation of the form

$$<\text{sentence}> \rightarrow <\text{subject phrase}><\text{verb}><\text{object phrase}>$$
$$<\text{subject phrase}> \rightarrow <\text{definite article}><\text{noun}>$$
$$<\text{object phrase}> \rightarrow <\text{definite article}><\text{adjective}><\text{noun}>$$
$$<\text{definite article}> \rightarrow \text{the}$$
$$<\text{noun}> \rightarrow \text{boy}$$
$$<\text{noun}> \rightarrow \text{ball}$$
$$<\text{adjective}> \rightarrow \text{blue}$$
$$<\text{verb}> \rightarrow \text{kicked}$$

The non-terminals are enclosed in angle brackets to distinguish them from the terminals. One of them, of course, is rather special, i.e. <sentence>. Each of the rules such as

$$<\text{sentence}> \rightarrow <\text{subject phrase}><\text{verb}><\text{object phrase}>$$

is called a production and it describes in some sense the composition (or decomposition) of the non-terminal <sentence>. It says that a sentence is composed of a <subject phrase> followed by a <verb> and then an <object phrase>.

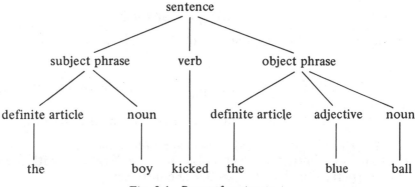

Fig. 2.1. Parse of sentence.

Let us now look at this set of productions from another point of view. They can be used to generate sentences of the English language. Starting from the rule for <sentence> apply the production beginning <sentence> and replace <sentence> by <subject phrase><verb> <object phrase>. By using the productions defining <subject phrase>, <verb> and <object phrase> each of these non-terminals can be replaced. Continuing in this way, sentences of the English language will eventually be produced. So these rules can serve a dual purpose: they

7

can act as a means of generating sentences and they also serve as the rules for parsing a sentence.

Unfortunately some of the sentences generated from the productions are not sensible, e.g.

The ball kicked the blue ball.

This sentence though grammatically correct must be dismissed on the grounds that it is not meaningful.

With these introductory remarks we now try to formalise the idea of a grammar with the intention of using it for describing programming languages.

2.1.2 The definition of a grammar

A grammar is a means of describing in a finite way a potentially infinite set of sequences of characters. These sequences of characters will have a certain (grammatical) structure and the reader should think of these as the set of legal programs that can be expressed in some programming language.

Before giving the formal definition of a grammar we introduce some notation. A set A of characters – sometimes also called symbols – will be termed a *vocabulary* or *alphabet*. A^+ denotes the set of non-empty words or strings formed from the items of A. Thus

$$A^+ = \{ a_1 a_2 ... a_n : \text{each } a_i \in A \text{ and } n \geq 1 \}$$

If the empty string ϵ is added to A^+ the set A^* results, thus

$$A^* = A^+ \cup \{\epsilon\}$$

If $\alpha \epsilon A^*$ the notation $|\alpha|$ is used to denote the length of α, the number of characters in α.

Formally a grammar is a quadruple (V_T, V_N, S, P) consisting of

(a) V_T, a finite set of symbols called *terminals*;

(b) V_N, a finite set of symbols called *non-terminals* with the property that $V_T \cap V_N = \emptyset$, the empty set;

(c) S, a special non-terminal called the *sentence* or *start* symbol;

(d) a finite set P of pairs (α, β) called *productions* or *rewriting rules*: each rule is written in the form

$$\alpha \to \beta$$

where, if $V = V_T \cup V_N$, $\alpha \in V^+$ and $\beta \in V^*$. With these conventions α is then the *left part* and β the *right part* of the production $\alpha \to \beta$.

To save having to repeatedly specify the precise nature of V_N, V_T and therefore V, we adopt the conventions that unless there is a remark to the contrary

- small letters denote terminals and capital letters denote non-terminals
- the symbol S will traditionally represent the sentence symbol
- the lower-case Greek letters $\alpha, \beta, \ldots$ denote elements of V^*, i.e. strings of terminals and/or non-terminals.

In using grammars to describe programming languages these simple conventions will become totally inadequate and more sophisticated schemes will have to be employed. For the moment however this simplicity is convenient.

To relate a grammar to the language it defines, we introduce the concept of a *derivation*.

Definition of immediate derivation
If $\alpha \rightarrow \beta$ is a production and $\gamma \alpha \rho$ is a string then

$$\gamma \alpha \rho \rightarrow \gamma \beta \rho$$

is an *immediate derivation*. The string $\gamma \beta \rho$ is obtained from $\gamma \alpha \rho$ by replacing α by β.

Definition of derivation
A *derivation* is a sequence $\alpha_0, \alpha_1, \ldots, \alpha_n$ with the property that each $\alpha_i \rightarrow \alpha_{i+1}$ ($i = 0, 1, \ldots, n-1$) is an immediate derivation. If $n \geq 0$ we write

$$\alpha_0 \rightarrow^* \alpha_n$$

and if $n \geq 1$ then

$$\alpha_0 \rightarrow^+ \alpha_n$$

Thus derivations result from repeated processes of rewriting using productions of the grammar.

We shall be especially interested in those strings which are derivable from the sentence symbol S. In particular, the set of such strings which contain only terminals will include, when we start looking at programming languages, the set of legal programs expressible in a particular language. With this in mind it is convenient to introduce more notation.

Definition of sentential form
If $\eta \in V^*$ has the property that

$$S \rightarrow^* \eta$$

where S is the sentence symbol then η is called a *sentential form*.

Definition of language
In the special case where η is a sentential form and $\eta \in V_T^*$, η is called

9

a *string* of the language. The set of such strings then constitute the *language, L(G)*, which the grammar *G* describes.

Example 2.1 Grammars

(i)   Let $V_N = \{E,T\}$, $V_T = \{(,),i,j,+,\times\}$, let E be the sentence symbol and let the set of productions be

$$E \to E+T$$
$$E \to E \times T$$
$$E \to T$$
$$T \to (E)$$
$$T \to i$$
$$T \to j$$

Then the set of sentences of the language defined by this grammar are just simplified arithmetic expressions involving only two operators + and × and two variables *i* and *j*.

(ii)   Let $V_N = \{S,B,C\}$, $V_T = \{a,b,c\}$ and let S be the sentence symbol.

Then if the set of productions are

$$S \to aSBC$$
$$S \to aBC$$
$$CB \to BC$$
$$aB \to ab$$
$$bB \to bb$$
$$bC \to bc$$
$$cC \to cc$$

the language so defined consists of strings of the form $a^n b^n c^n$, i.e. a number of *a*s followed by the same number of *b*s and then the same number of *c*s.

To overcome the problem of stating several productions with the same left part it is often convenient to use the abbreviation

$$\alpha \to \beta_1 |\beta_2| \dots |\beta_n$$

for the set of productions

$$\alpha \to \beta_1 ; \alpha \to \beta_2 ; \dots \alpha \to \beta_n$$

The stick, |, can be read as 'or'.

The rule that results from this extension we refer to as a *syntax rule* or a *production rule*; it is not a production unless there is only a single right part.

Example 2.2   Production rules
The productions of example 2.1(i) can be written in the form

$$E \rightarrow E+T|E \times T|T$$
$$T \rightarrow i|j|(E)$$

Note that within a right part the various terminals and non-terminals are concatenated. Using this new notation the various right parts are themselves separated by the stick. Thus one could now imagine that there are two operators on the right-hand side of one of these more general productions: there is 'concatenation' (implicit) and 'or' (explicit). The mathematical properties of these operators can then be investigated and a kind of algebra results.

Traditionally grammars have been used in connection with the syntax of programming languages and indeed this is their main area of application. But their use is not restricted to this application. They can be used in any area where structure is involved and has to be formalised. Thus there are uses in artificial intelligence and in computer graphics to describe objects of the real world, they can be used to describe the commands of an operating system or editor, etc. One particular application relates to the form of a grammar itself. A grammar can be described by a set of productions or production rules all of which have a particular structure. Therefore the method of writing a grammar can be described by a kind of higher-level grammar.

2.1.3   The Chomsky hierarchy
For most purposes the above idea of a grammar is too general. It is convenient to add successively stronger restrictions – which have a theoretical basis – to the nature of the productions that can occur in a grammar, and thereby obtain correspondingly simpler grammars. The classification was originally given by Chomsky, hence the name.

type 0:   a grammar of the form already described is a type 0 grammar

type 1:   a grammar all of whose productions are of the form $\alpha \rightarrow \beta$ where $|\alpha| \leq |\beta|$ is said to be of type 1 or *context-sensitive*

type 2:   a grammar all of whose productions are of the form $\alpha \rightarrow \beta$ where $\alpha \epsilon V_N$ is said to be of type 2 or *context-free*

type 3:   (*a*)   if all the productions of a grammar are of the form

$$A \rightarrow a \quad \text{or} \quad A \rightarrow aB$$

where $A,B \epsilon V_N$ and $a \epsilon V_T$ the grammar is said to be of type 3 (or *regular*) and *right-linear*
(*b*)   if the productions are all of the form

$$A \rightarrow a \quad \text{or} \quad A \rightarrow Ba$$

where the notation is as above the grammar is again of type 3 or *regular* but now *left-linear*.

The adjectives used in describing these grammars can also be used in describing the language generated by the grammars. Thus there are type 0 languages, context-free languages, etc.

Another formulation of the definition of context-sensitive grammars states that all productions of the grammar must be of the form

$$\alpha A \beta \rightarrow \alpha \gamma \beta$$

where $\alpha, \beta, \gamma \epsilon V^*$, $\gamma \neq \epsilon$ and $A \epsilon V_N$. The set of languages so defined is the same in both formulations. The latter however explains the phrase 'context-sensitive'. For A can be replaced by γ only if it has the correct context, i.e. α on its left and β on its right. In context-free grammars no such context is required and A can be replaced by its right part regardless of the context in which it occurs.

If G_1 and G_2 are two different grammars it may well happen that they describe the same language, i.e. $L(G_1) = L(G_2)$. Under these conditions G_1 and G_2 are said to be *equivalent* grammars. Though G_1 and G_2 may be of different types it will usually be advisable to describe a language in terms of the simplest possible grammar and thus refer to it as a type-2 language rather than a type-1 language, for example.

The Chomsky hierarchy does not give a special classification to a very simple type of grammar. A grammar, all of whose productions are of the form

$$A \rightarrow a$$

where $A \epsilon V_N$ and $a \epsilon V_T$, is called a *finite-choice grammar*.

2.2 Parsing

2.2.1 The parsing problem

Given a sequence of symbols, supposedly a sentence of a language, the task of a syntax analyser or recogniser is to determine whether or not this is a sentence and, if so, how it was derived. In so doing, the basic structure of the sentence as described by the underlying grammar will be found. Essentially then a recogniser must reconstruct in some way a sequence of immediate derivations that produced the given sentence. Now the same sentence can usually be derived in various different ways, but these differences are usually irrelevant since the derivations impose the same basic structure. For context-free languages this structure can be represented in a convenient way by a *derivation tree* or *parse tree*.

To illustrate take the grammar

12

$$S \rightarrow AaS|A$$
$$A \rightarrow b|c$$

and consider the sentence

$$bacab$$

This can be parsed as shown in figure 2.2 and this represents derivations

$$S \Rightarrow AaS \Rightarrow baS \Rightarrow baAaS \Rightarrow baAaA \Rightarrow bacaA \Rightarrow bacab$$

or

$$S \Rightarrow AaS \Rightarrow AaAaS \Rightarrow AaAaA \Rightarrow baAaA \Rightarrow baAab \Rightarrow bacab$$

etc.

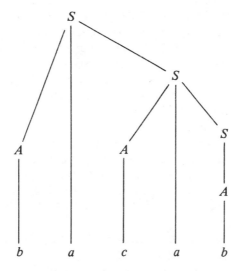

Fig. 2.2. Parse tree for *bacab*.

Note that

· the root of the tree is the sentence symbol S
· if $X_1, X_2, ..., X_n$ are the labels of descendant subtrees of a node labelled R then

$$R \rightarrow X_1 X_2 \ldots X_n$$

is a production of the language (note that each X_i may denote either a terminal or non-terminal).

These properties then typify the derivation tree or parse tree. Consequently it illustrates the structure of the sentence without reference to the alternative ways in which it might be derived.

13

Having said this, there are two particular derivations and parses that merit special mention. In a right derivation the rightmost non-terminal of each sentential form is replaced to form the next sentential form. The right derivation of the sentence *bacab* with respect to the grammar given above is

$$S \Rightarrow AaS \Rightarrow AaAaS \Rightarrow AaAaA \Rightarrow AaAab \Rightarrow Aacab \Rightarrow bacab$$

More formally a right derivation $\alpha_0, \alpha_1, \dots$ is such that

$$\alpha_{i-1} = \gamma A \rho \rightarrow \gamma \omega \rho = \alpha_i$$

where $\rho \epsilon V_T$, γ and $\omega \epsilon V^*$ and $A \epsilon V_N$. A right parse is the reverse of the sequence of productions which constitute a right derivation.

Similar definitions result in left derivations and the reverse of this sequence is a left parse. In left derivations the leftmost non-terminal of each sentential form is replaced on each occasion.

The parsing problem for these languages should be likened to the parsing problem for natural languages such as English. In natural languages the non-terminals correspond to subjects, objects, verbs and so on.

So far we have said nothing about how the parse tree might be formed automatically. We have merely described the parsing problem as the task of determining such a parse tree. This topic of designing parsers or recognisers we leave until the next section.

We conclude this section by noting that part of the task of a compiler is to perform precisely this recognition or parsing of text, supposedly legal programs, to be compiled. Compilers are usually divided into several phases. There are three main phases which are common to most compilers.

The lexical phase or the lexical analyser typically reads the source program and groups together sequences of characters which naturally go together, it removes irrelevant spaces and ideally commentary, it produces listings, etc. Thus the characters which form an identifier are grouped together, and in a similar way numerals, reserved words and multi-character symbols such as :=, .LE., are all isolated. To carry the analogy to natural languages, the task of the lexical phase is basically to separate the words of a sentence. The output from the lexical phase is typically a sequence of tokens all of the same size, one token for each identifier, reserved word, number, etc.

The syntax analysis phase takes as its input the sequence of tokens from the lexical phase. It then attempts to perform the recognition or parsing of the input; it thus attempts to determine the basic structure of the given program.

The parse tree, or something similar to it, is then used by the third phase, the code generator, to produce the machine code to be executed eventually on some computer.

The above is a grossly oversimplified view of compiler design. Often there are other phases: compilers must be prepared to recover from errors; often the compiler does not produce machine code but perhaps assembly code or some other code; etc. Moreover the concept of a phase has not been precisely described. However, for the purposes of this book the above explanation will suffice.

2.2.2 Recursive descent

In this section we introduce a simple technique for producing an analyser or recogniser for a language, given a suitable grammar for that language. The method is called *recursive descent.* In its simplest form, recursive descent is applicable only to grammars of a rather limited kind but further considerations will allow us to extend the class of grammars that may be employed.

Recursive descent involves associating with each non-terminal in the grammar a procedure for recognising strings belonging to the set represented by that non-terminal. Moreover, the syntax rule for a non-terminal N is used in a direct way to describe how the procedure corresponding to N should be written.

To elucidate consider the following simple grammar whose sentence symbol is A:

$$A \to aB|bc$$
$$B \to bAA$$

Assume we have to write procedures to recognise strings in this language. Then we will make use of a character variable ch whose successive values will be the various characters appearing in the input stream.

The procedures for A and B – we denote these by A and B themselves – are written as follows in an ALGOL 68 notation:

```
proc A = void:
if ch = "a"
    then read(ch); B
    elif ch = "b"
    then read(ch);
        if ch = "c"
            then read (ch)
            else print ("error")
        fi
    else print ("error")
fi,
```

```
proc B = void:
if ch = "b"
        then read(ch); A ; A
        else print ("error")
fi
```

These declarations can then form part of a program to recognise strings of the language:

```
begin char ch;
        proc A = void: ...,
        proc B = void: ...;
        read(ch); A
end
```

Take the sentence *abbcbc* of the above grammar. The program given will correctly interpret this as a legal sentence. But what kind of parse is produced? Because of the initial *a* in *abbcbc* the recursive descent process and, in particular, the procedure *A* will assume that $A \Rightarrow aB$ has occurred. The next input symbol is *b* and procedure *B* will assume $aB \Rightarrow abAA$. The next input symbol is *b* and procedure *A* assumes that the production $A \rightarrow bc$ is applicable.

From the nature of this process it should be apparent that at all times the leftmost non-terminal is replaced. A left parse is thus obtained.

In the example given above all the procedures associated with the non-terminals are of mode **proc void**. But there are other variations. One alternative is to have procedures of mode **proc bool**. These deliver **true** if a string in the set represented by that non-terminal has been recognised, otherwise they deliver **false** (thus **true** represents success and **false** failure). Another variation is to have each procedure delivering a structure which becomes part of an internal representation such as a tree of the object being recognised.

In writing the above procedures a mechanical translation from the syntax rules of the grammar was performed. In scanning a syntax rule from left to right either terminals, non-terminals or vertical bars will be encountered:

- non-terminals are replaced by a call of the corresponding procedure
- vertical bars are replaced by **elif**
- terminals are replaced by a test to check that the correct terminal is indeed present in *ch*; if it is, then the next character is read; if not an error message is printed.

Since this translation process is so mechanical it should be apparent that it is possible to perform the same translation by program. We therefore have the possibility of a program which accepts as input a grammar and outputs a program to recognise strings of the language defined by the grammar.

From what has been said it should be noted that the technique in its present form is applicable only to a limited set of grammars. To be precise, the grammars must be context-free and each production for a given non-terminal must start with a different (non-empty) terminal. Such grammars are sometimes referred to as s-grammars.

The recognisers produced by the technique of recursive descent are fairly efficient. However, it may be possible to increase their efficiency by imposing a careful ordering on the various tests that must be performed. Thus

$$A \rightarrow aB|bc$$

implies that $ch = $ "a" is tested before $ch = $ "b". On the other hand

$$A \rightarrow bc|aB$$

implies the converse. The choice that is made can affect the efficiency of the resulting recogniser. If the recogniser is to be produced automatically care should be exercised in deciding on the best way to present syntax rules. From an implementation point of view the vertical bar is not commutative! Further evidence of this will appear later.

The approach outlined here is so attractive that it is enticing to consider the possibility of examining ways of extending the ideas involved and the range of grammars to which it can be applied. We shall do this assuming at each stage that we require an automatic method of producing analysers/recognisers.

One immediate extension to the idea of an s-grammar would allow the inclusion of productions which have the empty string as their right part. But it is necessary to impose the restriction that it should still be possible to make a decision on which alternative production to follow on the basis of the then current character. From an implementation point of view the basic idea is that if the right parts of all other productions are unsuitable then ϵ must have been present and this can be implemented as the **else** part of a conditional.

Example 2.3 Recursive descent
The grammar represented by

$$S \rightarrow \epsilon \mid cA$$
$$A \rightarrow bSc|d$$

could not be recognised by a program built using the techniques described. In the string $cbc...$ the recogniser would not know on encountering the second c whether this started an S or followed an S (in the latter case ϵ would have been present).

So this new extension can be used but it leads to certain problems. From an implementation point of view two consequences arise: the previous methods must be extended to cope with ϵ; it would be convenient to have an algorithm to decide automatically whether ϵ would lead to trouble of the kind described in the above example. Indeed it is possible to derive an algorithm of the required kind.

The idea behind looking at the simple notion of recursive descent is to show that parsers or recognisers can be, and usually are, built in such a way that their structure reflects the structure of the underlying grammar. As such they are then said to be syntax-directed.

The basic idea behind recursive descent can be extended to deal with a much wider class of grammars. In these cases the programmer is able to write pieces of program of the form

> **if** a particular construction now appears
> **then** attempt to recognise the corresponding right part
> **elif** the construction ... appears
> **then** ...
> **fi**

In the process of performing the recognition the programmer might build a parse tree, generate code, interpret the various commands, and so on. Some of these extensions will be examined later in section 2.3.

2.2.3 Ambiguity in grammars

In what follows we restrict our attention to the set of context-free grammars since these are most commonly used for describing programming languages and this is our particular area of interest.

Given a grammar there are normally certain properties which that grammar would be expected to possess. Included in these properties would be:

· there is no production of the form $L \to L$
· there is at most one non-terminal which appears in the left part of a production but in no right part of any production
· there are no undefined non-terminals
· there are no unused terminals
· every non-terminal can be expressed eventually in terms of terminals.

There are, however, more subtle qualities that are desirable. One of these is that the grammar should not be ambiguous. To explain, consider the grammar

$$S \rightarrow Ac|aB$$
$$A \rightarrow ab$$
$$B \rightarrow bc$$

and the string *abc*. This can be parsed in two different ways – see figure 2.3.

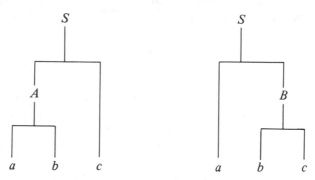

Fig. 2.3. Alternative parses of *abc*.

A context-free grammar which allows a string to be parsed in at least two different ways is said to be *ambiguous*. If every grammar generating a context-free language is ambiguous then that language is said to be *inherently ambiguous*.

In programming language design the grammars should not be ambiguous and the language should certainly not be inherently ambiguous. For ambiguity might imply that the meaning to be attributed to a sentence is not well defined. To take an analogous situation in natural language consider the sentence

The boy kicked the light blue ball.

Does the word 'light' refer to the colour or to the weight of the ball? The sentence could legitimately be interpreted in either way and the meanings of the two interpretations are quite different. So we shall want to avoid this type of situation.

In practice it does sometimes happen that ambiguity is harmless but the occasions are rare and as a general rule ambiguity should be avoided.

2.3 Grammars for parsing

The task of producing parsers is of course one of the main concerns of the compiler writer. He would like to be provided with a grammar which makes his task simple and his parser efficient, in terms of both the time and space taken by the parser. In what follows we shall look

19

briefly at two common classes of grammars, the LL(k)-grammars and the LR(k)-grammars. These have the important advantage that a parse of input text can be performed using a single scan over the text. We want to exclude the possibility of the parser reaching a certain point in the text and only then realising that a wrong decision was made earlier. For this requires the parser to return to an earlier point in the text, to remember what stage it had reached in the parsing process when it previously passed this point, to remember what possibilities it had checked and excluded and to re-read the text to test for the next possible structure. Backtracking, as this is called, can be very costly and inefficient and often unnecessary if a suitable choice of grammar is made. The time and space required by these LL(k)- and LR(k)-parsers are both linear functions of the size of the input; in short, they are efficient.

Another considerable advantage that these grammars possess is that parsers can be automatically generated. We shall refer to a parser for an LL(k)- (or an LR(k)-) grammar as an LL(k)-parser (or an LR(k)-parser). Consequently it is possible to devise a program which, given an arbitrary LL(k)-grammar G, will produce as output another program which is a parser of sentences of the language $L(G)$. The same is true of LR(k)-grammars.

The basic idea behind the design of LL(k)-parsers is a generalisation of the process of recursive descent; as parsing is progressing the left parse of the input is being constructed. LR(k)-parsers attempt to find the right parse in performing a left-to-right scan of the source text.

2.3.1   LL(k)-grammars

Informally a grammar is said to be LL(k) if the following condition is satisfied: a parser can make a decision, based on at most the next k symbols of input, about which production applies at any stage of the parsing process. We say that k symbols of lookahead can be used. Given a rule

$$A \rightarrow \alpha_1 \,|\, \alpha_2 \,|\, ... \,|\, \alpha_n$$

from the grammar a decision about whether the production $A \rightarrow \alpha_1$, $A \rightarrow \alpha_2$, etc. applies can be made on the basis of the first k symbols on the input stream. Having come to a decision the parser can then proceed to look for α_1, α_2, ... or whatever. As parsing progresses the input text is scanned from left to right (hence the initial 'L' of 'LL') and the process results in the deduction of the left parse of sentences of the language (hence the second 'L'). Parsers for LL-grammars are constructed in a manner similar to the recursive descent approach which, as we saw earlier, itself produces a left parse.

The generalisation that occurs can be described as follows. Given an LL(k)-grammar it is possible to deduce from the grammar the set of terminals that can start each instance of a non-terminal. There are convenient ways of remembering this information. In the case $k = 1$, for example, a Boolean matrix or table with each non-terminal to a row and each terminal to a column can be used. If the $(i.j)$th entry is set to true the ith non-terminal can start with the jth terminal. Then when a symbol is read the tables can be examined to determine which of the alternative productions to follow. The tables themselves and the parser can be constructed automatically from the given grammar.

Definition
A language that can be described by an LL(k)-grammar is itself said to be an LL(k)-language.

One very common class of grammar is the set of LL(1)-grammars which use just one symbol of lookahead. Unfortunately some very simple grammars are not LL(1). Take the grammar described by

$$A \rightarrow a \mid Ab$$

Such a rule is said to be *left-recursive* since a production of a non-terminal has a right part starting with that non-terminal. This would be LL(1) only if it were possible to decide on the basis of a single character of lookahead whether the production $A \rightarrow a$ or the production $A \rightarrow Ab$ applies in a particular situation. Unfortunately the single letter a could start the right part of either production and so no decision can be made. The grammar is not therefore LL(1). Nor is the grammar specified by

$$A \rightarrow aB \mid aC$$

since a can again start the right part of either production.

In the two examples given above the decision that the grammar is not LL(1) is easily deduced. In general the decision is much more complex but there are algorithms which will perform the test.

It would appear that the class of LL(1)-grammars is rather limited, and this is so. Fortunately there are standard techniques for overcoming some of the difficulties outlined above. There are standard transformations which can be applied to important classes of non-LL(1)-grammars to produce equivalent LL(1)-grammars.

Left-recursive rules such as

$$A \rightarrow a \mid Ab$$

can be replaced by two rules

$$A \rightarrow aX$$
$$X \rightarrow \epsilon \mid bX$$

21

where ϵ is the empty symbol. The language generated by the new grammar is that generated by the original grammar. The new grammar has the advantage of being LL(1). Similarly

$$A \to aB \mid aC$$

can be replaced by

$$A \to aX$$
$$X \to B \mid C$$

thereby removing the problem caused by the double appearance of a at the start of the two right parts. The process exhibited by this last example is, for obvious reasons, referred to as *factorisation*.

The removal of left recursion exhibited above can always be accomplished and the task can be performed automatically. Even when mutual left recursion (A has a production starting with ... which in turn starts with A) is involved as in

$$A \to Bc \mid ...$$
$$B \to Ad \mid ...$$

the recursion can be automatically removed. The factorising described above can also be automated to a considerable extent but in general there is no guarantee of success – the automatic process may not terminate. But for large classes of grammars these transformations can be applied and will produce LL(1)-grammars.

LL(k)-grammars have an advantage in that as parsing is in progress the parser knows exactly what has been recognised and the context in which it occurred. Accordingly as parsing is progressing it is possible to perform other actions, e.g. produce machine code for the piece of program just parsed. These actions can be imbedded in the grammar and a parser can arrange to have these actions executed after the appropriate construct has been recognised. To illustrate consider the following definition of the non-terminal <integer> in terms of the non-terminal <digit>

$$\text{<integer>} ::= \text{<digit>} \mid \text{<integer>} \text{<digit>}$$

A program may wish to calculate the integer represented by a particular numeral by evaluating

$$r : = val\,(ch)$$

for the first character ch encountered (val delivers 0, 1, 2, ... according as the character read is 0, 1, 2, ...) and

$$r : = r \times 10 + val\,(ch)$$

for all subsequent characters. This can be described in a more natural way by surrounding the action with brackets { } and writing

$$\langle\text{integer}\rangle ::= \langle\text{digit}\rangle \; \{ \, r := \text{val} \, (ch) \, \} \; | $$
$$\langle\text{integer}\rangle \langle\text{digit}\rangle \; \{ \, r := r \times 10 + \text{val} \, (ch) \, \}$$

Now the grammar given above is not LL(1) since it is left-recursive. But transformations of the kind described earlier will produce an LL(1) grammar. It can be arranged that these transformations take actions of the kind described above into account. Consequently automatic transformations might produce

$$\langle\text{integer}\rangle ::= \langle\text{digit}\rangle \; \{ \, r := \text{val} \, (ch) \, \} \; X$$
$$X ::= \epsilon | \; \langle\text{digit}\rangle \; \{ \, r := r \times 10 + \text{val} \, (ch) \, \} \; X$$

Although the parse tree for an integer is now different the various actions are performed in the correct order and the correct result is obtained.

2.3.2 LR(k)-grammars

Again informally, a grammar is said to be LR(k) if each sentence that it generates can be parsed in a single scan from left to right (with no backtracking) using at most k symbols of lookahead.

A parser for an LR(k)-grammar will attempt to reconstruct the derivation tree in a bottom-up fashion by looking for the reverse of the rightmost derivation; hence the R of LR – again the initial L implies a left-to-right scan of the text. LR-parsing itself is founded on the premise that the parser will enter only a finite number of different states and all these states and the transitions between them can be calculated in advance from the initial grammar. Basically a state is nothing more than information indicating the position that a parser has reached within a grammar. This alone does not represent an accurate history of the parser's previous actions since it does not take account of depth of nesting and so on. But a list of the states that have been entered, hopefully condensed to avoid irrelevances, would provide such information.

As parsing progresses the LR-parser will absorb text and in the process move through the grammar in its attempt to recognise a sentence. Given a production such as

$$A \to \alpha_1 \; \alpha_2 \; ... \; \alpha_n$$

· it will have to recognise α_1 then α_2 and so on until α_n is recognised; the process of moving through the right part of a production in this way – one way of changing state – is called *shifting* and a *shift* is a single move, e.g. from before α_1 to before α_2

· having recognised a complete right part such as $\alpha_1 \; \alpha_2 \; ... \; \alpha_n$ the parser will realise that an A has been recognised; the corresponding move on behalf of the parser is to replace α_1 $\alpha_2 \; ... \; \alpha_n$ by A - effectively part of the parse tree is built; such a move through the grammar by the parser is a change of state called a *reduction* or a *reduce* move
· perform an *accept* move when it realises that a sentence has been successfully recognised
· perform an *error* move when it realises that the text supplied is not a legal sentence of the language.

To illustrate take the grammar described by

1. $S \rightarrow A$
2. $A \rightarrow a$
3. $A \rightarrow Ab$

This is just a simple left-recursive grammar in which the various productions have been numbered for referencing purposes. The string *abb* would be parsed by a set of actions (which we explain later)

shift a; reduce by $A \rightarrow a$, production 2
shift b; reduce by $A \rightarrow Ab$, production 3
shift b; reduce by $A \rightarrow Ab$, production 3
finally, reduce by $S \rightarrow A$, production 1

| | | Terminals/non-terminals | | | |
		a	b	S	A
	1	s3		accept	s2
States	2	r1	s4	r1	r1
	3		r2		
	4		r3		

Table 2.1. *Table for LR-parser*

An LR-parser would make use of a table constructed, possibly automatically, from the initial grammar – see table 2.1. If a dot is used to denote the position in the grammar that the parser has reached then

· state 1 is characterised by three productions, all of which denote possible starts

$S \rightarrow \cdot A$; an A will now lead to state 2
$A \rightarrow \cdot a$; an a will lead to state 3
$A \rightarrow \cdot Ab$; an A will lead to state 2

In effect this is the initial state.

·state 2 is characterised by
   $S \rightarrow A \cdot$; now reduce by production 1
   $A \rightarrow A \cdot b$; a b will lead to state 4
·state 3 is characterised by
   $A \rightarrow a \cdot$; reduce by production 2
·state 4 is characterised by
   $A \rightarrow Ab \cdot$; reduce by production 3

As regards the various entries in the table

·shift entries such as s3 indicate shift and move to the new state 3
·reduce entries such as r2 indicate reduce using production number 3

All other entries should never be used and are error situations.

The parser starts in state 1. On encountering a terminal or non-terminal it will perform the action indicated in the corresponding' table entry. It will now enter a new state and read a new symbol. The table is again examined for the next action. In this way parsing proceeds.

For a complete understanding of the workings of the parser we describe its actions in parsing the string *abb*. Use is made of a stack onto which are pushed alternatively state numbers and either terminals or non-terminals. The topmost state will indicate the current state of the parser.

The initial state is 1. This is pushed onto the stack. The first character read is *a*. The table indicates s3. Accept the *a* by pushing it onto the stack together with the new state, state 3. The stack now contains 1*a*3 and the remaining input is *bb*.

Read the next symbol, *b*. The table indicates r2. Remove from the stack twice as many symbols as there are in the right part of production 2 and replace these with the left part. The stack has then 1*A*. When the parser is in state 1 and receives an *A* it moves to state 2 which now becomes the new state. This state combined with the *b* that has been read produces on the stack 1*A*2*b*4 leaving one further *b* on the input.

The entire parsing process can be summarised by noting the various changes in the stack and the corresponding changes in the input stream. The final *accept* shows that the given input is indeed a string of the language. See figure 2.4 where $ merely terminates the input. In this way then strings can be parsed.

What characterises LR(k)-grammar is the fact that tables such as that used above can be constructed. Taking lookahead by k symbols into account each table entry must be unique. There can be no clashes, no

Stack	Input stream
1	abb$
1a3	ȧbb$
1A	
1A2	
1A2b4	ȧ̷ḃb$
1A	
1A2	
1A2b4	ȧ̷ḃ̷ḃ$
1A	
1A2	
1S	
accept	

Fig. 2.4. History of LR-parse.

conflicts between shifting and reducing or between reductions. These remarks indicate the kind of grammar construct which will cause a grammar to fail the LR(k)-test. Given productions

$$A \rightarrow a \qquad A \rightarrow aB$$

the LR-ness of the grammar will depend on what can appear to the right of an a. For from the next few symbols of input the parser must be able to decide on encountering an a whether to reduce thereby supplying production $A \rightarrow a$ or merely to shift thereby assuming $A \rightarrow aB$.

Unfortunately not all aspects of programming languages are LR in nature. One common example that causes trouble arises from the nature of procedure calls and the nature of array subscripting. Given a construct such as $A(I,J)$ it is often not possible to tell if this is a procedure call or an array being subscripted without knowing the type or mode of A. A solution to this kind of problem is to re-arrange the grammar and to introduce a non-terminal that covers both situations; there are however dangers in this, and if possible it should be avoided.

2.3.3 Comparing LL- and LR-grammars

The question of the relative merits of LL- and LR-parsers deserves some mention. Both have considerable advantages in that they are one-pass, require no backtracking and are efficient in terms of space and time. Both will detect errors at the earliest possible opportunity, i.e. when the first erroneous character is encountered, and so they permit good error reporting. But in favour of LR-parsers, LR-grammars form a larger class than LL-grammars and LL-grammars tend to be unnatural and difficult to devise. On the other hand, it can be argued that LL-grammars can be automatically constructed from more natural grammars, and can permit semantic actions to be embedded in a natural way in the grammar (the automatic transformations can be modified to ensure that the semantic actions will occupy their proper place in the new grammar). Advocates of LR-parsers might at this stage counter with a remark that semantic actions can be incorporated into LR-parsers. Indeed this is so but their use is less natural than for the LL-parsers.

2.4 Theoretical results

In this section we shall describe and discuss some important theoretical results from grammar theory. This will help to explain something about the kinds of grammars used for describing certain aspects of programming languages. We omit mention of finite-choice grammars because of their extreme simplicity. For proofs of these results see the references (section 2) at the end of this book.

In discussing theoretical results about grammars or languages some questions will be solvable or unsolvable. If a question is solvable this will mean that it is possible to devise an algorithm which will resolve the question, i.e. will give the answer 'yes' or 'no'. Algorithms always terminate, they cannot loop. Moreover they will operate correctly for all valid data. If, on the other hand, some question is not solvable then it is not possible to devise an algorithm to answer the question in the general case. But in particular cases it may be possible to reach some conclusion.

We begin by looking at the most general kind of language, the type-0 language. For these languages it is not possible, in the general case, to write a recogniser which will always terminate no matter what input text is supplied. Consequently it would not, in general, be possible to guarantee the termination of a compiler built for such a language. It would therefore appear that the unrestricted type-0 grammar is too powerful to be used in defining programming languages. For completeness we also mention that the problems of deciding whether a type-0 grammar describes a type-1, type-2 or type-3 language are all unsolvable.

Let us now turn to context-sensitive grammars and languages. These do not suffer from the drawback described above for type-0 languages; recognisers can be built and their termination can be guaranteed no matter what form of input is supplied. But traditionally context-sensitive grammars have not been used in language definition. There are no very sound theoretical reasons for this though lack of convenience could be cited – there are no known simple methods such as recursive descent for constructing recognisers. Moreover, in using context-sensitive grammars there is a kind of implication that certain constructions may be syntactically valid in some contexts but not in others. From the teaching and learning points of view, and even from efficiency of recognition and parsing, this kind of restriction would appear to be undesirable in programming languages.

Context-free grammars are very commonly used in defining certain aspects of programming languages and consequently they have received a great deal of attention. Some of the important results concerning context-free languages and grammars are given below:

(a) recognisers can be built using a single stack
(b) if G_1 and G_2 are two context-free grammars it is unsolvable whether $L(G_1) = L(G_2)$
(c) it is unsolvable whether a context-free grammar is ambiguous
(d) it is unsolvable whether a context-free grammar generates an inherently ambiguous language
(e) it is unsolvable whether a context-sensitive language is in fact context-free.

All of the above results are of course general. In particular cases it is often possible to obtain answers to particular questions. In this connection we mention a result regarding ambiguity. Any grammar containing a production of the form

$$A \to A\gamma A$$

will be ambiguous ($A \in V_N$ and $\gamma \in V^*$ in the notation of section 2.1.2). In particular an attempt to define expressions E by a rule of the form

$$E \to E+E|E-E|\ldots$$

results in ambiguity.

Much of the work on context-free grammars and languages has revolved around the problem of finding efficient methods of recognising strings of the language. Recursive descent has highlighted s-grammars but there are also the LL(k)- and LR(k)-sets of grammars and languages.

The last class to be considered are the type-3 or regular grammars and languages. For these some relevant results are

(a) these languages can be recognised by a finite-state machine
(b) if G_1 and G_2 are regular then the question of whether $L(G_1) = L(G_2)$ is solvable
(c) the question of whether or not a context-free language is regular is unsolvable

(*d*) the question of whether a regular grammar is ambiguous is solvable

(*e*) no regular language is ambiguous.

In connection with (*a*) above, there are algorithms for minimising the number of states in the machine for performing the recognition. Consequently a 'best-possible' finite-state machine can be devised.

For completeness we mention some theoretical results associated with the class of LL(k)- and LR(k)-grammar and languages:

(*a*) each LL(k)-grammar is also LR(k)

(*b*) there are LR(1)-grammars which are not LL(k) for any k

(*c*) there are algorithms for deciding whether grammars are LL(k) and LR(k)

(*d*) there are no algorithms for deciding if languages are LL(k) or LR(k).

(*e*) LR(k) grammars are not ambiguous.

It has already been mentioned that there is no algorithm for deciding if an arbitrary context-free grammar is ambiguous. Consequently the algorithm mentioned in (*c*) for detecting LR(k)-grammar, will, in the light of result (*e*), catch many ambiguous grammars.

3

EARLY ATTEMPTS AND SOME DEVELOPMENTS

In this chapter we look for the first time at some language definitions. We begin with the definitions of FORTRAN, ALGOL 60 and LISP. All these languages were defined in the early 1960s and they represented the first attempts at language definition. The actual timing of the definitions of these languages is not in itself very important. These three definitions have been selected for inclusion in this early chapter because they either started trends or provided valuable lessons in language definition and had considerable influence on the development of the subject and on the definitions that followed subsequently.

It will suit our purpose to criticise these attempts somewhat severely since the realisation of their deficiencies led to the later developments in language definition. This, of course, is no reflection on the authors of these language definitions. Around twenty years later our knowledge and appreciation of these matters ought to be more developed.

3.1 The definitions of FORTRAN

Before making some remarks about the document which defines the FORTRAN language it is convenient to review briefly the historical development of FORTRAN.

3.1.1   The history of FORTRAN
The FORTRAN project began in the summer of 1954. Around that time IBM had just produced their new IBM 704 computer. A team under the direction of John Backus was given the task of developing a new programming language for this computer. This effort resulted in the production of FORTRAN, one of the most notable developments so far in computing.

About two-and-one-half years after the project began a language had been designed and a compiler produced. The compiler had many faults and the use of the language and its translator did not gain widespread acceptance till sometime later. FORTRAN as it is now known first came into use in the late 1950s. The language itself was designed in such a way that compilers for the language could produce efficient object code using the techniques then available. One of the consequences of this preoccupation with efficiency was that the language reflected the hardware constraints of the IBM 704, e.g. the DO and the IF statements. The reason for this preoccupation with efficiency was that, at that time, the alternative means of programming was assembly code or machine code. Users had to be persuaded therefore of the wisdom of programming in FORTRAN and one crucial aspect of this was convincing them that efficient object code could be produced by a compiler.

Some years later, in 1962, a working party of the then American Standards Association (ASA) was given the task of producing a specification of FORTRAN. At that time IBM FORTRAN IV and IBM FORTRAN II were the most important dialects of FORTRAN in use. In 1966 the working party produced two FORTRAN standards which were finally approved by ASA. These documents, ASA FORTRAN and ASA BASIC FORTRAN, were closely related to FORTRAN IV and FORTRAN II respectively. Moreover, BASIC FORTRAN was a subset of FORTRAN. Since 1966 the American Standards Association has undergone some changes in title, and the titles of the FORTRAN standards have altered accordingly. But the contents of the FORTRAN documents remained unaltered over the years. FORTRAN thus became the first programming language to be adopted as an American Standard.

In 1978 the 1966 FORTRAN Standard was repealed and replaced by the FORTRAN 77 Standard. This defined a new language and was more sophisticated than its predecessor. We shall look at this later. For the moment we concentrate on the first FORTRAN Standard with a view to learning some of the lessons it taught.

It is of interest to look at the early objectives of the Committee who eventually produced the 1966 FORTRAN Standard. The criteria that they were to use in considering and evaluating the various aspects of the language were (see Heising, 1964)

(a) ease of use by humans
(b) compatability with past FORTRAN use
(c) scope of application
(d) potential for extension
(e) facility of implementation, i.e. compilation and execution efficiency.

There was moreover a statement of intent by the Committee:

The FORTRAN Standard will facilitate machine to machine transfer of programs written in ASA Standard FORTRAN. The standard will serve as a reference document both for users who wish to achieve this objective and for manufacturers whose programming products will make it possible. The content and method of presentation of the standard will recognise this purpose.

In order to achieve widespread acceptance and recognition of their product, the FORTRAN Committee published draft reports to inform interested parties of their progress and to invite comments, criticisms, reactions, etc.

It is significant that the specification of the FORTRAN language appeared several years after the language itself had been designed and after the first compilers had appeared. The method of definition was definitely not used as an aid in designing the language. There were therefore problems in making the language seem natural.

The specification of the language itself was written in an informal style using ordinary English and is quite readable. Illustrations are given by looking at part of the definitions of assignment statements and DO statements.

7.1.1 **Assignment Statements.** There are three types of assignment statements:

(1)   Arithmetic assignment statement
(2)   Logical assignment statement
(3)   GO TO assignment statement

7.1.1.1 *Arithmetic Assignment Statement.* An arithmetic assignment statement is of the form:

$$v = e$$

where v is a variable name or array element name of type other than logical and e is an arithmetic expression. Execution of this statement causes the evaluation of the expression e and the altering of v according to Table 1.

7.1.1.2 *Logical Assignment Statement.* ...

Further sections go on to describe the logical assignment statement (the wording closely follows that of the arithmetic assignment statement) and the GO TO assignment statement.

The definition of the DO statement takes the form:

7.1.2.8 *DO Statement.* A DO statement is of one of the forms:

$$\text{DO } n \; i = m_1, m_2, m_3$$

or

$$\text{DO } n \; i = m_1, m_2$$

where:

(1) n is the statement label of an executable statement. This

statement, called the terminal statement of the associated DO, must physically follow and be in the same program unit as that DO statement. The terminal statement may not be a GO TO of any form, arithmetic IF, RETURN, STOP, PAUSE, or DO statement, nor a logical IF containing any of these forms.
(2) i is an integer variable name; this variable is called the control variable.
(3) m_1, called the initial parameter; m_2, called the terminal parameter; and m_3, called the incrementation parameter, are each either an integer constant or integer variable reference...

Further paragraphs describe the meaning of a DO statement in the same informal style.

The action succeeding execution of a DO statement is described by the following six steps:
(1) The control variable is assigned the value represented by the initial parameter. This value must be less than or equal to the value represented by the terminal parameter.
(2) The range of the DO is executed.
(3) If control reaches the terminal statement, then after execution of the terminal statement, the control variable of the most recently executed DO statement associated with the terminal statement is incremented by the associated incrementation parameter.
(4) ...

A total of six steps define the meaning of a DO statement.
The attitude that the FORTRAN standard adopted to the question of conforming can best be described as permissive.

A processor shall conform to this standard provided it accepts, and interprets as specified, at least those forms and relationships described herein.

Thus to conform, an implementation had only to accept and properly interpret a minimal set of programs. A compiler writer was therefore free to add other features and still remain within the Standard. This permissive approach was one of the crucial reasons for the Standard becoming widely accepted. Manufacturers could freely add their own features but they had to provide a minimal level of facility.
There is always a serious conflict associated with the production of any standard. The case of FORTRAN was no exception. If standardisation is undertaken too soon, people will argue that insufficient time has been devoted to exploring alternatives and it is possible that ill-considered decisions will be taken and then prematurely frozen. On the

other hand, if freezing is not performed early enough then different irreconcilable alternatives will tend to appear and become accepted. The FORTRAN group overcame this dilemma by taking their permissive approach.

But permissiveness (as always!) brought its own problems. The most obvious of these was that different dialects of the language still arose and portability of FORTRAN programs was impeded. A less obvious problem arose from the combination of the permissive attitude and the fact that BASIC FORTRAN was a subset of full FORTRAN. This had the consequence that implementors could add extensions to BASIC FORTRAN in a way that made the resulting language similar in form to full FORTRAN but with a different meaning.

We shall now look at the FORTRAN specification and indicate the reasons for some of the restrictions in FORTRAN.

3.1.2 Implementation considerations

The Standard has gained something of a reputation as 'a careful documentation of the bugs in the earliest compilers'! For there are many irregularities and peculiar restrictions in the language. To take just one example, the variables local to a subprogram become undefined on leaving the subprogram. This restriction is stated to allow for the possibility of overlays taking place between subsequent calls of a subprogram.

Many of the irregularities in FORTRAN 66 exist because of attempts to make sure that efficient object programs could be produced. Thus, for example, there are restrictions on the forms of the initial parameter, the increment and the terminal parameter in a DO statement, the lower bounds of arrays, etc. Perhaps the form of subscripts should also be mentioned. Recall that these are of the form $c*v+k$, $c*v-k$, $c*v$, $v+k$, $v-k$, v, k where c and k are integer constants and v is an integer variable. These restrictions were imposed because of the possibility of having an array element accessed inside a loop. In all these cases, if v happens to be the control variable of some DO statement, then successive elements of the array can be accessed by performing addition, not multiplication. For

$$[c * (v+s) - k] - [c * v - k] = c * s$$

and this is constant for all the values of v.

FORTRAN 66 was designed with static storage allocation in mind. A compiler can deduce at compile-time a run-time address for each variable, array, etc. used in a program. Consequently efficient object code can be produced. The static allocation is made possible by insisting that the number and size of each object is known at compile-time and by ensuring that no recursion can occur. All arrays therefore have to be of known size and dynamic arrays cannot be permitted.

We now look at some further irregularities in FORTRAN 66 and explain these from the compilation point of view. In this we follow Larmouth (1973).

Take the restriction which states that array elements cannot appear in statement functions. Statement functions were introduced so that they could be compiled efficiently. Now compilers often arrange that the value of the same variable should reside in two places at the same time, e.g. in a location in store and in a register. In certain circumstances it may be necessary for the compiler to check that these two values are not incompatible. When loops are being executed the value of the control variable is usually held in two positions. In the light of these remarks consider

```
      REAL ARRAY (10)
      F(X)=ARRAY(I)+X
      DO 2 I=1,10
      ...
      Y=F(D)
      ...
    2 CONTINUE
```

To ensure correct execution of this the compiler would have to arrange that before a call of F is activated the location for I is updated with the contents of the register holding the value of the control variable I. But in the interests of efficiency it may fail in this and hence the restriction in the standard.

Some of the restrictions on DO statements can also be explained by realising that when loops are executed control variables, and perhaps even increments and initial and terminal parameters, may be held in registers. When a DO loop commences the registers have to be initialised in an appropriate way. It should be immediately obvious that in general jumping into a DO loop is liable to cause chaos since the appropriate actions connected with the registers will not have been performed. A special case of this is that

```
      DO 7 ...
      ...
      GO TO 7
      ...
      DO 7 ...
      ...
    7 CONTINUE
```

is not allowed since it can be argued that the GO TO causes a jump to the end of an inner loop. Such a jump is legal only if it is contained in the innermost loop.

However, there is one situation in which it is legal to jump into a loop. If there is a set of nested DO statements the FORTRAN 66 Standard says that it is legal to jump completely out of that nest from the innermost range and then back into that range. The set of statements which lies completely outside the nest and is liable to be executed in this way is called the extended range of the DO statement.

Now care must be taken to ensure that the registers which were previously being used are still intact when control returns to the innermost loop. For this to be the case certain restrictions have to be placed on the nature of an extended range. The particular restriction we have in mind is that an extended range may contain another DO statement but not a DO statement which itself has an extended range. If this restriction did not exist consider what would happen to the contents of the original registers if an extended range included the original nest of DO statements, for example. (Remember that FORTRAN 66 was designed in such a way that it could be implemented using a static storage allocation policy.)

The problem of having a variable whose value is liable to reside in at least two places has already been mentioned. It could occur again, for instance, when a subroutine is called. If the dummy argument is a simple variable it can happen that the compiler introduces a new (hidden) location

- to receive the initial value of the variable when the subroutine is called
- from which a value is returned to the original store location when control returns after the subroutine call.

This same value may thus be held in two places, the original location and the location set aside for the dummy argument. But how can this original location be accessed? Answer: FORTRAN does have COMMON and EQUIVALENCE statements. The necessary restrictions imposed by the FORTRAN Standard are:

- dummy arguments may not appear in EQUIVALENCE, COMMON or DATA statements in the subroutine
- if an actual argument appears in a COMMON block then it is illegal to write to either the dummy argument or the location in the COMMON block
- if an actual argument becomes associated with a dummy argument that is written to, then that actual argument must be either a variable, an array element or an array itself – when an expression is passed as an actual argument, call by value occurs and it is not sensible to write to the dummy argument.

36

This then completes an explanation of some of the restrictions in FORTRAN. Of course, it tells only part of the story. But it is of interest to see what resulted from attempts at specifying a language after that language had existed for several years. Compare this with what we earlier saw as the desirable features of a definition of a programming language.

The previous discussions may have implied that the only criticisms that could be made of the standard were criticisms about the restrictions in the FORTRAN language itself. But this is not so.

3.1.3 The 1966 FORTRAN Standards

The Standard did serve to remove inconsistencies from the language and formalise the existing practices of the time.

Its effect on interchangeability of programs has been somewhat limited. Standard FORTRAN was, as it happened, somewhat inadequate for some of the work in progress at the time the Standard was being prepared. Consequently users made use of manufacturers special features to achieve their aims. Moreover, from an education point of view, few people learned FORTRAN from the Standard. Instead they made use of manufacturers' manuals which did not emphasise those aspects of the language which were standard. In this respect textbooks were (and are) little better. So the permissive attitude which was adopted with a view to enhancing acceptability had the effect of working against interchangeability of programs. (Of course, few people worry about interchangeability till they themselves attempt the transfer of a program.)

Although the FORTRAN 66 Standard remained unaltered over the years its informal character did lead to various comments, questions and criticisms. To allow time for the original document to be properly studied, to give time for information to be collected and to give proper consideration to the various questions, the FORTRAN Committee waited until 1969 before publishing a first clarification document. A second appeared in 1971. The clarification documents mentioned eight mistakes, fifty-two topics selected for interpretation and three corrections to typographical or transcription errors. To give the flavour of the kind of topic which required clarification:

> · does the Standard describe Standard-conforming programs or does it describe Standard-conforming processors?
> · what does 'type of expression' mean? Does it mean the kind of expression, arithmetic or logical? Or does 'type' refer to the result produced by the expression?
> · does FORTRAN have reserved words?
> · what is the position concerning the mixing of formatted and unformatted records on output?

- does the 'size of an array' mean the number of array elements or the number of storage units occupied by the array?
- does the Standard provide an interpretation of the empty statement?
- are 'leading blanks' to be considered as before or after the sign when a sign is present in a numeral?
- may an individual subscript expression exceed its declared maximum value provided it does not exceed the 'maximum subscript value'?

There is a public-relations side associated with the promotion of any programming language. Almost all initial documents on programming language definition will contain errors of some kind, though every attempt must be made to minimise these. The designer(s) of a language must consider carefully initial reactions, comments, criticisms, questions, etc., act as judge and jury and provide an interpretation about the meaning, or intended meaning, of some part of the language, hopefully in an unambiguous way. Thus design committees must be followed by maintenance committees and usually there will be some overlap in the membership. In the case of FORTRAN that committee produced the clarification documents and thereby brought to an end (it appeared) the major part of their work on the original FORTRAN standard.

The clarification work had involved much more time and effort than the original work of standardisation. Since FORTRAN was the first programming language to obtain American National Standards Institute (ANSI) approval it naturally happened that the FORTRAN Committee encountered all kinds of trouble caused by the fact that ANSI was not geared to dealing with highly complex programming language standards – its typical standards were much shorter and involved the sizes and shapes of screws, etc. In 1970 the FORTRAN Standards Committee decided to abandon further work on clarification. They decided that their energies would best be spent on producing a new revision of FORTRAN. The most pessimistic estimate for the date of completion of this revision was then around the end of 1971. In fact, the revision, FORTRAN 77, was finally approved by ANSI in April 1978.

It has been of considerable interest to look carefully at the 1966 FORTRAN Standard. Although the document is now obsolete it did have enormous influence on the future directions of language definition. It merited a great deal of attention and taught many lessons.

3.1.4 The FORTRAN 77 Standard
In April 1978 the previous FORTRAN Standards, both the standard for FORTRAN and for BASIC FORTRAN, were withdrawn and the new Standard was approved (and superseded the old). The FORTRAN

77 Standard – its technical development ended in 1977 – was one document which contained two levels, FORTRAN and Subset FORTRAN. As the name implied Subset FORTRAN was a sublanguage of the larger FORTRAN language, i.e. any program written in Subset FORTRAN was also a program in FORTRAN. The sublanguage was chosen with the intention of reducing storage requirements and of developing and maintaining supporting software. Extensions of the sublanguage were not allowed to produce a conflict in meaning with aspects of the full language.

The FORTRAN 77 designers attempted to produce a language whose programs would be easy to compile, would produce efficient object code and would remain upward compatible with programs written in 1966 FORTRAN. The criteria they used in deciding whether or not to include features not contained in FORTRAN 66 were:

- new features should be chosen only if they have proved useful
- new features to encourage portability should be added
- there should be as little increase as possible in the complexity of the language or of processors for the language
- there should be upward compatibility, if possible, with FORTRAN 66
- there should be elimination of features from FORTRAN 66 only if there are good reason for doing so
- there should be a more precise and accurate definition of the language.

The concept of an extended range, for example, does not exist in FORTRAN 77.

Several changes were made to encourage portability and hence the cost of transferring programs from one machine to another. For example,

- the Hollerith data type was removed and replaced with the more useful character data type
- the READ and WRITE statements did not require unit numbers
- it became simpler to change a complete section of program from performing single precision arithmetic to performing double precision arithmetic.

The main extensions attempted to remove some of the peculiar restrictions of its predecessor: it permitted

- the use of integer, real or double precision expressions in array subscripts, in the control parameters of DO loops, as the selection values for computed GO TOs, etc.

- the ability to execute loops zero or more times, negative incrementation parameters in DO loops, functions with zero arguments, multiple entry points to subroutines, arrays to have as bounds negative, zero or positive integer expressions and to have from one to seven dimensions, the specification of symbolic constants (e.g. to use PI for 3.14159), the use of fixed-length character strings and it provided appropriate operators for their manipulation
- more ambitious input/output facilities including direct access, additional formats for tabbing, etc., standard input and output which do not have to be explicitly identified, the ability to open and close files and to enquire about file status, etc.

The new language is more regular than its predecessor and does not contain so many strange restrictions. However some persist and the introduction of new features into the language introduce a new set of peculiarities. The following illustrate the kind of restrictions that remain:

- mixed mode arithmetic is allowed but certain combinations of types are not permitted, e.g. mixing double precision and complex
- integer expressions can appear in positions where formerly only integer constants were allowed; but in the PARAMETER statement, for example, integer constants, and not expressions, must appear
- in character string manipulation, zero-length character strings or substrings are not allowed
- in FUNCTION statements there are restrictions on the kind of character expression that can be passed as an actual parameter; moreover a function statement may not be of character type.

Other restrictions in the FORTRAN tradition include: statements could not have more than nineteen continuation lines (or nine in Subset FORTRAN), arrays can have at most seven dimensions (or at most three in Subset FORTRAN), a statement must not contain more than 1320 characters (or 660 in Subset FORTRAN), symbolic names have at most six letters and/or digits starting with a letter. Expressions involving '*' and '/' are evaluated from left to right; since '/' denotes integer division when supplied with integer operands $7/2*6.5$ produces 19.5 and $6.5*7/2$ produces 22.75. Dynamic arrays are not permitted.

The new standard is much weightier and more comprehensive than its predecessor; it has about 200 pages compared with the 35 pages of the 1966 Standard. The authors claim that much of the extra verbosity has been caused by an attempt to make the document easier for a programmer or user to understand. It was very definitely aimed at users but also attempted to give compiler writers enough freedom for them to supply efficient implementations.

The FORTRAN 77 document had similar aims to its predecessor. It specified the form of a program and rules for interpreting the meanings of well-formed programs and their data, and the form of input and of output. But it made no attempt to discuss or deal with errors, the maximum size or complexity of a program, the range and precision of numbers, methods of rounding, or the physical properties of input/output devices or stores.

Although the design of the new language (or rather the extension of the old language) and the production of its definition went essentially hand-in-hand, the Standard again adopted a permissive approach to the question of conforming. But this decision was in keeping with the philosophy of upward compatability. A program conformed to the Standard if it used only those statements, etc. described and given a meaning in the Standard. On the other hand, a processor, i.e. implementation, conformed if it executed programs that conformed and gave them the intended meaning. A processor could then provide extra facilities provided the meaning of Standard programs was unaffected.

The style of the FORTRAN 77 document was similar to that of the 1966 document though more comprehensive and more helpful. The document had the same informal style, thus

> The form of a DO statement is
> $$DO \ s \ [\ , \ ] \ i = e_1, e_2, [,e_3]$$
> where s is the statement label of ...
> > i is the name of an integer, real or double precision variable, ...
> > e_1, e_2 and e_3 are each an integer, real or double precision expression.

The square brackets implied that the enclosed forms are optional. Meaning was described using the same informal style as its predecessor..

The Standard ended with several sections of interest:

(a) a set of syntax diagrams which describe the syntax of the FORTRAN language (see section 3.2)
(b) a set of some twenty known conflicts between FORTRAN 77 and its predecessor
(c) a set of notes explaining aspects of the language
(d) a list of items which inhibit portability
(e) a set of recommendations for enhancing portability

(b) demonstrates that though it was intended that FORTRAN 77 would be upward compatible with its predecessor this aim was not achieved. In fact, most of the known conflicts related to features of the language that are rarely used.

Further information on the various aspects of the FORTRAN Standards can be obtained from the reference at the end of this book.

3.2 The Revised ALGOL 60 Report

The algorithmic language ALGOL 60 was originally described around 1960 by an international group of language designers. These designers formed Working Group 2.1 of IFIP, the International Federation for Information Processing, and were concerned with the advancement of the design of programming languages and their methods of definition. In April 1962, in Rome, the group again met to remove 'apparent ambiguities in and otherwise clarify the ALGOL 60 Report'. The document produced as a result of this meeting was the Revised ALGOL 60 Report. For a detailed history of the ALGOL 60 story see Naur (1978) and Perlis (1978).

In contrast to the FORTRAN Standard, the design and definition of the language proceeded in effect in parallel. The language was defined using essentially just syntax and semantics: the syntax sections described the set of admissible strings of characters; the semantics sections associated a meaning with syntactically correct sequences of characters. Apart from the syntax and semantics sections of the Report, there were other sections which included illustrative examples, imposed certain other restrictions on the set of syntactically admissible sequences of characters, discussed such topics as values and types, subscripts, etc.

The Report contained five chapters. It was structured in such a way that

- chapter 1 described the BNF formalism for describing the syntax (see section 3.2.1)
- chapter 2 described the basic symbols together with identifiers, numbers, strings, etc.
- chapter 3 dealt with expressions, both arithmetic and logical
- chapter 4 contained a description of the different kinds of statements
- chapter 5 dealt with declarations
- at the end were examples of various kinds and an index.

Note that the chapters were carefully structured so that they contained increasing levels of syntactic complexity – chapter 5 contained procedure declarations.

3.2.1 The ALGOL 60 syntax

The syntax is expressed in the form of a context-free grammar using the metalanguage employing Backus–Naur Form, BNF notation for short. This makes use of the characters $<, >, ::=, |$. Non-terminals appear as strings of characters surrounded by $<$ and $>$, e.g. $<$identifier$>$, $<$unsigned integer$>$. Terminals such as **begin**, :=, are referred to as basic symbols. The symbol ::= indicates 'is defined to be'. Thus the rules

- (a) $<$program$>$::=$<$block$>$ | $<$compound statement$>$
- (b) $<$block head$>$::=**begin** $<$declaration$>$ | $<$block head$>$;
  $<$declaration$>$
- (c) $<$identifier$>$::=$<$letter$>$ | $<$identifier$><$letter$>$ | $<$identifier$>$
  $<$digit$>$

define the non-terminals $<$program$>$, $<$block head$>$ and $<$identifier$>$ respectively:

> • a program is either a block or a compound statement; other rules define $<$block$>$ and $<$compound statement$>$ in terms of other non-terminals and the basic symbols
> • a block head is either the terminal **begin** followed by a declaration or it is a block head followed by a semi-colon and then a declaration
> • an identifier is either a letter, a (different) identifier followed by a letter or a (different) identifier followed by a digit; again $<$letter$>$ and $<$digit$>$ are defined in other rules in terms of just the basic symbols $a,b,c,...,0,1,2,...$

Now it is possible to have many grammars which will generate the same language. Consequently some choice can be made and the grammar therefore chosen to exhibit certain particularly useful characteristics or to be suitable for some special purpose. In particular, a grammar to describe the syntax of a programming language may be used as a

- (a) device to generate syntactically legal strings of the language, i.e. syntactically legal programs
- (b) means of recognising or parsing pieces of text submitted as programs
- (c) framework on which to hang meaning; this in turn is related to a compiler's task of generating object code
- (d) means of arguing about theoretical aspects of the language, e.g. the nature of the programming language.

Most grammars used in the definition of a programming language will be chosen with (c) in mind – after all, one of the most important functions of a language definition is to explain meaning. A grammar would not normally be chosen with a view to satisfying (*b*), for example, for there are many different methods of recognising or parsing programs and different kinds of grammars are needed for these different methods.

Note that the grammars used in the definition of programming languages are important. They are needed by compiler writers for the design of their compilers. If for some reason, the grammars used are unsuitable it means that equivalent but suitable grammars have to be deduced. The task of finding such grammars can be very awkward and the process is liable to be error-prone. Errors can be obscure and mean that the language accepted by the new grammar is either a subset or superset of the original language.

The BNF definition of ALGOL 60 is for the most part quite accurate though objections could be levelled at it on several grounds. For instance, it is incomplete. In the section on commentary there appears the non-terminal <any sequence not containing ;> and this has not been defined. In the definition of strings there appears <any sequence of basic symbols not containing 'or'> and again this has not been defined. Note, however, that these deficiencies could have been overcome by including the appropriate definitions. They represent a fault, not in the method of definition, but in the application of that method.

Ambiguities of another kind are also present. In the definition of strings there appear the rules

> <proper string>::=<any sequence of basic symbols not containing 'or'> | <empty>
> <open string>::=<proper string> | '<open string>' | <open string> <open string>
> <string>::='<open string>'

There is a syntactic ambiguity here – only the first two rules are relevant. The string '' can be derived, and therefore parsed, in various ways, e.g.

(*a*) <string> ⇒ '<open string>' ⇒ '<proper string>' ⇒ '<empty>' ⇒ ''

(*b*) <string> ⇒ '<open string>' ⇒ '<open string> <open string>' ⇒ '<proper string> <open string>' ⇒ '<proper string> <proper string>' ⇒ '<empty> <proper string>' ⇒ '<empty> <empty>' ⇒ '<empty>' ⇒ ''

Other derivations are also possible. The problem can be overcome by replacing the syntax rule for <open string> by

<open string>::=<proper string> | <open string> <string>
   <proper string>

In this case again the fault that has been illustrated lies not in the method of definition but in the application of the method. It is, perhaps, questionable whether this should be classified as a fault. But from the compiler writer's point of view, and from the point of view of many other users of a formal definition, the presence of the syntactic ambiguity is extremely unfortunate. Most people would agree that it should not be there.

It is of interest to look at some of the uses of BNF notation in the definition of ALGOL 60. The syntax of expressions is, briefly,

<factor>::=<primary> | <factor> ↑ <primary>
<term>::=<factor> | <term> <multiplying operator>
   <factor>
<simple arithmetic expression>::=<term> | <adding operator>
   <term> | <simple arithmetic expression> <adding
   operator> <term>

The adding operators include + and −, the multiplying operators are × and /, and the primaries include unsigned numbers, variables, function designators and bracketed expressions.

The entire implied bracketing of arithmetic expressions and the precedence given to operators is contained within this piece of syntax. For example, it indicates that $a-b-c$ must be parsed as $(a-b)-c$ and not as $a-(b-c)$. Note that the right part of a production of <term> starts with <term>; similarly for <factor>. The presence of left recursion is crucial to the inclusion of the proper implied bracketing in arithmetic expressions. The basic reason for left recursion is connected, therefore, with the meaning of arithmetic expressions.

Left recursion appears in other places also, e.g.

<identifier>::=<letter> | <identifier><letter> | <identifier>
   <digit>
<unsigned integer>::=<digit> | <unsigned integer><digit>

It might be argued that in the first of these examples the use of left recursion is perfectly natural. For removing the rightmost letter or digit from a multi-character identifier leaves an acceptable identifier; removing the first character need not.

But in the second case would it not have been just as natural to employ right recursion as left recursion, i.e. could the rule not have been written as

<unsigned integer>::=<digit> | <digit><unsigned integer> ?

Another argument suggests that all the digits should be placed on an equal footing and the first and last should not be highlighted by using recursion at all. However BNF as used in the formal definition of ALGOL 60 did not use phrases such as <digit list> or <digit sequence> in these circumstances nor did it make use of the { } notation of section 3.2.3. Terminology of this kind was introduced after the formal definition of ALGOL 60 had appeared.

Why then left recursion and not right recursion? One possible answer comes from observing what actions a compiler would have to perform in calculating the value represented by an integer, or more precisely a numeral, given the sequence of characters for representing that integer. If we express a number as

<start of numeral><last digit>

then the value of the numeral, *val*(*numeral*) can be expressed as

$$val(\textit{start of numeral}) \times 10 + val(\textit{last digit})$$

Such a simple formula cannot be obtained if instead we write the numeral as

<first digit><rest of numeral>

In the case described above, and in other similar cases, the particular grammar that is chosen can be justified since it makes the task of associating a meaning with a sequence of characters much simpler and more natural.

3.2.2 Deficiencies in BNF notation

The deficiencies previously described were related to the ALGOL 60 Report and related to the application of a particular method of defining syntax. In this section we look at some deficiencies of a more fundamental nature, deficiencies in the method itself. The first point is perhaps a borderline case (see section 3.2.3) but is nevertheless important.

Consider the syntax rule

<relational operator>::=<|≤|=|≥|>|≠

The symbols < and > enclose a sequence of characters. These could justifiably be interpreted as a non-terminal – there is nothing in the Report to exclude this. Thus there is an ambiguity caused by the interplay between the programming language being defined and the metalanguage being used to define the programming language; there is an interplay between ALGOL 60 and BNF notation.

Note that the problem described above would become more pronounced if the vertical bar, as happens in other programming languages, is used as a terminal to denote the Boolean operator **or** or for operations on strings. The general form of a grammar expressed in BNF notation can itself be expressed in BNF notation. This is an extreme situation in which it is important to be careful to avoid confusion between the language and the metalanguage.

Other deficiencies in the syntactic specification of ALGOL 60 stem from the fact that too large a set of syntactically legal but erroneous programs are defined by the syntax of the Report. We illustrate this remark with some examples.

The assignment statement

$$x:=y$$

though syntactically acceptable, is meaningful only if x and y have been suitably declared within the current or an enclosing block. This kind of restriction is not contained in the BNF syntax of the ALGOL 60 Report, nor can this be done without some extension to the notation.

There are other kinds of restrictions that must be enforced. If a sub-scripted variable is used then the number of subscripts must relate to the number of dimensions in the array. If procedures are called, the number and type of the actual parameters must agree at least to some extent with the number and type of the corresponding formal para-meters. If a declaration of x, say, appears, then it is legal only if there is no other declaration of x within that same block.

In summary, many of the ALGOL 60 constructions are legal only if they appear in a suitable context, the context being defined by the declarations of identifiers accessible from within the current block. These context-sensitive requirements are not present in the syntax of ALGOL 60.

A close inspection of the ALGOL 60 syntax rules reveals that several sets of rules are similar. Take the following examples:

- the rules for arithmetic expressions and the rules for Boolean expressions
- the rules for <integer> and <number>
- the rules for <decimal number> and <unsigned number>
- <procedure identifier>, <variable identifier>, <switch identifier>, <array identifier>.

Perhaps some economy of notation could have been used but this could not have been done using the BNF notation of the ALGOL 60 Report.

3.2.3 Extensions to BNF notation
It is of interest to take a brief look at some of the extensions to the

BNF notation used in the Revised ALGOL 60 Report. Many extensions were introduced later because they were found for various reasons to be useful, convenient or natural but they added nothing new to the power of BNF notation. The extensions we look at are taken from Wirth (1977).

In the following discussion we describe essentially just three extensions. We let capital letters denote (possibly null) strings of terminals and/or non-terminals; the letter A will always represent a single non-terminal. All the examples used in the illustration of the various extensions show alternative methods of writing non-terminals which are used in the ALGOL 60 Report.

The first extension allows a kind of factorisation within syntax rules. To be more precise the rule

$$A ::= SBT|SCT|...|SZT$$

can be written as

$$A ::= S(B|C|...|Z)T$$

This extension would allow the following:

<identifier>::=<letter> | <identifier>(<letter> | <digit>)

The next extension allows for optional parts in a syntax rule. In more general terms

$$A ::= ST|SBT|SCT|...|SZT$$

can be written as

$$A ::= S[B|C|...|Z]T$$

Thus we could write

<signed integer>::=[+|-]<unsigned integer>

and the two rules

<actual parameter part>::=<empty> | (<actual parameter list>)
<procedure statement>::=<procedure identifier><actual parameter part>

could be replaced by the single rule

<procedure statement>::=<procedure identifier>[(<actual parameter list>)]

The third extension allows for multiple repetition of symbols from particular classes and the notation employed has its origins in the notation used for regular expressions in finite-state machine theory. Thus

$$S ::= U|ST \quad \text{can be written as} \quad S ::= U \; \{T\}$$

indicating that each element of S must consist of an element of U followed by a sequence of zero or more elements (not necessarily all identical) from T. A similar notation allows

$$S := U|TS \quad \text{to be written as} \quad S ::= \{T\} \; U$$

and

$$S := TU|TS \quad \text{to be written as} \quad S ::= T \; \{T\} \; U$$

This latest extension allows the following possibilities

<identifier>::=<letter> { <letter> | <digit> }
<unsigned integer>::=<digit> { <digit> }

The reader might assume (correctly) that these new symbols ( ), [ ], { } might further aggravate the problem of the interference between the programming language itself and the metalanguage used in the definition. Following Wirth (1977) this difficulty can be overcome by enclosing any terminals inside quotes, the quotes symbol itself appearing as a repeated set of quotes. Thus

<procedure statement>::=<procedure identifier>["("<actual parameter list>")"]

On a different level, the introduction of BNF notation gave rise to another representation of syntax, a graphical form. The major advantage of this approach was that the entire syntax could be represented on a single sheet and, if properly documented so as to allow cross-referencing and so on, was very convenient. In figure 3.1 we illustrate part of a more complete chart – see Taylor, Turner & Waychoff (1961) – the part describing a <factor>. Ellipses or rectangles surround non-terminals and circles surround the basic symbols. Ellipses are used for a non-terminal when the non-terminal is being defined; rectangles are used when a non-terminal is used essentially in the right part of a production.

Superimposed on the basic syntax chart is a grid, like longitude and latitude on a geographical map, and thus references could be made to different parts of the chart. These references could be made even from within the chart itself. The non-terminal <arithmetic expression>, for example, appeared twelve times in the chart but, of course, its definition appeared only once. It was convenient therefore to reference the definition of <arithmetic expression> wherever it appeared elsewhere in the chart by including appropriate coordinates in the rectangles, i.e. $(K,41)$ in the given section of the chart.

This use of a graphical representation of syntax started a trend.

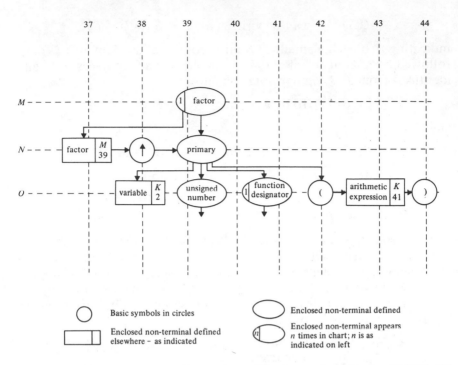

Fig. 3.1. Syntax of factor (from chart of Taylor *et al.*, 1961, for ALGOL 60).

Examples of parts of other syntax diagrams are given in figures 3.2–4. The PASCAL chart appears in Hoare & Wirth (1973), the FORTRAN chart in FORTRAN (1978) and the ALGOL 68 chart in Watt, Peck & Sintzoff (1974) and McGettrick (1978*a*).

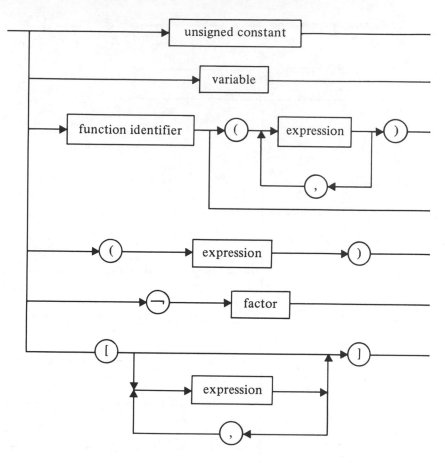

Fig. 3.2. Syntax chart for factor (PASCAL).

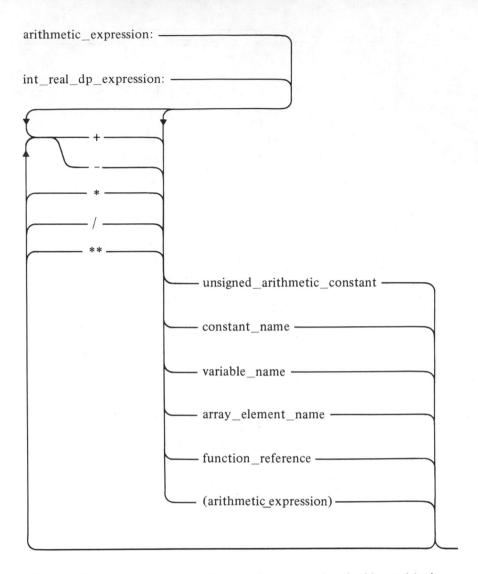

Fig. 3.3. Syntax chart defining arithmetic (integer, real or double precision) expressions for the FORTRAN 77 Standard.

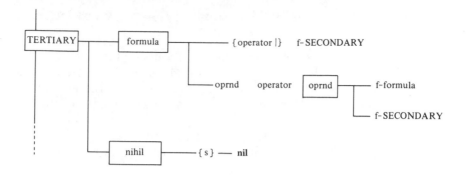

1. The boxes enclose items being defined.
2. Prefixes s-, f- indicate strong, firm syntactic positions.
3. { operator | } denotes a sequence of one or more operators.
4. { s } indicates that **nil** can appear only in a strong position.

Fig. 3.4. Part of a syntax chart for ALGOL 60.

3.2.4 Semantics and other sections

The semantics sections and other sections of the ALGOL 60 Report
were described for the most part in an informal manner in English.
This is where most of the blemishes and inaccuracies in the definition
occurred.

At the outset let it be said that the most glaring omission from the
ALGOL 60 Report is a section on input and output. No mention was
made of this at all, neither in the syntax, the semantics nor any other
section of the Report. The result was that manufacturers designed their
own input/output routines and this severely hindered portability, etc.
Some of the chief advantages of a language definition were lost in one
stroke.

A careful examination of the Report will reveal two different kinds
of semantics. Koster (1974) calls these the dynamic semantics and the
static semantics, though this distinction does not appear in the Report
itself; in fact they do not even appear consistently in the sections
headed 'Semantics'.

The dynamic semantics is concerned with what happens when a program is being executed. It contains a description of the meaning and
effect to be attributed to each construction in the language. Thus there
are sections devoted to the meaning, etc. of assignment statements, for
clauses, procedure statements, the use of expressions in switch lists, etc.

Static semantics on the other hand relate to what happens when a
program is being compiled. This includes the context-sensitive restrictions which we have already noted were missing from the syntax of

ALGOL 60. Included in static semantics therefore are restrictions of the following nature:

- a **go to** cannot cause a jump from outside into a block
- the types associated with all variables and procedure identifiers in a left-part list must be the same; and there are corresponding restrictions on the types of expressions in the right part
- the type of the value of a particular variable is defined in the declaration of the variable or the corresponding array identifier.

Note now the implication that syntax and static semantics are concerned with compile-time, dynamic semantics is concerned with run-time.

Inaccuracies occur in both these aspects of the semantics. We give below some illustrative examples but the list is by no means complete.

The first set of examples are taken from the semantics sections of the Report and concern the dynamic semantics. Ambiguities arose from the failure to define precisely

- the order of evaluation of operands, subscripts, bound pairs in block heads and value parameters; ambiguities result when the evaluation of an item causes side-effects (which alter the values of other variables)
- the effect of conditionals; for it states that essentially

    if b **then** s

is equivalent to the dummy statement if b is false – this also fails to take account of side-effects
- the effect of jumps out of functions, for this can result in partially evaluated expressions (whose partial evaluation may have caused side-effects!)
- the **own** concept; trouble was caused by failure to define what happens when dynamic **own** arrays are used and when **own** variables or arrays appear in recursive procedures.

As regards the static semantics, the following could be cited as examples:

- the syntax of the Report allows a program to be labelled; the semantics talk about labels being local to a block
- it is not stated clearly whether repeated formal parameters are allowed in procedure or function declarations; thus could a, for example, appear in two positions as a formal parameter?

Many of the remaining blemishes occur not in the semantics sections as such but in the sections devoted to remarks of an explanatory nature. Into this category fall the following:

- the Report does not state to what extent actual parameters must agree with their specification in a procedure declaration
- the Report states that the operator / is defined for all combinations of types integer and real and fails to exclude division by zero; similarly for integer division
- the Report states that in the outermost block of a program any array declarations must have constant bounds; it therefore fails to recognise that arithmetic expressions such as 2+3 could appear as bounds.

There are other aspects of the ALGOL 60 semantics which are worthy of note. Apart from informal English sections there were other places in the ALGOL 60 Report where another technique was used. We cite two examples:

- there is a remark that

  else <*unconditional statement*>

  is equivalent to

  else if true then <*unconditional statement*>

- statements of the form

  A **step** *B* **until** *C*

  are equivalent to

  $V := A$;
  Ll: **if** $(V-C) \times sign(B) > 0$ **then go to** *Element exhausted*;
      statement S;
      $V := V+B$;
      go to *Ll*;

  Here *S* is the statement that has to be repeated, *V* is the control variable and *Element exhausted* refers to the next statement in the program. Similar definitions are given for other kinds of for-statements.

This technique of describing more complex constructions in terms of simpler constructions (sometimes called *definition by substitution*) has its uses. If the semantics of the simpler constructions has already been described there will then be no need to describe the semantics of the complex construction. But there are some disadvantages. Should the equivalence of the two pieces of program be taken literally? Take the statement

A **step** B **until** C

described above. If we assume this is equivalent to the piece of program set out above then

- if B is a procedure call, it must in general be evaluated twice each time round the loop
- if the control variable V is a subscripted variable then in general the subscript must be evaluated three times per circuit of the loop
- the labels *Element exhausted* and *Ll* can be accessed inside the statement S.

The fundamental problem is perhaps one of over-specification – the meaning may have been described in too specific a manner.

Much of the previous discussion has been involved in illustrating the disadvantages of using English text as a means of describing aspects of the definition of a programming language, in particular of FORTRAN 66 and of ALGOL 60. On a more general level it is possible to mention some of the particular difficulties inherent in the use of natural languages for this purpose. The examples given below highlight some genuine problems – see Hill (1972):

Problems involving numbers
- compare 'twelve and a half' and 'a million and a half'
- the phrase 'positive and negative' excludes zero
- given the question 'how often can 5 be taken away from 17?' it would be perfectly legitimate to reply 'as many times as you like, the result is always 12'

Scope problems
- people in different parts of the world will associate different meanings with a word
- sometimes words are used with a technical meaning, and sometimes they are used with their normal meaning; the two should not be confused
- phrases such as 'all the above', 'the previous section', etc. are often ambiguous – it might not be clear where the boundaries lie

Particular problems
- words such as 'repeat' and 'again' are often used imprecisely and can be interpreted to imply that closed loops are present (and a process therefore never terminates)

- conditionals (especially nested conditionals) are often ambiguous; does an 'if ... then ...' or an 'if ... then ... else ...' form of construction apply?
- words such as 'and' and 'or' can be ambiguous; is 'or' an inclusive or exclusive 'or'?
- when are definitions properly stated, are terms well defined or are they circular in nature?

3.2.5 *Further comments*

The BNF approach to defining syntax tends to result in a regular programming language. ALGOL 60 has no peculiar restrictions on the number of characters in an identifier, the number of dimensions in an array, the depth to which blocks can be nested, and so on. But it would be wrong to suggest that there are no irregularities in the language. We mention three – the commentary facilities, the dangling **else** problem and the type-checking problem.

Comments in ALGOL 60 programs can be included in three different ways:

- they can occur between **comment** and the next semi-colon and then they can appear immediately after a **begin** or a semi-colon; in this case the commentary can contain any sequence of symbols other than a semi-colon
- they can occur between an **end** and the next semi-colon and can consist of any sequence of characters other than an **end**, an **else** or a semi-colon
- they can occur in a procedure declaration when the comma can, in effect, be replaced by

) any sequence of letters : (

Note that the rules in the three cases are all different and there is no obvious reason in the third case for restricting the characters to be letters. Moreover, it is not possible to put explanatory comments in declarations immediately following the occurrence of the identifier. From a programmer's point of view these restrictions are all undesirable. They are also highly undesirable from a compiler writer's standpoint. Comments cannot be removed from programs until a complete syntax analysis has been performed; it is preferable if they can be removed by the initial lexical scan.

Irregularities of another kind arise because of the possibility of undesirable interactions between two constructs which begin in the same way and have no suitable terminator. These are the **if ... then ...** construct and the **if ... then ... else** construct. If both appear side-by-side which **then** should accompany the single **else** – hence the name 'the dangling **else** problem'. There are two special cases to consider:

(a) **if** $b1$ **then if** $b2$ **then** $s1$ **else** $s2$
(b) **if** $b1$ **then**
        for $i := 1 \ldots$ **do**
        if $b2$ **then** $s1$ **else** $s2$

These difficulties are resolved purely by the syntax of ALGOL 60. Thus

<if clause> ::= **if** <Boolean expression> **then**
<unconditional statement> ::= <basic statement> |
    <compound statement> | <block>
<if statement> ::= <if clause><unconditional statement>
<conditional statement> ::= <if statement> | <if statement>
    else <statement> | <if clause><for statement> |
    <label>:<conditional statement>

The irregularities caused by the dangling **else** problem – necessary to avoid ambiguity – appear in the syntax in the sense that only statements of a particular kind can follow **then.**

The last irregularity we mention relates to the types of identifiers occurring in ALGOL 60 programs. In many cases the types of all identifiers are clear and well defined. But if identifiers appear as parameters of procedures this need not be the case. Can an array be used in some cases as a one-dimensional array and in other cases as a two-dimensional array, e.g.

    if $bool$ **then** a $[i]$ **else** a $[i,j]$?

Can procedures be used on different occasions with different numbers and different types of parameters? If a parameter is called by name it need not appear in the specification part; moreover if it is assigned to within the procedure body this places certain restrictions on the nature of actual parameters. Thus although most type checking can be done at compile-time there are cases where some type checks (and some syntax checks) have to be done at run-time. It has been suggested that difficulties such as these can be overcome by allowing the language definition, the language design and its implementation to proceed hand-in-hand.

Some people would add further criticisms and comments about the Revised ALGOL 60 Report. The definition does not distinguish between symbols and their representation. For example, the less-than-or-equal-to operator appears as just $\leq$. No mention is made of alternative representations such as **le**, <=, .LE., etc. No distinction is made between number and numeral – a numeral is a representation in character form of the abstract mathematical concept of number; thus 3,03,003,... are all numerals representing three.

BNF notation itself can be criticised further on the grounds that it highlights the way in which programs are written, i.e. the way they actually appear on paper. It does not highlight their structure, and this is a more important aspect of a program. People who regard structure as important argue that the one grammar should encompass any representation of a program, including, for example, a program expressed in reverse Polish notation. For in all cases the essential structure of the program is the same; only the representation differs. Thus some form of abstract syntax would be preferable to the concrete syntax exhibited by BNF notation.

Consider now the compilation process. If one takes the lexical analysis phase then this is concerned with representations. Should a formal definition therefore provide a description of the structure one might expect after the lexical analysis phase, after the syntax analysis phase, or what?

3.2.6 Conclusions

Although the definition of ALGOL 60 has been criticised rather severely it should be remembered that it was a fine piece of work (and only seventeen pages in length). It was essentially the first programming language to be formally defined. It preceded the FORTRAN 1966 Standard and brought about advances of many kinds in computer science. Indeed a measure of its success is precisely the amount of attention and criticism it attracted.

Because of the absence of hardware representations and because of the lack of input/output the Report did not lend itself either to portability or to standardisation, surely desirable aims of a definition. Thus some of the advantages of a complete definition were lost.

The formal syntactic sections were much more successful than the informal sections. The formal approach meant less ambiguity and indeed there was less room for trouble of the kind we have discussed. The Report led therefore to a move towards formality in the definition of programming languages. It started a trend towards including in the syntax more aspects of the formal definition, i.e. moving material from the (static) semantics into the syntax. It also resulted in attempts at providing a more formal approach to the task of describing semantics.

An important lesson to be learned from the 1966 FORTRAN Standard and the ALGOL 60 approach to semantics relates to the danger of using informal methods in language definition. Such methods just do not encourage precision or accuracy. When used in discussing or describing abstract ideas they are particularly unwieldy and tend to result in ambiguity or overspecification/underspecification. There is a very real danger of appealing to intuition, to preconceived meanings of words which are then used in a technical sense. Formalism alone, of course, is no cure for all ills. But abstract ideas are more easily described and it is more likely that problems will be revealed.

We shall not dwell further on the dangers of informality. In some of the language definitions we examine later in this book informal methods are again used. Again difficulties of the kind mentioned occur but there is little further insight into methods of language definition to be gained by dwelling on them.

Finally, let it be said that the Revised 60 Report begins with a quotation from the philosopher Ludwig Wittgenstein. Translated it states:

> 'what we can resolve must be reported clearly; and what we cannot resolve must be passed over in silence'.

It summarises in a nice way the spirit of the authors of Revised ALGOL 60 and explains the omission of any aspect of input and output. It also explains that the designers themselves were aware of certain difficulties (side-effects, call by name, the **own** concept, the for statement, the conflict between specification and declaration) but rather than create further difficulties they left these topics for future consideration.

3.2.7 The Modified Report on ALGOL 60

In a more recent document, the Modified Report on the Algorithmic Language ALGOL 60 published in 1976, many of the deficiencies mentioned above were corrected or amended (see De Morgan, Hill & Wichmann, 1976). This document was published because the language was still used to a significant degree. The defects of the Revised Report had resulted in variations in implementation and the Modified Report sought to define a standard interpretation. But it went somewhat further.

Briefly, we mention some of the amendments: all formal parameters had to be specified; own variables were regarded as static and own arrays had to have fixed bounds – they were also initialised automatically to zero in the case of numeric variables or **false** for Boolean variables; in a for statement the step expression was evaluated only once each time round a loop, the control variable could not be subscripted and it retained its value on exit from a loop.

The Modified Report introduced input and output routines and so filled a significant gap. It did this by stating that any program should be assumed to be contained in an outer or environmental block which contained standard declarations. These would include input and output routines for integers, reals, characters and strings together with variables

·*maxreal* holding the maximum allowable real number
·*minreal* holding the smallest positive real
·*maxint* holding the largest allowable integer
·*epsilon* holding the smallest real for which 1.0 and
 1.0 + *epsilon* differ and 1.0 and 1.0 –*epsilon* also differ

and among other items a procedure called *fault* which would be called
when run-time error situations (caused by division by zero, etc.)
occurred.

The Modified Report also defined subsets of the language. The full
language was called level 0; two subsets called levels 1 and 2 were defined, level 2 being a subset of level 1. The motivation behind the
introduction of these was the removal from the full language of features
which would cause implementation problems. The kind of restriction
embodied in these subsets were that **own** variables were removed, actual
parameters had to be of a specific kind, only the first twelve symbols of
identifiers were significant, etc.

Unfortunately even this Modified Report has not been without its
difficulties, and further modifications ensued!

3.3   The definition of LISP

LISP was designed around 1960 by J. McCarthy at Massachusetts
Institute of Technology. The language was a significant development
in the field of programming languages and it has been used extensively
in areas such as artificial intelligence, theorem proving and mathematical logic. Basically it is a language for list processing and hence
its name.

The novel feature of the definition of LISP is the way in which the
semantics of the language were described, namely by a program which
acts as an interpreter of other LISP programs. The interpreter is written
in LISP itself. Consequently a brief introduction to LISP will precede a
study of the interpreter. In fact various versions of LISP have existed
but we concentrate on LISP 1.5, the most common.

3.3.1   S-expressions
The language is used basically for symbol manipulation. All items of
data take the form of a single atom or a group of atoms. Atomic symbols or *atoms* (they cannot be decomposed into simpler parts) consist
of a string of capital letters and/or digits starting with a letter. Thus
an atom is nothing more than a traditional identifier. Items of data are
then referred to as S-expressions, i.e. symbolic expressions.

Programs in LISP take the form of (usually recursive) procedures
which act upon S-expressions. Programs are not written in terms of
S-expressions themselves but in terms of other expressions,

M-expressions, i.e. programs are written in a metalanguage, hence M-expressions.

Definition of S-expressions
An S-expression is either

(i) an atomic symbol, or
(ii) left parenthesis, S-expression, dot, S-expression, right parenthesis.

Example 3.1 S-expressions
Each of the following is a legal S-expression:

(i) *ABC*
(ii) *((ABC.C).(A.B))*

The above method of representing S-expressions is usually referred to as the dot-notation. S-expressions can be written in another manner which does not require such frequent use of the dot or brackets. It tends to be more readable and more convenient:

$$(m_1\ m_2\ m_3\ ...\ m_n)$$

can be written in place of

$$(m_1.(m_2.(...(m_n.NIL)...)$$

where *NIL* acts as a terminator for lists and is equivalent to the list containing no elements, i.e. ( ).

Example 3.2 Equivalent representations of S-expressions
(i)   *(A B C D)* and *(A.(B.(C.(D.NIL))))*
(ii) *(A)*   and *(A.NIL)*
(iii) *(A (B C))* and *(A.((B C).NIL))*, i.e. *(A.((B.(C.NIL)).NIL))*

The dot-notations and this new notation can be intermingled if desired and S-expressions such as

(A.(B C))

become syntactically legal.

In defining the syntax of S-expressions a form of BNF notation was used:

<LETTER>::=*A*|*B*|*C*| ... |*Z*
<number>::=0|1|2| ... |9
<atomic symbol>::=<LETTER><atom part>
<atom part>::=<empty> | <LETTER><atom part> |
   <number><atom part>

$$\text{<S-expression>::=<atomic symbol> |}$$
$$\text{(<S-expression>.<S-expression>) |}$$
$$\text{(<S-expression>...<S-expression>)}$$

Certain comments should be made about these definitions

· in the syntactic definition of <LETTER> and <number> the three-point ellipsis has its obvious meaning
· in the definition of <S-expression> three dots imply an arbitrary number, including zero, of S-expressions; note the similarity between this LISP convention and { } used earlier
· <number> as defined above is essentially just a digit
· a restriction (given in English) states that atomic symbols are limited to at most thirty characters in length.

In fact LISP does allow a wider class of atomic symbols than mentioned above. For example, symbols starting with signs or digits are classified as numbers and are treated as such. In the remainder of this discussion 'number' will take on its more usual meaning.

3.3.2 M-expressions

M-expressions are just basically the functions which act upon the S-expressions. There are three elementary functions which are used to break down and put together S-expressions. There are two other functions which test for atoms and test atoms for equality.

The first function is *cons*. Basically it builds or constructs (hence *cons*) a new S-expression from two smaller S-expressions. More precisely

$$cons \ [S_1 ; S_2] \qquad \text{yields} \quad (S_1 . S_2)$$

Thus

$$cons \ [A ;(B \ C)] \quad \text{gives} \quad (A.(B \ C)), \text{i.e. } (A \ B \ C)$$

The next two functions decompose suitable S-expressions. The first function, *car*, detaches the first S-expression of a pair and the second, *cdr*, detaches the second S-expression. Thus

$$car \ [(S_1 . S_2)] \qquad \text{yields} \quad S_1 \text{ and } cdr \ [(S_1 . S_2)] \text{ yields } S_2$$

If an attempt is made to apply *car* or *cdr* to S-expressions which are atomic, the results are not defined.

Example 3.3 car and cdr
  (i) *car* [*cons*[A;B]] gives A
  (ii) *cdr* [*cons*[A;B]] gives B

There is a convenient abbreviation which can be used when *car* and *cdr* have to be applied repeatedly. It is exemplified by the following:

$$cadr[s] \qquad \text{denotes} \qquad car[cdr[s]]$$
$$cadddr[s] \qquad \text{denotes} \qquad car[cdr[cdr[cdr[s]]]]$$

Thus the number and order of the *a*'s and *d*'s denote the number and order of applying the functions *car* and *cdr* respectively.

The origin of the terms *car* and *cdr* is not important. It is tied to the original implementation of LISP on an IBM 704 computer; *car* and *cdr* refer to the contents of the address and decrement parts of an IBM 704 word.

Before describing the next function note that in LISP the symbol T denotes **true** and F **false**. The function *eq* takes two parameters which are both atoms. It yields T if the two atoms are equal and F if they are not. Its value is undefined if neither parameter is an atom. The last function *atom* is used to decide if an S-expression is an atom.

Example 3.4 eq and atom
  (i) $eq[A;A]$ yields T and $eq[A;B]$ yields F
  (ii) *atom* $[A]$ yields T and *atom* $[(A\ B)]$ yields F

These five elementary functions are the only standard functions supplied for the manipulation of S-expressions. Other functions acting on S-expressions must be built from these and this is done using conditional expressions and the lambda notation. Other basic functions are present in the LISP system for other purposes. For instance, there are functions to help in the performing of arithmetic calculations. For example,

$lessp[x;y]$ is T if $x<y$ and F otherwise
$plus[x_1;x_2;...;x_n]$ yields the sum of all the arguments.

These have arguments which are numbers and in some of the definitions that follow these will actually be replaced by arithmetic operations such as $<$, $+$. But it should be remembered that in practice the functions should be called.

Conditional expressions in LISP are written as

$$[p_1 \rightarrow e_1; p_2 \rightarrow e_2; ...; p_n \rightarrow e_n]$$

where each p_i is an expression whose value may be T or F and each e_i is any expression. The result of such a conditional expression is obtained as follows:

if p_1 is true the result is e_1; otherwise
if p_2 is true the result is e_2; otherwise
... and so on. If no p_i yields T the result is undefined.

Thus the various p_i are scanned from left to right. If p_i is the first expression yielding **true** then the result determined by the conditional is e_i.

Example 3.5 Use of conditionals
Conditionals can now be used to define functions, e.g.

$$ff[x] = [atom[x] \rightarrow x; T \rightarrow ff[car[x]]]$$

selects the first atomic symbol of an S-expression.

We now introduce a special notation for simplifying the task of defining functions.

3.3.3 The lambda notation

Lambda expressions, or λ-expressions for short, are used for defining functions as follows:

$$\lambda[[x_1;...;x_n];e]$$

where e is any expression, denotes the function f of n variables such that

$$f[x_1;...;x_n] = e$$

The variables $x_1,...,x_n$ are known as *dummy* or *bound variables*. Any other variable occurring in e but not in the list $x_1,...,x_n$ is called a *free variable*.

Example 3.6 Lambda notation
The function of x and y whose value is $x^2 + y^2$ is written in the λ-notation as

$$\lambda[[x;y];x^2+y^2]$$

The lambda notation has the effect of making cleaner and more precise the distinction between an expression, or in LISP terminology a form, and a function. An expression or form e such as x^2+y^2 is *not* itself a function. But it can be used in defining a function, the function associated with the form, namely

$$\lambda[[x;y];x^2+y^2]$$

Recursive functions are expressed in the lambda notation by means of a special notation. If the function to be defined is denoted by the dummy variable f and if e is an expression involving f then one writes

$$label[f;e]$$

65

Example 3.7   Use of label
The factorial function defined as follows

$$f[n] = [n{=}0 \to 1; T \to n \times f[n{-}1]]$$

is written using *label* as

$$label[f; \lambda[[n]; [n{=}0 \to 1; T \to n \times f[n{-}1]]]]$$

Functions are central to the task of expressing programs written in LISP. Recall that programs are written in terms of M-expressions. Consequently we can now give the syntactic definition of M-expressions described in terms of BNF notation (below <number> is synonymous with <digit> and dots have the meaning they had in defining S-expressions):

```
<letter>::=a|b|...|z
<identifier>::=<letter><id part>
<id part>::=<empty> | <letter><id part>
          |<number><id part>
<form>::=<constant> | <variable> |
          <function>[<argument>;...;<argument>] |
     [<form> → <form>;...;<form> → <form>]
<constant>::=<S-expression>
<variable>::=<identifier>
<argument>::=<form>
<function>::=<identifier> |
     λ[<var list>;<form>] |
     label[ <identifier>;<function>]
<var list>::=[<variable>;...;<variable>]
```

Note that these rules define the class of objects which are called *forms*. A form is just an expression which can be evaluated when, if appropriate, actual parameters have been supplied.

3.3.4   Conversion from M-expressions to S-expressions
It was mentioned earlier that the definition of the semantics of LISP appeared as a LISP program, namely the LISP interpreter. Programs themselves are written as functions or M-expressions which act on S-expressions. The interpreter, being itself a function, must act on S-expressions. It follows that it is necessary to have a means of converting M-expressions to S-expressions so that the interpreter can properly interpret all programs. The conversion is done as follows. Consider first functions.

· if the function is represented by a name it is translated by changing all lower-case letters to capital letters, e.g. *car* is

66

replaced by *CAR*

· if the lambda notation such as $\lambda[[x_1;x_2;...;x_n];e]$ is used this is replaced by $(LAMBDA\ (X1\ ...\ XN)\ e*)$, where $e*$ denotes the appropriate translation of expression e

· if a function begins with *label* as in $label[f;e]$ its translation is $(LABEL\ f*\ e*)$ where again $f*$ and $e*$ denote the translation of f and e respectively.

Forms are treated in a similar kind of way. The class of forms includes constants, variables, conditionals and function calls. These are translated as indicated below.

· a variable is translated by replacing lower-case letters by capital letters

· the function call $f[x_1;...;x_n]$ is translated to $(f*\ x_1*\ ...\ x_n*)$ where again the star denotes the translation of the appropriate item

· using the star convention $[p_1 \rightarrow e_1;p_2 \rightarrow e_2;...;p_n \rightarrow e_n]$ is translated to $(COND\ (p_1*\ e_1*)\ ...\ (p_n*\ e_n*))$

· finally consider constants. One cannot simply use X for X since X could be a translation of x and ambiguity would result. The constant X is translated to $(QUOTE\ X)$.

Before considering the design of the LISP interpreter it is convenient to introduce some preliminary functions which will be used in its definition.

· $null[x]$ yields T if and only if x is *NIL*

· $pairlist[x;y;a]$ gives the list of corresponding elements of lists x and y and appends this to list a:

$$pairlist[x;y;a]=[null[x] \rightarrow a;T \rightarrow cons[cons[car[x];car[y]];$$
$$pairlist[cdr[x];cdr[y];a]]]$$

The list as formed by this function is usually called an *association list*. Typically x might be a list of variables and y a list of the values of these variables. The list so formed is then a list of pairs containing a variable and its corresponding value

· $assoc[x;a]$: if a is an association list as formed by *pairlist* above, the *assoc* produces the first pair whose first term is x:

$$assoc[x;a] = [equal[caar[a];x] \rightarrow car[a];$$
$$T \rightarrow assoc[x;cdr[a]]]$$

3.3.5 *The LISP interpreter*
The LISP interpreter takes the form of a function called *evalquote*. This function has the property that if f is a function of n arguments

$x_1, x_2,...,x_n$ then

$$evalquote[f^*;(x_1\ x_2...x_n)] = f[x_1;x_2;...;x_n]$$

Now *evalquote* is defined using two main functions called *eval* and *apply*. The first of these, *eval*, defines the evaluation of forms and *apply* defines what happens when functions are applied to arguments. Each of these function definitions makes use of an extra list, x, an association list which holds variables and their current values:

$$evalquote[fn;x] = apply[fn;x;NIL]$$

where

$apply[fn;x;a] =$
$\qquad [atom[fn] \rightarrow [eq[fn;CAR] \rightarrow caar[x];$
$\qquad\qquad eq[fn;CDR] \rightarrow cdar[x];$
$\qquad\qquad eq[fn;CONS] \rightarrow cons[car[x];cadr[x]];$
$\qquad\qquad eq[fn;ATOM] \rightarrow atom[car[x]];$
$\qquad\qquad eq[fn;EQ] \rightarrow eq[car[x];cadr[x]];$
$\qquad\qquad T \rightarrow apply[eval[fn;a];x;a]];$
$\qquad eq[car[fn];LAMBDA] \rightarrow eval[caddr[fn];$
$\qquad\qquad pairlist[cadr[fn];x;a]];$
$\qquad eq[car[fn];LABEL] \rightarrow apply[caddr[fn];x;$
$\qquad\qquad cons[cons[cadr[fn];caddr[fn]];a]]]$

To explain consider some examples. Take first the evaluation of

$$car[(A.B)]$$

To evaluate this one has to invoke

$$evalquote[CAR;((A.B))]$$

Since *CAR* is a function this call of *evalquote* invokes in turn

$$apply[CAR;((A.B));NIL]$$

Following through the definition of *apply* we obtain

$atom[CAR]$ yields T
$eq[fn;CAR]$ yields T

The result is therefore $caar[x]$ where x is $((A.B))$. This produces the required result, A.

The function *evalquote* invokes *apply* in the case of functions. For forms it invokes *eval* where

$eval[e;a] = [atom[e] \rightarrow cdr[assoc[e;a]];$
$\qquad atom[car[e]] \rightarrow$
$\qquad\qquad [eq[car[e];QUOTE] \rightarrow cadr[e];$

$$eq[car[e];COND] \rightarrow evcon[cdr[e];a];$$
$$T \rightarrow apply[car[e];evlis[cdr[e];a];a]];$$
$$T \rightarrow apply[car[e];evlis[cdr[e];a];a]]$$

This makes use of two extra functions: *evcon* evaluates conditionals, i.e. evaluates the predicates in the required order, and when it finds the first producing T it yields the corresponding result.

$$evcon[c;a] = [eval[caar[c];a] \rightarrow eval[cadar[c];a];$$
$$T \rightarrow evcon[cdr[c];a]]$$

The other function, *evlis,* is defined as

$$evlis[m;a] = [null[m] \rightarrow NIL;$$
$$T \rightarrow cons[eval[car[m];a];evlis[cdr[m];a]]]$$

Basically this evaluates all the elements of list m using the association list a. The results are placed on a new list which is the result produced.

This completes the brief discussion of the design and the mechanics of the LISP interpreter. In some respects the result is very satisfactory. The interpreter itself is relatively compact yet not too complex.

3.3.6 Commentary

The formal definition of LISP represented a first attempt at describing in a formal manner the semantics of a programming language. The method used was to describe or write an interpreter for the language. Given a list P representing a LISP program and a list D representing the data then *apply* would compute the result of applying P to D.

This definition of LISP acted as a model on which to base subsequent attempts at describing programming languages in terms of interpreters. In the case of LISP the definition of *apply* was given in terms of LISP itself. In other cases the interpreter was written in some other (previously defined) programming language. In yet other cases, the formal definition took the form of a compiler producing object code in, perhaps, some abstract object language. For with the introduction of a neat syntactic notation, in the form of the BNF notation used for ALGOL 60, compilers could be produced in a syntax-directed manner employing an approach akin to recursive descent.

In general, programs such as interpreters and compilers tend to be long, involved, not transparent and full of often irrelevant details. But interpreters and compilers for describing program semantics should ideally be short (relatively), transparent, stable and not cluttered with details. The process of describing semantics then involves just programming, but programming of a rather special kind. No account need be taken of such considerations as efficiency, size of store needed, etc.

In the work which followed the initial description of LISP,

69

J. McCarthy argued that the meaning of a program should be defined by its effect on a state vector. In this, he was making a commitment to an interpreter- or compiler-oriented approach to language definition. The most notable progress in this direction has been the work of the definition of the programming language PL/I (see chapter 5).

However, some people have raised objections to this method of language definition, what they call an *operational approach,* since the meaning of a piece of program is obtained by essentially running the interpreter or compiler. Instead they favour a mathematical approach, intended to avoid all irrelevancies attributable to implementation. They argue as follows: who should decide whether an interpreter or compiler is correct? For a decision to be made it is necessary to have some clear statement, a mathematical definition, of the semantics of a programming language and this will be independent of interpreters or compilers. This line of reasoning led to the mathematical semantics of Scott and Strachey (see chapter 8).

4

SOME FURTHER DEFINITIONS

In this chapter we look at the definitions of ALGOL W, COBOL and
BASIC. These definitions represent developments on the earlier work
outlined in the previous chapter. ALGOL W and its definition reflected
the views of Working Group 2.1 of IFIP around 1965; COBOL developed over a number of years but began life around 1960; although
BASIC was originally designed around 1964, its definition finally began
to emerge only in 1978.

The definition of all these languages owed much to earlier efforts in
language definition, especially to ALGOL 60. Again, the precise timing
of these documents is not so significant but the maturity of the ideas
expressed in them is more important as are the differing approaches
taken to some old problems.

4.1 ALGOL W

4.1.1 History
The programming language ALGOL W came into existence around
1965. It arose from the work which followed the design of ALGOL 60
and it reflected the state of thinking of the ALGOL movement at this
time. The language itself did not receive formal approval in the sense
that ALGOL 60 and later ALGOL 68 received formal approval from
IFIP. For it was felt that the language did not represent a sufficient
advance on the previous ideas. Consequently the details of the new
language appeared as a private publication under the names of N. Wirth
& C.A.R. Hoare.

The language and its method of definition represented, in retrospect,
a kind of half-way house between ALGOL 60 and ALGOL 68. It had
been realised that there were deficiencies in ALGOL 60: there were no
records or structures, character handling was limited, etc., and, of
course, certain ambiguities and uncertainties had been unearthed. The
language which emerged had as its aims:

> · to serve as a means of programming a digital computer; it
> should be possible to build efficient compilers, and program-
> mers should be encouraged to produce effective programs

· to serve as a means of communication between people engaged in problems with algorithmic solutions both in numeric and non-numeric areas of computing, including simulation, symbolic manipulation, graph theory and linguistics

· the language constructs should be chosen in a very careful manner reflecting the fundamental and abstract concepts in programming; these would be carefully unified and would not appear as a set of poorly integrated facilities.

It had been realised that the definition of ALGOL 60 had been successful in many respects including brevity, clarity, rigour, its style and the quality of its notation. Accordingly these features should be retained. Yet around that time ideas of orthogonal design of programming languages and ideas on two-level grammars were starting to emerge.

It will be of interest then to look at some aspects of the definition of ALGOL W in detail. This exercise will pave the way for a close look at the later definition of ALGOL 68. Many of the ideas which appeared in a simple form in ALGOL W were extended and developed almost beyond recognition in the subsequent definition of ALGOL 68.

Our description of the definition of ALGOL W is based on the definition which appears in Eve (1972). This is clearly based in turn on the original definition in Wirth & Hoare (1966) though some slight but significant differences make it somewhat closer to the ALGOL 68 definition than the original.

4.1.2 Syntax
The syntactic definition of ALGOL W was in many senses similar to the syntactic definition of ALGOL 60. But there were some noticeable differences. By comparison with ALGOL 60 the syntactic specification was formalised into a kind of grammar containing

· a set V of basic constituents of the language (basic symbols or terminal symbols)
· a set U of syntactic entities (or non-terminals)
· a set P of syntactic rules or productions.

Syntactic rules were of the form

$$<a>::=x$$

where $<a>$ is a member of U and x is a sequence of basic constituents and syntactic entities, i.e. elements of U and V.

At this juncture it would be natural to introduce the notation which makes use of the vertical bar to separate alternatives on the right of a production. But in the programming language ALGOL W the vertical bar was used for selecting strings from substrings. Its use in syntactic rules would produce a high degree of confusion between the programming language and the metalanguage used in the definition. To overcome this difficulty a rule

<bar>::= |

was introduced. It was then stipulated that, wherever the vertical bar had to appear as an operator, the non-terminal <bar> would appear. Other appearances of the vertical bar would then be regarded as part of the metalanguage and not the programming language. With this reservation

<a>::= $x|y| \dots |z$

could be regarded as an abbreviation for the set of rules

<a>::=x
<a>::=y
....
<a>::=z

The use of the vertical bar represented one possible area of confusion between the programming language and the metalanguage. Another area of confusion was the use of the operators '<' and '>'. The stipulation that syntactic entities should be denoted by a sequence of letters, digits and hyphens rendered rules such as

<inequality-operator>::= $<|\leqslant|\geqslant|>$

unambiguous.

The formal definition of the syntax had been expressed as a kind of context-free grammar. The appeal to grammar theory went further; the definition defined terms such as 'directly produces' and 'produces'.

Many of the syntax rules of ALGOL W were similar to the corresponding rules of ALGOL 60. Thus

<identifier>::=<letter> | <identifier><letter> |
    <identifier><digit> | <identifier>_

But there appeared also various rules such as

<identifier-list>::=<identifier> | <identifier-list>,<identifier>

Other rules defined the non-terminals <bound-pair-list>, <for-list>, <statement-list>, etc.

The language ALGOL W was on the whole much more type conscious than its predecessor. Thus integers, or more accurately constructs producing integer values, were expected to appear in certain places, as subscripts or as bounds in arrays, as the increment, the initial value or the limit value in a **for** statement and so on. Real numbers were expected to be produced in other positions, e.g. as the operand of **round** or **entier**. The formal definition reflected this and consequently the syntax contained such non-terminals as <integer-expression>, <real-expression>, <logical-expression>.

To illustrate this type consciousness note the following definitions:

> *in array declarations*
>   <bound-pair>::=<lower-bound>::<upper-bound>
>   <lower-bound>::=<integer-expression>
>   <upper-bound>::=<integer-expression>
> *in case statements*
>   <case-clause>::=**case** <integer-expression> **of**
> *in iterative statements*
>   <initial-value>::=<integer-expression>
>   <increment> ::=<integer-expression>
>   <limit>   ::=<integer-expression>

and so on.

To be sensible and realistic, this type-information had to be carried through the entire syntax in a consistent manner. Consequently integer expressions would have to be defined in terms of operators and operands and these operands would themselves have some type. The operator '+', for example, would require integer operands to produce an integer result and the syntax would have to insist on this. Eventually, of course, operands would be either constants, functions or variable identifiers, and in the latter two cases the type information would have to relate to the declarations of the appropriate identifiers. Unless some convenient notation could be introduced there would have to be a large number of syntax rules which would be essentially the same; there would be, for instance, one syntax rule for each type of variable identifier.

4.1.3 The T-notation
In an attempt to maintain brevity the T-notation was introduced, T denoting type. Thus there were rules such as

> <T-variable-identifier>::=<identifier>

Here T could be replaced by any one of the words

integer	real	long-real	complex	long-complex
logical	bit	string	reference	

and on each substitution a new syntax rule would result. Thus replacing T by 'integer' would produce

<integer-variable-identifier>::=<identifier>

A subsequent definition of <identifier> combined with this substitution rule would then give a meaning to all of the nine non-terminals covered by <T-variable-identifier>.

In certain rules the T appeared more than once. For example, there was the production

<simple-T-variable>::=<T-variable-identifier> |...

It clearly made sense when replacing T by some type to replace each occurrence of T in the rule by that same type. Thus

<simple-integer-variable>::=<integer-variable-identifier>

was sensible but

<simple-integer-variable>::=<real-variable-identifier>

was not sensible. Accordingly, associated with the T-notation as used in this form was a *consistent substitution rule* which stated that each occurrence of T had to be replaced consistently throughout the same rule by the same type.

Another example of the use of the T-notation was

<simple-T-variable-declaration>::=<T-type><identifier-list>

Consistent substitution meant that declarations of simple integer variables, simple real variables, etc. were all embodied in the one rule. Subsequent syntax rules gave the definition of <integer-type>, <real-type>. Thus

<integer-type>::=**integer**
<real-type>   ::=**real**

So far the T-notation was neat and simple. But it did not remain so. Consider, for example, the assignment statement. ALGOL W realistically permitted integer values (derived from integer expressions) to be assigned not just to integer variables but also to real variables, complex variables, etc. Consequently possibly the same but also different types could be associated with the left and right parts of assignments. On the other hand, it was illegal to assign real expressions to integer variables and so the combinations of types that could appear in the separate parts of assignments were not arbitrary.

To cope with differing types T0, T1, T2,... could be used to denote differing types within the one syntax rule. Hence

<T0-assignment-statement>::=<T0-left-part><T1-expression> |
    <T0-left-part><T1-assignment-statement>

75

$$<\text{T-left-part}>::=<\text{T-variable}>:=$$

The rules regarding the permitted combinations of the types T0 and T1 then read

> For each left part variable, the type of the expression or assignment variable immediately to the right must be assignment compatible with the type of that variable.
>
> A type T1 is said to be assignment compatible with a type T0 if either
>
> (1) the two types are identical (except that if T0 and T1 are **string**, the length of the T0 variable must be greater than or equal to the length of the T1 expression or assignment), or
>
> (2) T0 is **real** or **long real**, and T1 is **integer**, **real** or **long real**, or
>
> (3) T0 is **complex** or **long complex**, and T1 is **integer**, **real**, **long real**, **complex** or **long complex**.
>
> In the case of a reference, the reference to be assigned must be null or refer to a record of one of the classes specified by the record class identifiers associated with the reference variable in its declaration.

These rules merely mirrored what one might expect. Yet they were no longer neat. Moreover they appeared in the definition of ALGOL W as part of the semantics. But the T-notation, even in the more complex form in which it appeared in assignment statements, acted merely as a convenient way of expressing several similar rules which could all be listed in the usual way. If this listing was done, the same information would be included in the syntax. The rules regarding permitted combinations of type could then be viewed as being of a syntactic and not a semantic nature.

4.1.4 Expressions

The problem of specifying the syntax of expressions became much more pronounced because of the variety of different operators and the wide range of the types of their operands.

Associated with each expression in the ALGOL W syntax were two attributes, type and precedence. The type was just the type of the result of that expression and the precedence was derived from the precedence hierarchy imposed on operators by the syntax rules. These are summarised in table 4.1. Thus examples of expressions from the ALGOL W syntax were

· $<\text{logical-expression-4}>$, which delivered a logical result and was essentially a comparison of some kind (the precedence 4 operators were the comparison operators)

· <integer-expression-5>, which delivered an integer result and was a sum of some kind.

In keeping with these and similar observations it became possible to associate a description of each <T-expression-i>. See table 4.2.

Precedence level	Operator
1	or
2	and
3	¬
4	<, <=, =, ¬ =, >=, >, is
5	+, −
6	*, /, div, rem
7	shl, shr, **
8	long, short, abs

Table 4.1. *Precedence of operators*

Syntactic entity	Description
<T-expression-1>	disjunction
<T-expression-2>	conjunction
<T-expression-3>	negation
<T-expression-4>	relation
<T-expression-5>	sum
<T-expression-6>	term
<T-expression-7>	factor
<T-expression-8>	primary

Table 4.2. *Description of expressions*

To keep the subsequent discussion relatively simple we begin by examining logical expressions. They were defined by

```
<logical-expression-1>::=
     <logical-expression-1> or <logical-expression-2>
<logical-expression-2>::=
     <logical-expression-2> and <logical-expression-3>
<logical-expression-3>::= ¬ <logical-expression-4>
<logical-expression-4>::= <relation>
<relation>::=
     <T6-expression-5><equality-operator>
          <T7-expression-5> |
     <T8-expression-5><inequality-operator>
          <T9-expression-5> |
     <reference-expression-5> is <record-class-identifier>
```

where

    <equality-operator> ::= = | ¬ =
    <inequality-operator> ::= < | <= | >=| >

Note that the definition of <relation> made use of T6, T7, T8 and T9. These were subject to the following rules:

   · T6 and T7 must be consistently replaced by any one of bit, string or reference, or by any of the words from the list, complex, long-complex, real, long-real, integer
   · T8 and T9 must be identically replaced by string or by any of real, long-real or integer.

From the various definitions given above a <logical-expression-1> seemed to be a sequence of operands separated by **or**, the operands themselves being items from <logical-expression-2>, i.e. operands separated by **and**, and so on. But to justify the fact that *a* **or** *b* was a <logical-expression-1> required an awareness of the rules

    <T-expression>::=<T-expression-1> |
       <conditional-T-expression>
    <T-expression-1>::=<T-expression-2>
    <T-expression-2>::=<T-expression-3>
    <T-expression-3>::=<T-expression-4>
      ...
    <T-expression-7>::=<T-expression-8>
    <T-expression-8>::=<T-variable> |
      <T-function-designator> | <T-constant> |
      (<T-expression>) | <T-block-expression>

This set of rules implied that an expression which was valid at one precedence level was also valid at all lower precedence levels provided the type was correct. These together with the earlier rules for logical expressions implied that, for instance, *a* **or** *b* was a legitimate <logical-expression-1>. In a similar way a sequence of variables separated by **and** was a <logical-expression-2>, and so on.

The same set of rules gave all the information about the implied bracketing in logical expressions. A similar set of rules existed for arithmetic expressions and performed a similar role:

    <T3-expression-5>::=+<T3-expression-6> |
       -<T3-expression-6>
    <T0-expression-5>::=<T1-expression-5>+<T2-expression-6> |
       <T1-expression-5>-<T2-expression-6>
    <T0-expression-6>::=<T1-expression-6>*<T2-expression-7> |
       <T1-expression-6>/<T2-expression-7>

<integer-expression-6>::=
    <integer-expression-6> **div** <integer-expression-7> |
    <integer-expression-6> **rem** <integer-expression-7>
<T4-expression-7>::=
    <T5-expression-7>**∗∗**<integer-expression-8>
<T4-expression-8>::= **abs** <T5-expression-8> |
    long<T5-expression-8> |**short**<T5-expression-8>
<integer-expression-8>::=<control-identifier>

These rules made use of T0, T1,..., T5 and there were rules regarding the permitted combinations of these. To understand these required knowledge of the ALGOL W *triplet rules*:

(*a*) If T1 and T2 had any of the qualities integer, real or complex, the corresponding quality of T0 was given by the table

T1 \ T2	integer	real	complex
integer	integer	real	complex
real	real	real	complex
complex	complex	complex	complex

(*b*) T0 had the quality long either if both T1 and T2 had that
    quality or if one had the quality long and the other was integer.
The rules regarding the use of T0, T1,..., T5 in arithmetic expressions were then

    · for the operator '∗' the second triplet rule was modified in that T0 had the quality long unless both T1 and T2 were integer
    · for the operator '/' the triplet rules applied except when both T1 and T2 were integers and then T0 was long-real
    · in the relevant syntactic rule, T3 had to be consistently replaced by integer, real, long-real, complex, or long-complex
    · in the syntactic rule involving ∗∗, T4 and T5 were replaced by any of the combinations given in the following

T4	T5
long-real	integer
long-real	real
long-complex	complex

T4 had the quality long whether or not T5 had this quality
·in the syntactic rule involving **abs**, T4 and T5 were replaced by any of the combinations given in the following

T4	T5
integer	integer
real	real
real	complex

Moreover, if T5 had the quality long so also did T4.

In conclusion note that the syntax of expressions made use of T0, T1,...,T9. There were a vast number of rules which stated the allowable combinations of the different types in particular situations.

4.1.5 *Conclusions on syntax*

The syntax of ALGOL W has been defined using an approach based on the syntax of ALGOL 60. But the formal idea of a grammar is more apparent and the non-terminals of the grammar have started to take on characteristics or attributes such as type and precedence level.

To cope with the increased prominence of type information the T-notation was introduced in an attempt to limit the number of syntax rules. The productions involving the T-notation were not syntax rules in the strict sense but instead they were used as a means of generating syntax rules by applying substitution.

Strictly speaking it was not necessary to introduce the T-notation. ALGOL W permitted only a finite number of types and consequently only a finite number of substitutions were possible. It was certainly convenient. But the rules regarding permitted combinations of T0, T1, etc. were very awkward. The one rule that was easy to remember and which was convenient to use was the consistent substitution rule. Though these were contained in the semantic section they were not semantic in nature, but were syntactical.

In our later discussion of ALGOL 68 it will be seen that that language permits an infinite number of possible modes or types. In these circumstances something resembling the T-notation but much more highly developed has to be introduced. The notation is then present not as a matter of convenience but as an essential. The pleasant aspects of the T-notation are retained but the awkward aspects are superseded.

Although the T-notation was introduced to reduce the number of syntax rules there were still sets of rules which were very similar in nature. We mention two such sets:

$\cdot$<T-variable-identifier>::=<identifier>
<T-array-identifier>::=<identifier>
<procedure-identifier>::=<identifier>
<T-function-identifier>::=<identifier>
<record-class-identifier>::=<identifier>
<T-field-identifier>::=<identifier>

etc.

$\cdot$<T-expression-1>::=<T-expression-2>
<T-expression-2>::=<T-expression-3>

...

<T-expression-7>::=<T-expression-8>

And, of course, there were the definitions of <identifier-list>, <bound-pair-list>, etc. It would seem that some technique for reducing the number of these would have been desirable.

Finally note that many of the criticisms of the ALGOL 60 syntactic notation were still valid. Context-dependent aspects of the syntax were still absent. Yet it would surely have been convenient to include these. The interplay between the language and the metalanguage had been reduced by careful screening but was still a nuisance.

4.1.6 Semantics

The semantics of ALGOL W was described in essentially the same style as the semantics of ALGOL 60. But there were some noticeable differences including, in conjunction with the relevant syntax, the definition of input/output routines.

As in ALGOL 60 the effect of certain constructs was defined in terms of other usually simpler constructs, with the inherent dangers. In the definition of logical expressions there appeared the following equivalences:

$\neg X$	**if** X **then false else true**
X **and** Y	**if** X **then** Y **else false**
X **or** Y	**if** X **then true else** Y

In the definition of arithmetic expressions there was the equivalence

$$X \text{ rem } Y \qquad X - (X \text{ div } Y)*Y$$

(Note the difficulty if X, for example, happened to be a procedure call.) In iterative statements it was explained that

$$\textbf{while } E \textbf{ do } <statement>$$

was exactly equivalent to

```
begin
    L: if E then
        begin <statement>; go to L end
end
```

and it was stated that L represented some identifier which was not in scope where the **while** statement occurred.

The standard functions were defined using either ALGOL W or explanatory comments and were assumed to be included in a block which encompassed each ALGOL W program. To illustrate, consider some examples:

```
integer procedure entier (real value x);
    comment the integer i such that
        i <=x<i+1;
real procedure sqrt (real value x);
    comment the positive square root of x,
        domain : x>=0;
```

Included also were certain declarations which would permit control of errors. Thus

```
record exception (logical xcpnoted;
    integer xcplimit, xcpaction;
    logical xcpmark; string(64) xcpmessage);
reference(exception)
    endfile,
    ovfl, unfl, divzero, intovfl, intdivzero,
    sqrterr, experr, lnlogerr, sincoserr;
```

These reference variables denoted end of file on input, overflow involving real or complex numbers, underflow involving real or complex numbers, division by zero, integer overflow, integer division by zero, negative argument for square root, and error in argument for the exponential function and successively *ln,log,sin* and *cos.* Briefly, if a variable had a null value the appropriate error condition would be ignored if it arose. Otherwise a procedure called *processexception* would be called with the appropriate reference variable as parameter, i.e. the reference variable associated with that error condition.

The definition of *processexception* was as follows

```
procedure processexception (reference (exception) value
    condition);
begin xcpnoted (condition) := true:
    xcplimit (condition) := xcplimit (condition) - 1;
    if (xcplimit (condition) < 0) or xcpmark (condition)
```

> then *write* ("*** *error near coordinate...-*",
> *xcpmessage (condition)*);
> if *xcplimit (condition)* < 0 then *endexecution* else
> if *specialcondition* then *resultant* := *default* else
> *resultant* := if *xcpaction (condition)* = 1
> then *adjustment* else
> if *xcpaction (condition)* = 2
> then ol else *default*

end *processexception*

Thus the

- *xcpnoted* field indicated that the exception had occurred
- *xcplimit* field indicated the maximum number of times the error could occur before the program would be terminated
- *xcpaction* field indicated the action to be performed when the error occurred – values of 1 or 2 produced standard responses
- *xcpmark* field indicated whether or not the error message had to be printed each time the error occurred
- *xcpmessage* field held the message to be printed
- ol indicated long-zero.

The nature of many of the identifiers used in the declaration of *processexception* need not concern us. But there were special procedures whose definitions could not have been given in ALGOL W, e.g. procedures to terminate the execution of the program.

A programmer then could supply his own record for each of these error situations and so take control of what happened in the event of errors; thus, for example,

> *ovfl* := *exception* (**false**, 1, 1, **true**, *"overflow occurred"*).

The various reference variables were all initialised in an appropriate way. All these variables, apart from *unfl* which was initialised to **null**, were made to refer to a special private record. Access to this could only occur indirectly through a call of the *processexception* procedure and then it caused the program to terminate.

4.2 COBOL

4.2.1 History
The programming language COBOL came into being as a result of an effort, initiated in America in May 1959, to devise a business-oriented

programming language. Around that time several different manufacturers were working on devising their own business programming language and it was generally felt that one common language would have many advantages. Not only were computer manufacturers involved, but also other groups from government establishments and academic institutions who had considerable interests in such a venture. The desire for a common language came from an awareness of the considerable benefits which would accrue from a machine-independent language – savings in time, money and reprogramming effort, availability of machine-independent programs and so on.

The group involved in the design of the language set up three committees, a Short-Range, an Intermediate-Range and a Long-Range Committee to look into the short-, medium- and long-range aspects of the development of the language. They were responsible to the CODASYL (Committee on Data Systems Language) Executive Committee which acted as a steering committee to coordinate the work of the various sub-committees. In fact, the Long-Range Committee was never properly established.

The initial intention of the designers of COBOL was to produce a language which 'favoured the maximum use of simple English language', was easy to use and would allow more people to become involved in programming. The language should be open-ended and capable of accepting change and modification, it should be problem-oriented and machine-independent, and it should make maximum use of English and avoid symbolism.

The Short-Range Committee was given a relatively brief time in which to produce a report. By December 1959 they produced a language which they definitely understood to be an interim language. Shortly thereafter this Committee was dissolved. In fact, their report turned out to be the basis of COBOL as it is known today. In the years that followed, COBOL underwent various stages of upgrading, refinement and alteration. Work on standardisation began in 1963 and in 1968 a Standard was approved by the American National Standards Institute. We shall look at this in some detail.

It should be emphasised that the Short-Range Committee saw their report as a first effort. They understood that the Intermediate-Range Committee would have the time and resources to produce a very worthwhile language. The deliberations of the Short-Range Committee were hampered by many non-technical considerations such as the short time they had to complete their work, the difficulty of achieving compatibility between various machines and the constraints imposed by manufacturers' equipment.

From an early stage, from the beginnings of the deliberations of the

Short-Range Committee, the COBOL designers were acutely aware of a need for maintenance. Accordingly comments and suggested alterations, enhancements, etc. to COBOL were channelled towards maintenance committees. This meant that major dialects of COBOL did not develop and the subsequent task of standardisation was therefore simplified.

4.2.2 The 1968 Standard

It was envisaged that the aims and objectives of the early COBOL designers would be realised in the following way:

> program text would appear in the PROCEDURE DIVISION; it would be written in words, sentences and paragraphs like normal English and paragraphs could be grouped into sections; commas, semi-colons and full stops would be used for punctuation

> data would appear in a separate DATA DIVISION and could be structured in a hierarchical manner

> machine-dependencies would be isolated in the ENVIRONMENT DIVISION so localising alterations needed to move programs to other machines.

The approach to machine-independence failed rather badly. For example: machine dependencies concerning files can appear in the FILE SECTION of the DATA DIVISION; formats of elementary items are often machine-dependent and users are often encouraged to take advantage of implementation details.

The COBOL Standard is based on the idea of *functional processing modules*; it consists of a Nucleus together with seven of these modules identified as Table Handling, Sequential Access, Random Access, Sort, Report Writer, Segmentation and Library. The Nucleus and modules are themselves divided into two or three levels, the lower levels being subsets of the higher levels. In five of the modules the lowest level is in fact empty.

The minimum standard COBOL consists of the lowest levels of the Nucleus and of each module. It thus consists of the lowest level of the Nucleus and the Table Handling and Sequential Access modules since the remaining modules have an empty lowest level. The full standard COBOL consists of the uppermost level of the Nucleus and the seven modules. We look briefly at the content of the Nucleus and the various modules.

The Nucleus contains these elements of the language necessary for the internal processing of information. It thus includes the definition etc. of verbs such as ADD, MOVE, PERFORM, IF and DISPLAY. Level 1 provides the more basic operations and the simple use of other operations. Level 2 provides the full facilities. To illustrate, the lower level permits full use of ENTER, EXAMINE, EXIT, GO, MULTIPLY, NOTE and STOP but only limited use of ACCEPT, ADD, ALTER, DIVIDE, DISPLAY, IF, MOVE, PERFORM and SUBTRACT. Moreover, level 1 does not permit the use of the full facilities for qualification, punctuation, data-name formats and figurative constants.

The Table Handling module is devoted to these aspects of the language which are used for defining, accessing and referencing items in a table. To give some flavour of the division between the different modules, the low-level module deals with fixed-length tables of one dimension, the middle-level module deals with fixed-length tables of up to three dimensions and the high-level module deals with variable-length tables.

As the names suggest, the Sequential Access module allows for the definition of and access to external sequentially ordered files and the Random Access module permits the random accessing of direct access devices. The lowest level of the Random Access module is empty. The two levels of the Sequential Access module and the two remaining levels of the Random Access module are similar in that the lower level provides basic operations and the higher level provides more sophisticated operations on input/output devices.

We summarise the content of the remaining modules:

- the Sort module provides for sorting in COBOL programs
- the Report Writer module permits the semi-automatic production of printed reports containing varying levels of detail
- the Segmentation module allows the overlaying at run-time of Procedure Division sections of program
- the Library module permits the inclusion of predefined libraries into user programs, more precisely predefined data descriptions and procedures

In preparing the Standard certain criteria were used in deciding whether language features should be included or excluded. To quote from X3.23, the ANSI COBOL Standard, the criteria used were

(1) General usefulness of an element or function in terms of
    (a) the degree of implementation shown by the Compiler Study (a study of the then-existing compilers)
    (b) acceptance by users ..., and the general experience of the committee's members
    (c) the degree to which a function is required as determined by the experience of the committee's members

(2) Functional capability of an element or function, considering redundancy

(3) Processing system capability

(4) Cost of implementation versus advantage of use

(5) Overall consistency of a defined level

(6) Upward compatibility within a module

The first two criteria were applied mainly in selecting language elements and functions for inclusion in the Standard as a whole, while the last four were especially important in assigning elements and functions to the various levels of a Functional Processing Module.

Like the FORTRAN Standard the COBOL Standard adopted a permissive approach to the problem of conforming. If extra facilities were provided by an implementation this did not render the implementation non-Standard; the Standard made no comment on what action would be taken by a compiler on encountering non-Standard features.

The main body of the COBOL Standard is divided into two sections, an introductory section and a second section containing the detailed specification of the various aspects of the language. In the second section, consecutive chapters describe Nucleus level 1, Nucleus level 2, Table Handling level 1, Table Handling level 2, Table Handling level 3 and so on through Sequential Access levels 1 and 2, Random Access levels 1 and 2, Sort levels 1 and 2, Report Writer levels 1 and 2, Segmentation levels 1 and 2 and Library levels 1 and 2.

The definition of each level of the Nucleus or of a module begins in the same manner. There is a description of the function of that module, then its level characteristics, i.e. the restrictions that distinguish that level from other levels, and finally a section on module interactions. There then follows a description of the effect of that module on the various divisions of a COBOL program.

4.2.3 The definition of clauses
Each statement is defined in much the same manner. There are usually four sections:

> Function – describes the role played by the particular clause being defined
>
> General Format – gives a kind of BNF definition of the syntax of the clause being defined
>
> Syntax Rules – imposes constraints of a context-sensitive nature
>
> General Rules – describes the semantics or meaning to be associated with a particular clause

The General Format sections are worth looking at in more detail. Terminals appear as words in capital letters or special symbols

- words in capitals which are underlined are key words and must appear when the appropriate function is used
- words in capitals which are not underlined are optional

Non-terminals appear as *generic terms* and are expressed as possibly hyphenated lower-case words sometimes with a number or letter added at the end to identify them in a discussion or explanation that follows.

Much of the definition of the COBOL language is given informally. Literals (both numeric and non-numeric), words, the statements and sentences of various kinds (conditional, compiler-directing and imperative), etc. are all defined informally using English text. Corresponding to these items are appropriate generic terms which then appear in the BNF-oriented discussion of the General Format sections.

As regards the actual use of BNF notation, the following remarks apply:

- the BNF notation does not make use of the traditional vertical bar. Whenever alternative forms of a clause are possible they are presented as Format 1, Format 2, etc.
- the brackets [ ] encompass optional portions of a format
- the brackets { } enclose a set of portions of a format from which one must be selected
- the ellipsis ... indicates repetition of the preceding section of a format
- commas and semicolons are used within formats as separators and there are rules for their admission

An example below illustrates the approach.

The syntax rules and general rules are both expressed informally in English, the former imposing further constraints on the strings of characters and the latter describing the meaning.

To illustrate the various possibilities consider the ADD statement. Its definition takes the form:

The ADD Statement
    Function. The ADD statement causes two or more numeric operands to be summed and the result stored.
General Format
Format 1

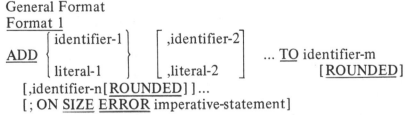

ADD $\left\{ \begin{array}{l} \text{identifier-1} \\ \text{literal-1} \end{array} \right\}$ $\left[\begin{array}{l} \text{,identifier-2} \\ \text{,literal-2} \end{array} \right]$ ... <u>TO</u> identifier-m [<u>ROUNDED</u>]

[,identifier-n[<u>ROUNDED</u>]]...
[; ON <u>SIZE</u> <u>ERROR</u> imperative-statement]

Format 2

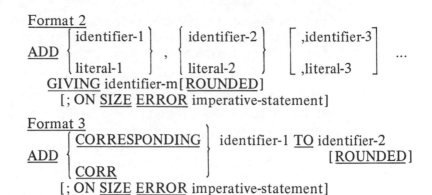

ADD { identifier-1 / literal-1 } , { identifier-2 / literal-2 } [,identifier-3 / ,literal-3] ...
GIVING identifier-m [ROUNDED]
[; ON SIZE ERROR imperative-statement]

Format 3

ADD { CORRESPONDING / CORR } identifier-1 TO identifier-2 [ROUNDED]
[; ON SIZE ERROR imperative-statement]

Syntax rules

(1) In Formats 1 and 2 each identifier must refer to an elementary numeric item, except that the identifier appearing only on the right of the word GIVING may refer to a data item that contains editing symbols

(2) Each literal must be a numeric literal

(3) The maximum size of each operand is eighteen (18) decimal digits. The composite of operands, which is that data item resulting from the superimposition of all operands, excluding the data items that follow the word GIVING, aligned on their decimal points, must not contain more than eighteen digits

(4) CORR is an abbreviation for CORRESPONDING

General rules

(1) ...

(2) If Format 1 is used, the values of the operands preceding the word T0 are added together, then the sum is added to the current value in each identifier-m, identifier-n,..., and the result is stored in each resultant identifier-m, identifier-n, ..., respectively

(3) If Format 2 is used, the values of the operands preceding the word GIVING are added together, then the sum is stored as the new value of identifier-m, which is the resultant-identifier

(4) If Format 3 is used, data items in identifier-1 are added to and stored in corresponding data items in identifier-2

(5) The compiler ensures that enough places are carried so as not to lose any significant digits during execution

The design of various clauses gives rise to certain anomalies within the syntax of COBOL:

> · since constructs have as a rule no terminator there are problems with the design of compound statements; in particular

difficulties with nested conditionals give rise to a classification of statements into imperative and conditional statements · the COPY statement is overspecified and causes difficulties both for implementors and for users.

4.2.4 The 1974 Standard

The 1968 COBOL Standard has not been the only attempt at standardising the programming language COBOL. More recently in 1974 a second Standard appeared and thereby rendered its predecessor obsolete. But there were some lessons which could be learned.

The new Standard presented a new enhanced language – extra facilities were provided including new modules and attempts were made at removing some of the inconsistencies and ambiguities in COBOL 68. The resulting language was more powerful than its predecessor but was also bigger in the sense that no serious efforts were made to improve consistency or simplicity.

The definition was again based on the idea of functional processing modules with various levels. Each module was described in a single section and not, as in the previous Standard, in separate chapters. Within a chapter, high-level features were boxed and restrictions at lower levels were described by further rules. To illustrate we look at part of the definition of the ADD statement.

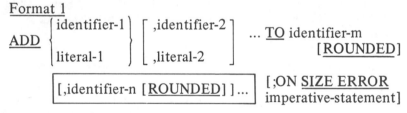

Format 1

$$\text{ADD} \left\{ \begin{array}{l} \text{identifier-1} \\ \text{literal-1} \end{array} \right\} \left[\begin{array}{l} \text{,identifier-2} \\ \text{,literal-2} \end{array} \right] \dots \underline{\text{TO}} \text{ identifier-m} \quad [\underline{\text{ROUNDED}}]$$

$$\boxed{[\text{,identifier-n } [\underline{\text{ROUNDED}}]] \dots} \quad \begin{array}{l} [;\text{ON } \underline{\text{SIZE ERROR}} \\ \text{imperative-statement}] \end{array}$$

Even within descriptive text certain parts are boxed. But this approach had the advantage that basically only one definition of ADD was required and not separate definitions for the different levels as in the previous Standard.

The general method of definition was, as the above example illustrates, similar to the previous approach though somewhat better organised and easier to follow. The various sets of brackets had their previous meaning as did underlining, etc.

Again there was a Nucleus but now eleven as opposed to seven other functional processing modules: Table Handling, Sequential I–O, Relative I–O, Indexed I–O, Sort–Merge, Report Writer, Segmentation, Library, Debug, Inter-Program Communication and Communication. Thus the two previous modules on Sequential Access and Random Access were replaced by three modules.

The Debug Module allowed a user to provide his own debugging algorithms in which to describe the conditions under which monitoring should occur at run-time. A programmer could indicate what information he required and in what detail. Level 1 provided selective debugging facilities, level 2 provided full facilities.

The Inter-Program Communication Module allowed a program to communicate with one or more other programs by permitting control to pass from one program to another and permitting access to common data items. In level 1 the names of the communicating programs had to be known at compile-time and space could be shared by such programs. In level 2 the names need not be known at compile-time; moreover a program had the ability to enquire about the availability of object-time memory of a program to which control was to be passed.

The Communications Module allowed a program to access, process and create all or parts of messages and to communicate them with local or remote communications devices. The two levels provided different levels of capability.

The criteria used in selecting items for inclusion within the 1974 Standard were similar to the criteria used for incorporating features in the earlier Standard. But there were some differences. The authors now sought overall consistency both within levels and within modules, they sought compatibility with the previous Standard, they thought about the usefulness of features in terms of the application requirements within each level of a module and they considered the state-of-the-art in compiler design and implementation.

Despite the avowed intention of making COBOL programs easily transferable the new Standard was not upward compatible with its predecessor. The list of reserved words had been extended; some facilities presented in COBOL 68 no longer existed in COBOL 74; some rules given in COBOL 68 had been clarified so that a particular implementation might no longer perform the correct action.

Further reading on COBOL Standards can be obtained from the references at the end of the book.

4.3 BASIC

The programming language BASIC is one of the most widely used and widely known programming languages. It was designed in Dartmouth College by J.G. Kemeny and T.E. Kurtz around 1964 and was intended to be friendly, easy-to-use, easy-to-learn, easy-to-remember and convenient for students. The students of Dartmouth were mainly from the social sciences and the humanities; they were not scientists. Accordingly there materialised a simple language in whose implementation the ideas of compiler, editor and operating system were merged – the distinction was unimportant for the majority of students using the system.

From within Dartmouth itself six different editions of the BASIC programming language emerged between 1964 and about 1974, because the language designers believed that for them the goals of their project were most important (i.e. the design of a simple, easy-to-use language) and they saw improvements that could be made on earlier editions. All over, BASIC flourished and numerous implementations appeared; the task of writing a compiler or interpreter was relatively simple. As might be expected the numerous implementations resulted in more versions of BASIC.

In 1973 some nine years after the original BASIC language was designed, initial efforts on standardisation began. The problems that then arose were severe and similar to the problems that faced those involved with the 1966 FORTRAN Standard. Fortunately, however, most editions of BASIC accepted a common set of statements, a common core, and provided further features to complement this core. This provided the clue or basis for the standardisation effort.

It was intended that the American National Standard for BASIC would take the form of a core or nucleus together with a series of upward compatible modules. These modules – enhancement modules – could then be implemented and each, when combined with the nucleus, would form a subset of the full BASIC language. These enhancement modules would contain facilities for the manipulation of files, strings, matrices, formatted input and output, etc. Note the similarity to the philosophy underlying the COBOL Standard.

The American National Standard for the core language appeared in 1978 – the core became known as Minimal BASIC. Like other Standards it defined the syntax of programs, the form of input and output and the semantics of syntactically legal programs. But it went further. It defined also:

- the precision and range of numeric quantities which would be acceptable on input or would be produced on output
- errors and exceptional conditions which had to be detected, and it stated the manner in which these should be handled

The precision of numbers had to be at least six significant decimal digits. The permissible range of numbers was defined in terms of a largest value, machine infinity, and a smallest positive value, machine infinitesimal. To conform to the Standard, machine infinity had to be at least 1E+38 and machine infinitesimal had to be at most 1E–38.

A program conformed to the Standard provided each statement separately and the combined set of statements were syntactically legal and had a meaning defined by the Standard. A processor conformed to the Standard provided that it accepted and properly interpreted programs conforming to the Standard. This included such considerations as dealing properly with numerical precision and magnitude and with errors and exceptions. Moreover a Standard processor had to

- report reasons for rejecting any program not conforming to the Standard (recall that enhancement modules would also become part of the Standard)
- include documentation covering the attitude of the implementation to undefined or implementation-defined features

The Standard defined the following statements:

LET, GO TO, GOSUB-RETURN, STOP, FOR-NEXT, PRINT, INPUT, DATA, READ, RESTORE, RANDOMIZE, IF-THEN, ON-GO TO, DEF-FN, DIM, REM

It did not define commands for the editing, listing, running, etc. of programs, nor did it contain matrix routines, etc. Consequently the Standard recognised the fact that BASIC could be used interactively or in batch mode.

Most of the statements defined in the Standard were explained in the same way. There were six types of section:

- general description sections indicated the statement(s) of the language to be treated and indicated the general syntactic form of those statements, e.g.

    LET variable = expression

- syntax rules for the statement under consideration were explained in a kind of BNF notation; it admitted that these defined too large a set of statements and that some syntactically correct statements would not have a meaning
- examples (valid) of the use of the current statement(s) were given
- semantics sections prohibited certain constructions which were syntactically correct but would not be given a meaning in the Standard; a meaning was then given to all the remaining syntactically correct constructions
- exceptions sections basically included mention of possible run-time errors
- remarks sections gave explanatory notes to users and recommendations to implementors

To illustrate the kind of material contained in the last two sections we give some examples. Included in exceptions sections were remarks about division by zero, evaluation of expressions resulting in overflow, assigning strings to numeric variables, executing a RETURN statement without having executed a GOSUB statement, passing a zero or negative number as an argument to the LOG function, and so on. Included in the

remarks sections were recommendations to implementors concerning
the accuracy of machine arithmetic, what to do if EXP(X) produced a
value less than machine infinitesimal and there were comments on using
step lengths of magnitude 0.1 in a loop.

We illustrate the nature of the BASIC Standard by quoting the section on assignment statements.

> *General description*
> A let-statement provides for the assignment of the value of an
> expression to a variable. The general syntactic form of the let-
> statement shall be
>
> > LET variable = expression
>
> *Syntax*
> 1. let-statement = numeric-let-statement/string-let-
>   statement
> 2. numeric-let-statement = LET numeric-variable equals-sign
>   numeric-expression
> 3. string-let-statement = LET string-variable equals-sign
>   string-expression
>
> *Examples*
> LET   P = 3.14159
> ...
> *Semantics*
> The expression is evaluated (see...) and its value is assigned to
> the variable to the left of the equals sign
> *Exceptions*
> A string datum contains too many characters (fatal)

Towards the end of the Standard were two sections of some interest:

> · there was a glossary of terms used within the Standard: it ex-
>   plained the meaning to be attributed within the Standard itsel
>   to phrases such as accept, batch mode, can, must, nesting, ove
>   flow, rounding, shall, significant digits, user interaction
> · there was a list of implementation-defined features of the
>   language: recalling that the Standard defined a *minimum*
>   level of precision for numbers and a *minimum* acceptable
>   range of numbers, the following were all implementation-
>   dependent – the precision and accuracy of numbers, the size
>   of printing zones, the pseudo-random number sequence, the
>   margin for output (i.e. the maximum number of columnar
>   printing positions per line), etc.

THE DEFINITIONS OF PL/I

5.1 The history of PL/I and its definitions

The programming language PL/I was born out of a desire by IBM to devise one all-purpose programming language which would satisfy the needs of all its customers, scientists, commercial users, systems programmers, real-time programmers and so on. Scientific users wanted floating-point arithmetic, arrays, subroutines and efficient object code; commercial users wanted decimal arithmetic, string handling, sophisticated input/output and, again, efficient object programs; other groups made use of variable-length facilities, pattern matching, list-processing facilities and fast responses for real-time applications.

The group involved in the initial design of the new language first met in October 1963 and produced their first document describing the language in March 1964. They had a mainly FORTRAN background and it was natural therefore that they should seek to extend FORTRAN and thereby achieve their desired aims. But they soon realised that this would be impractical. In the event, the new language took

- from FORTRAN, the ideas of separate compilation, subroutines, sharing common data, and the DO loop
- from COBOL, the data structures, input/output facilities and report generating facilities
- from ALGOL 60, block structure and recursion

and seemed to be oriented to use on OS/360, the operating system for the IBM System 360 series of computers.

In its initial stages the language was called NPL (New Programming Language). Its initial design was carried out by a joint IBM/SHARE Committee (SHARE was an IBM users' group). They saw as their objectives the production of a language which would permit

- freedom of expression, i.e. if some sequence of characters seemed sensible then it should be allowed and given its expected meaning
- full access to machine and operating system facilities; then the programmer should have no reason to resort to machine code

- machine-independence; thus programs should be capable of being moved to other machines
- modularity, i.e. to omit without penalty in terms of compile-time or run-time efficiency certain aspects of the language; this had the effect of making readily available subsets of the language which would be convenient for teaching purposes
- simplicity for novice programmers by allowing default attributes which need not be specified
- ease of programming by allowing a free-format in the writing of programs and by trying to take decisions which would reduce typing or punching errors.

These objectives were also governed by a desire to achieve efficient object code.

In its initial stages the language was designed in a very pragmatic fashion. The reference documents of the time contained many omissions, ambiguities and inconsistencies. No attempt had been made to produce a formal definition of any kind, and the reference documents were similar to user manuals.

After the initial design phase the responsibility for the language and its compilers moved to the IBM Laboratories at Hursley in England. There work began on removing irregularities and on improving the language. At Hursley and in the IBM Laboratories in Vienna (Austria) work on the definition of the language proceeded. These efforts, as might be expected, unearthed many deficiencies in the initial design, and the language that eventually emerged bore little resemblance to the original language. The new language even had a different name, PL/I, since in Britain NPL referred to the National Physical Laboratory. Thus the work of formal definition and the work of defining, or rather regularising, the language went hand-in-hand.

Work on producing a formal definition of PL/I began around 1969, some years after the first PL/I manuals and texts had appeared. Since PL/I was an IBM language, the major efforts of producing a formal definition were concentrated in IBM Laboratories, in Vienna and in Hursley.

The Vienna group's approach was based on some earlier work of J. McCarthy, P.J. Landin, C.C. Elgot and A. Robinson. As far as the syntax was concerned a distinction was made between *concrete syntax* (which effectively described the way in which programs appeared on paper) and *abstract syntax* (which more closely resembled the internal parse-tree representation of programs and was devoid of irrelevant detail).

The Vienna group also provided a formal definition of the semantics of PL/I. Their work in this area was based on the observation that semantics could be defined by a particular implementation; the effect produced by an implementation described the semantics. At first sight this was not a particularly useful observation since, in general, different implementations would accept different sets of programs or interpret the same program in different ways. This might be due to errors in the compiler but it might also be due to such considerations as the particular size of machine (and therefore the maximum size of symbol tables, etc), the permitted magnitude of numbers, and so on. However, if the implementation that was chosen to define the semantics of a programming language could be idealised in some sense then this approach did have some merit. This has come to be known as the *operational approach* to the definition of formal semantics and has origins in McCarthy's work on LISP.

The Vienna group then described the semantics of PL/I by describing in detail the effect of executing a PL/I program on a hypothetical computer, an abstract machine. The particular machine they chose was a rather strange model and was quite unlike any real computer. Rather conveniently and understandably it did not possess annoying limitations on the size of store, etc. But its architecture was also quite peculiar. The semantics of PL/I were described by writing instructions which indicated the way in which the state of the machine was altered when a particular instruction or piece of program was executed. These instructions were themselves defined formally in terms of their effect on the machine state.

The methods used by the Vienna group for describing programming languages have come to be known as the *Vienna Definition Language,* VDL for short.

The Hursley group, on the other hand, did not adopt such a rigorous approach to defining semantics although their basic idea was similar. They also made use of an underlying abstract machine and aimed to describe the semantics of PL/I by describing the effect of executing a program on this machine. The machine they used had an architecture which, though still unrelated to any particular computer hardware, more closely resembled normal computer architecture. Instead of writing instructions for their machine to describe semantics, a more informal and less rigorous approach was taken. The changes to the machine state were described by machine instructions; but these instructions were described in algorithmic terms using English. These algorithms in turn made use of a small set of standard basic instructions, akin to the microcode of a real computer. Any particular implementation did not need to perform the algorithms as described in the definition but would be permitted to optimise for greater efficiency.

The ANSI PL/I Standard that was eventually produced in August

1976 was based on the Hursley work. It was felt that the strict formality of the Vienna group would impede acceptance of the Standard, even though it was realised that a rigorous definition was essential. With its acceptance as an ANSI Standard came the implication that if a US government agency wished to buy a computer with a standard PL/I compiler then that compiler had to conform to the ANSI Standard.

In this chapter we shall look closely at both the Vienna and Hursley approaches to language definition. The Hursley work we shall study by looking at the PL/I Standard; its importance immediately follows from the widespread use and importance of PL/I itself. The VDL is also important and has had a considerable influence on methods of language definition.

5.2 The PL/I Standard

We begin by reviewing briefly the overall method adopted in the Standard for describing the programming language PL/I. Basically it involves a complete definition of the form of PL/I programs together with a description of their meaning. The latter takes the form of a description of the effect of running a program on an abstract machine.

In the Standard every detail of PL/I is specified in one of three ways:

- the precise specification is given
- the matter is 'implementation-defined', e.g. the maximum value of numbers
- the matter is explicitly 'undefined', e.g. the order of evaluation of subscripts.

Thus there are no gaps present and it is claimed that the definition is complete.

To conform to the Standard an implementation must provide all the facilities specified in the Standard. Moreover any extension of the language provided by a particular implementation should not affect any program not making use of such extensions. Note therefore that the Standard does not insist that a given program (and its accompanying data) should produce the same result with different implementations.

In looking at the various aspects of the definition below it should be noted that there are strong similarities between the definition and many aspects of the traditional compilation process. There is an idealised computer, an abstract machine, which corresponds to the usual concept of a computer: it has input and output; its memory holds both programs and data; it possesses instructions or operations defined by algorithms which make use of a small set of standard basic instructions

– the latter can be likened to the microcode of a normal computer, and programs are executed on it. The programs we look at are essentially parsers, interpreters, etc. and these run on this abstract machine.

5.2.1 Summary of the definition method

Source programs are presented as a sequence of characters or symbols. The form of these programs is described by a concrete syntax which imposes on the input a tree structure; this is then referred to as the *concrete form* of the given input. The translation from a string of symbols to a concrete form is performed by a parser program.

As with the syntax of many other languages, the concrete syntax describes too large a class of programs. A variant of BNF notation is used and so context-sensitive and other restrictions are not imposed at this stage.

The concrete forms of programs are then processed by a constructor program which performs tasks such as re-organising statements, including default options, removing irrelevant detail such as delimiters (e.g. the equals symbols in assignment statements) including checks of various kinds, and so on. The output is an *abstract form,* a version of the original input suitable for interpreting. The set of abstract forms is described by an abstract syntax, again expressed in a variant of BNF.

All the programs used in the Standard are defined within the Standard. In particular, there are definitions of the parser and the constructor and these together combine to form the translator. The translator therefore runs on the abstract machine, it accepts sequences of symbols as input and eventually produces as output an abstract form. It essentially performs the traditional lexical and syntactic phases of the compilation process including certain kinds of context-sensitive checks.

The next stage in the definition process is to interpret the abstract program. This is done by an interpreter which has as inputs the abstract program together with the input datasets, i.e. the data of the source program, and it produces a set of output datasets. The abstract machine has locations for program variables and it holds instructions and essentially possesses a program counter. As the interpretation of an abstract program progresses the state of the abstract machine, i.e. the contents of the variable locations and the program counter, change. The sequence of changes in state describes the meaning of the original source program.

All the information inside the abstract machine is represented as a single tree structure. Just as grammars can be used to describe a set of possible parse trees so also a grammar can be used to describe the various possible machine states. The resulting grammar is called the *machine-state grammar.*

To describe the programming language completely then, it becomes necessary to describe several quantities in complete detail. Firstly there are the three sets of syntax: concrete, abstract and machine-state. Moreover the translator (containing the parser and constructor) and interpreter need to be carefully described.

The Standard is organised in such a way that chapter 1 gives an introduction of the method of definition including the metalanguage, the machine states and what it means to conform to the Standard. Chapters 2 to 9 then describe successively the concrete syntax, the abstract syntax, the translator, the PL/I interpreter, flow of control, storage and assignment, input and output and finally expressions and conversion.

The main aim of the Standard was to describe the semantics of PL/I in terms of state changes of an abstract machine. In defining these changes the interpreter defines a particular order in which the various changes should take place.

An implementation of PL/I conforms to the Standard if and only if, given a standard program, the implementation makes the same state changes as defined in the definition; if a program is in some sense illegal or invalid any interpretation whatsoever is permitted. The Standard also permits certain carefully specified deviations from this: it permits different orders for the evaluation of expressions, limitations on the size of programs, on the size of data, certain restrictions with regard to input and output, etc.

Certain aspects of the definition are implementation-defined. There are forty six such aspects of the definition and these include such features as the length of file titles, items output by PUTDATA, results of numeric conversions, the number of digits in the exponent part of floating-point numbers, the precision of integers.

5.2.2 Syntactic notation

As mentioned previously there are three sets of syntax that have to be described, the concrete, the abstract and the machine-state syntaxes. These are all expressed in a variant of BNF notation. To distinguish clearly between the three, different kinds of metalinguistic brackets are used:

- the concrete syntax uses ⊰ and ⊱
- the abstract syntax uses < and >
- the machine state syntax uses ⩽ and ⩾

The terminal symbols of the concrete syntax are just letters, digits, and so on – in fact any of the fifty seven characters in the PL/I character set. These are just the characters which a programmer writes or types in preparing a program. The terminals for the other two sets of syntax

100

are surrounded by the appropriate kind of metalinguistic bracket and are underlined, thereby distinguishing them from non-terminals.

The concrete syntax of PL/I is in fact split into three different levels, low, middle and high: the low-level syntax deals with the formation of identifiers, constants and delimiters; the middle-level syntax deals with sentences, i.e. the phrases that can occur between semi-colons in a PL/I procedure; the high-level deals with procedures and executable units such as conditionals, ON-statements, blocks etc. The parser which deals with the concrete syntax is constructed in such a way that it operates at three levels, corresponding to the different levels of syntax.

Accordingly five different sets of syntax can now be envisaged. In the Standard the different rules are marked CH (concrete, high-level), CM (concrete, middle-level), CL (concrete, low-level), A (abstract) or M (machine-state) to distinguish the part of the syntax to which that rule belongs. The five sets are of course interrelated and together form one large syntax.

As previously mentioned the syntax is written in a variant of BNF notation. Non-terminals ending with '-list' are used to denote any non-zero number of items. Similarly '-commalist' denotes any non-zero number of items separated by commas. As an illustration, consider

CL15. ⟨integer⟩ ::= ⟨digit-list⟩

The right-hand side of a syntax rule may make use of the concatenation of terminals and non-terminals together with the use of the vertical bar | (the or-symbol) with the usual meaning. But also used is the bullet symbol '·'; this indicates that the terminals and/or non-terminals which appear on either side of it can appear in either order – it thus indicates permutation and is useful in indicating that order does not matter. Its use reflects the fact that PL/I permits options, declarations, etc. to appear in an arbitrary order.

The right-hand sides of productions are referred to as *syntactical expressions*. The metalinguistic operators in these expressions are *concatenation, permutation* and *or,* and they are given a descending order of precedence. The operands are either terminals or non-terminals or bracketed expressions. The brackets { and } are used to imply that one of a set of options should be chosen; the brackets [and] surround an optional piece of syntax which can be either included or excluded.

To illustrate some of the ideas outlined above we give some examples.

CH7. ⟨begin-block⟩::= ⟨begin-statement⟩ [⟨unit-list⟩] ⟨ending⟩

CM3. ⊰prefixed-clause⊱::= [⊰prefix-list⊱]
{ ⊰if-clause⊱ |
ON ⊰condition-name-commalist⊱
[SNAP] }
CL8. ⊰identifier⊱::= ⊰letter⊱ | ⊰identifier⊱ { ⊰letter⊱ |
⊰digit⊱ | _ }
CM107. ⊰write-statement⊱::= WRITE { ⊰file-option⊱ ·
⊰from-option⊱ · [⊰keyfrom-option⊱] } ;

But not all of the syntax rules are so well formed. The abstract syntax in particular contains some peculiarities. To illustrate some of the exceptional rules we look at examples.

A187. <integer>::=

Following this rule is a statement that the category A187 is defined as a ⊰symbol-list⊱ corresponding to the sequence of characters in an ⊰integer⊱.

A37. <number-of-digits> ::= <integer>
Constraint: the <integer> must not be zero.

(The stated constraint appears within the syntax section.)

A48. <options> ::=
This category is implementation-defined.

Again the above remark is included within the syntactic description.

In the usual way a grammar defines a parse tree. The definition of PL/I makes such frequent reference to these trees that a special notation for the representation of these trees is introduced. We illustrate the notation for the *enumeration of trees,* as it is called, by example.

A tree with root node <a>, and with immediate subnodes <b>, <c>, <d> would appear as

<a> :
<b>
<c>
<d> ;

The above typographical layout is not essential but acts as an aid in visualising the tree. The colon follows the root and the list of subtrees is terminated by a semicolon.

Trees of greater depth can be represented in a similar fashion. For example

```
<a>:
    <b>:
        <c>
        <d>;
    <e>:
        <f>;
;
```

is an enumeration of the tree

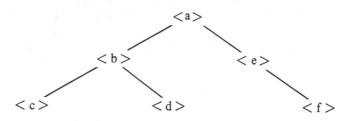

In certain circumstances it is convenient to be able to talk about sub-trees of larger trees. A convenient way of doing this is to give the sub-trees names. This feature can be incorporated in a tree enumeration by following a node with a comma and then its name. Thus

```
<a>:
    <b>, tree 1
        <c>
        <d>;
    ...
```

permits tree 1 to refer to the subtree whose root is <b> and whose two descendent nodes are <c> and <d>.

The notation used for the enumeration of trees is not restricted in application to the abstract syntax of the language but can be applied in discussing trees of any kind.

One new feature of the PL/I syntax is the appearance of context-sensitive information in the description of the abstract syntax – it would not make sense to use this in the concrete syntax of the Standard. It appears in two forms. Consider

A80. <goto-statement>::= <value-reference> (scalar & label)

The information in round brackets is of a context-sensitive nature referring to the <value-reference>. Consider also

A170. <variable-reference>::=
       [<locator-qualifier>] <declaration-designator> (variable)
       [<identifier-list>] [<subscript-list>]
       [<by-name-parts-list>] <data-description>

A designator node – as exemplified by <declaration-designator> – is essentially the name of another node and should be interpreted as a pointer to that node. In the particular example illustrated here the node would be pointer to a declaration of some kind in another part of the syntax tree.

5.2.3 The concrete and abstract syntaxes

We illustrate the difference between the concrete and the abstract syntaxes of PL/I by giving some illustrative examples. As might be expected many parts of the two sets of syntax are similar. See figures 5.1–3. One area of noticeable difference, however, is the declaration section of the syntax: the translator goes to great lengths to ensure that the abstract syntax is more complete than the concrete – default options are made explicit, etc.

Concrete syntax
CM 82. ⟨assignment-statement⟩ ::= ⟨reference-commalist⟩ = ⟨expression⟩
[, BY NAME];

Abstract syntax
A90. <assignment-statement> ::= <target-reference-list> <expression>

Fig. 5.1. Assignment statement syntax.

Concrete syntax
CH4. ⟨if-statement⟩ ::= ⟨if-clause⟩ { ⟨executable-unit⟩ |
⟨balanced-unit⟩ ELSE ⟨executable-unit⟩}

Abstract syntax
A75. <if-statement> ::= <test> <then-unit> [<else-unit>]

Fig. 5.2. If statement syntax.

Concrete syntax
CM110. ⟨get-statement⟩ ::= GET { ⟨get-file⟩ | ⟨get-string⟩};

Abstract syntax
A118. <get-statement> ::= <get-file> | <get-string>

Fig. 5.3. Get statement syntax.

The process of going from the concrete to the abstract is performed by the translator and the definition of this translator is given in the PL/I Standard. We reproduce it here:

104

Operation: translate(t)

          where t is a ⊰symbol-list⊱.

          result: an <abstract-external-procedure>.

Step 1. Perform parse(t,⊰procedure⊱) to obtain a ⊰procedure⊱, cep. Append a ⊰concrete-external-procedure⊱: cep; to the ⊰translation-state⊱.

Step 2. Perform complete-concrete-procedure.

Step 3. Let aep be an <abstract-external-procedure>.

Step 4. For each ⊰declaration⊱,d which is a block-component of the ⊰concrete-external-procedure⊱ perform create-declaration(d) to obtain a <declaration>,ad, and append ad to the <declaration-list> in aep.

Step 5. For each <declaration>,d which is a block-component of aep and which contains at least one ⊰expression-designator⊱ or ⊰reference-designator⊱, perform replace-concrete-designators(d).

Step 6. Let p be the ⊰procedure⊱ immediate component of the ⊰concrete-external-procedure⊱. Perform create-procedure(p) to obtain a <procedure>,ap, and attach ap to aep.

Step 7. Delete the ⊰concrete-external-procedure⊱.

Step 8. Perform validate-procedure(aep).

Step 9. Return aep.

This indicates the manner in which the various operations are defined. The approach is semi-formal. In the translator there are nine separate steps and these in turn invoke other programs. Step 1 for example invokes the parser. Its definition is given later. The other steps carry out the tasks of the constructor. Due to the number of default options in PL/I programs the first phase of the constructor is to complete declarations by inserting all the default attributes, adding default options on statements and making explicit some declarations which were previously only implicit. The result of these actions is a tree in a standard form. The next phase of the constructor is to check certain context-sensitive requirements. Finally an abstract tree is produced.

    The design of the parser differs from that of the translator in the sense that it consists of a sequence of cases rather than a sequence of steps. In these circumstances only one of the cases is executed. However, recursive calls of the parser can occur. If, for example, the parser is asked to produce a syntax tree for a non-terminal of the high-level syntax, it does this by first finding a tree for a non-terminal of the middle-level syntax, namely ⊰sentence-list⊱, and then invoking the high-level parser to produce from this the required syntax tree. In effect, therefore, there are three different parsers corresponding to the three different levels of syntax.

Operation: parse(sl,n)
                where sl is a ⟨symbol-list⟩,
                       n is a tree with a single node, whose type is
                       a non-terminal category in the Concrete
                       Syntax.
                result: a complete tree with respect to the Concrete
                       Syntax for n.

Case 1. The type of n is a non-terminal of the high-level syntax.
Perform parse(sl,⟨sentence-list⟩) to obtain a ⟨sentence-list⟩,snl. Perform high-level-parse(snl,n) to obtain nt.
Return nt.

Case 2. The type of n is a non-terminal of the middle-level syntax.
Perform parse(sl,⟨pli-text⟩) to obtain a ⟨pli-text⟩,pt.
Perform middle-level-parse(pt,n) to obtain nt.
Return nt.

Case 3. The type of n is a non-terminal of the low-level syntax.
Perform low-level-parse(sl,n) to obtain nt.
Return nt.

The low-level parser is an example of an operation which does not make use of any other operations and so can be examined in isolation. Essentially it performs the task of a lexical analyser.

Operation: low-level-parse(sl,n)
                where sl is a ⟨symbol-list⟩,
                       n is a tree with a single node, whose type is
                       a non-terminal category-name at the low-
                       level syntax.
                result: a complete tree with respect to the low-
                       level syntax for n.

Step 1. There must exist one and only one tree, nt, which is a complete tree with respect to the low-level syntax for n, such that the following conditions are true:

(1) the concrete-representation of nt is exactly the same as the concrete-representation of sl, and

(2) every occurrence of ⟨/*⟩ or ⟨*/⟩ in the concrete-representation of nt must be such that the ⟨/⟩ and ⟨*⟩ are nodes of a ⟨comment⟩ category or are contained in a ⟨non-delimiter⟩, and

(3) of all possible trees satisfying conditions (1) and (2), nt is that one containing the least number of ⟨delimiter-pair⟩s and ⟨delimiter⟩s.

Step 2. Return nt.

Note that the various operations of the abstract machine make frequent use of words such as 'let', 'perform', 'if'. These all indicate different forms of instructions – thus there are perform instructions, etc. – and the way in which these have to be executed is described informally; the obvious interpretations apply.

At any given time precisely one operation in either the <control-state> or the <program-state> of the machine is active. If the <program-state> is non-empty the active operation is the rightmost operation in the <operation-list> of the <program-state>. If the <program-state> is null the active operation is the rightmost operation in the <operation-list> of the <control-state>.

Operations can cause various effects. They can invoke other operations (like procedures or subroutines), they can cause changes in the <machine-state>, they can change operands, return results or produce any combination of these effects. The individual operations of the machine are not defined in a formal sense. They are defined semi-formally in the manner used in defining the operations, parse, etc., which we looked at earlier.

5.2.4 The interpreter
During the interpretation phase the abstract machine has a form described by the syntax rule

> M1. <machine-state> ::= <program>
> <control-state>
> <interpretation-state>

where

> M2. <control-state> ::= <operation-list>

and

> M6. <interpretation-state> :: <program-state>
> < allocated-storage >
> [<dataset-list>]

The machine operates as follows. The abstract program <program> is interpreted by the instructions or operations which constitute the <control-state>. The internal run-time state of the machine is reflected in the combination of the <program-state> and the <allocated-storage>. The former contains instructions and the latter represents the data areas in main store. The input/output appears in the form of <dataset-list> where each dataset makes use of <alpha> and <omega> for the starter and terminator respectively.

Both the <control-state> and the <program-state> contain instructions. To draw a distinction between them the <control-state> contains instructions analogous to those belonging to the system software of the

107

normal computer system. It therefore contains instructions for the parser, constructor, etc. When the object program has to be interpreted control is passed to the instructions in the ＜ program-state ＞. On completion of this, control returns again to the instructions in the ＜control-state＞.

To understand the way in which the abstract machine operates, each ＜operation＞ has associated with it an operation subtree which contains the name of the operation, the name of the parameters, etc. and control information indicating how far execution has progressed, a kind of program counter. When an operation has to be performed a new operation tree is appended at the rightmost end of the currently active ＜operation-list＞, execution of the current operation is suspended temporarily and the new operation invoked. On the other hand, when an operation ends its operation tree is deleted and control moves to the next or invoking operation. In this way the functioning of the abstract machine progresses.

We demonstrate the actions of the interpreter by looking at two kinds of statements whose syntax we have already discussed. These are the conditional and the assignment statements. These are interpreted by the execute-if-statement and the execute-assignment-statement respectively; in so doing the meanings of conditionals and assignments are thereby defined.

Operation: execute-assignment-statement(ast)
            where ast is an ＜assignment-statement＞.
Step 1. Perform Steps 1.1 and 1.2 in either order.
   Step 1.1. Let tr be the leftmost ＜target-reference＞ of the ＜target-reference-list＞ of ast. Perform evaluate-target-reference(tr) to obtain the ＜evaluated-target＞,et.
   Step 1.2. Let e be the ＜expression＞ of ast. Perform evaluate-expression(e) to obtain an ＜aggregate-value＞,v.
Step 2. Perform assign(et,v,d), where d is the ＜data-description＞ immediately contained in e.
Step 3.
   Case 3.1. ast contains no unevaluated ＜target-reference＞. Perform normal-sequence.
   Case 3.2. ast contains one or more unevaluated ＜target-reference＞s.
            Let tr be the leftmost unevaluated ＜target-reference＞. Perform evaluate-target-reference(tr) to obtain the ＜evaluated-target＞,et. Go to Step 2.

108

Operation: execute-if-statement(ifs)
            where ifs is an <if-statement>.
Step 1. Let e be the <expression> immediate component of
        the <test> of ifs. Perform establish-truth-value(e) to
        obtain tv.
Step 2.
    Case 2.1. tv is <true>.
               Replace the immediate component of the current
               <executable-unit-designator> by a designator of
               the <executable-unit> of the <then-unit> of ifs.
    Case 2.2. tv is <false> and ifs simply contains an <else-
               unit>,eu.
               Replace the immediate component of the current
               <executable-unit-designator> by a designator of
               the <executable-unit> of eu.
    Case 2.3. tv is <false> and ifs does not simply contain an
               <else-unit>.
               Perform normal-sequence.

Although we have not specified the meaning of every aspect of these
definitions the intention should be clear. Note in the assignment statement definition the use of the assign operation. Hidden within this are
all kinds of details regarding the type conversions necessary before a
value can be planted in a particular location.

5.2.5   Combining the different aspects of the PL/I definition
We have looked at the manner of operation of both the translator and
the interpreter. These have been presented as separate entities which in
a sense they are. The translator produces an abstract program from a
given source and the interpreter interprets this. To be more accurate
the interpreter and translator are operations which are invoked by the
operation define-program.

Operation: define-program
Step 1. Perform translation-phase.
Step.2. Perform interpretation-phase.
Step 3. No action. (Reaching this point indicates the successful
        completion of the definition algorithm.)

During the two phases of translation and interpretation the machine
state differs.

M1. <machine-state>::= <program>
                        <control-state>

$$[<\text{translation-state}> \mid$$
$$<\text{interpretation-state}>]$$

M2. $<\text{control-state}>::= <\text{operation-list}>$

M3. $<\text{translation-state}>::= [<\!\!\!\prec\text{concrete-external-procedure}\succ\!\!\!>]$

M4. $\prec\text{concrete-external-procedure}\succ::= [\prec\text{declaration-}$
$$\text{commalist}\succ]$$
$$\prec\text{procedure}\succ$$

M5. $<\text{operation}> ::=$

The exact structure of $<\text{operation}>$ is left unformalized and unspecified. It must have adequate structure and capacity to represent the carrying out of the actions of an operation. This includes designating the particular operation and the current position within it, holding the operands given to the operation, and holding the values of any variables used by the operation.

Note that the different syntaxes, the concrete and the abstract, now appear under the one syntax, namely the definition of a $<\text{machine-state}>$. Initially the machine is set in a state represented by the tree.

$<\text{machine-state}>$:
  $<\text{program}>$
  $<\text{control-state}>$:
     $<\text{operation-list}>$:
        $<\text{operation}>$ for define-program.

Note that at first the $<\text{translation-state}>$ is empty. The $<\text{operation}>$ for define-program is then set in motion. From the definition of define-program it can be seen that the first action is the invoking of the translation-phase operation. This is thus added to the rightmost end of the $<\text{operation-list}>$ and becomes the active operation. In this way execution progresses.

For completeness we now give the definitions of translation-phase.

Operation: translation-phase

Step 1. Append $<\text{translation-state}>$ to the $<\text{machine-state}>$.

Step 2.

   Step 2.1. Obtain, from a source outside this definition, a sequence of characters composing a putative PL/I external procedure, constructed in the form of a $\prec\text{symbol-list}\succ$,sl.

   Step 2.2. Perform translate(sl) to obtain an $<\text{abstract-external-procedure}>$,aep. Append aep to the $<\text{abstract-external-procedure-list}>$ in the $<\text{program}>$.

Step 2.3. Optionally go to Step 2.
Step 3. Perform validate-program.
Step 4. Delete the <translation-state>.

At the end of the translation phase there is now an abstract program <program>. The last action of the translation phase is to delete the <translation-state>. Then the operation tree for translation-phase is itself deleted and control returns to the define-program operation which then invokes the interpretation-phase operation.

The definition of the interpretation-phase is given below. The datasets are obtained, a suitable entry-point for the program is obtained, and control is passed to the interpret operation which

· sets up appropriate input and output datasets
· attaches to the <machine-state> an <interpretation-state>
· attaches to the <program-state> component of the <interpretation-state> a <program-control> which contains an <operation-list>
· passes control to the rightmost operation in the <operation-list>.

Operation: interpretation-phase
Step 1. Obtain, from a source outside this definition, the following items:
  (1) A collection of information to be used for input/ output, constructed in the form of a suitable <dataset-list>,dl.
  (2) A designation, as the first to be activated, of one of the <entry-point>s of a <procedure> simple component of <program>, constructed in the form of a suitable <entry-value>,ev. Such an <entry-point> must exist and must not have <parameter-name-list> or <returns-descriptor> components.
Step 2. Perform interpret(dl,ev.)

On successful completion of the program, or on abnormal termination, control will return to the <operation-list> of the <control-state>.

5.3 The Vienna Definition Language

As mentioned in the introduction to this chapter the Vienna Definition Language (VDL) was designed at the IBM Laboratories in Vienna with a view to describing in a formal way the programming language PL/I. The method is applicable to a wide range of programming languages.

Many of the ideas were first applied to LISP.

The VDL, like the formalism for language definition used in the PL/I Standard, makes use of concrete syntax, abstract syntax and an interpreter. In the same kind of way parsers, interpreters, etc. are all required for a complete definition. But the mechanism is different and in what follows we examine it closely.

The concrete syntax in the VDL is described in a form of BNF notation. It describes the form of source programs and imposes on them a tree structure. The abstract syntax, on the other hand, describes a form of the source program which is more suitable for the interpreter. Irrelevant details are removed and only the essential structure of a program remains. The abstract programs are described as trees. The mechanism for their definition is not BNF notation but is a completely new mechanism which we now introduce.

The abstract syntax will be defined in such a way that it will portray the essential structure of constructions in the programming language, not the way these are written on paper. Thus for assignment statements, for example, it matters only that there is a left part or destination and a right part or source. It is irrelevant whether in an actual program the assignment is written as, for example,

> destination = source
> destination ← source
> source → destination

or even as

> destination, source,:=.

In fact, the constructions will be represented by an object which can be depicted as a tree, the various phrases or branches of the tree being selected by appropriate selectors. The above assignment statement, for example, might appear as either of the trees in figure 5.4. Note that source and destination are selectors which select appropriate parts of the assignment statement construction; in fact the two trees in the diagram are equivalent.

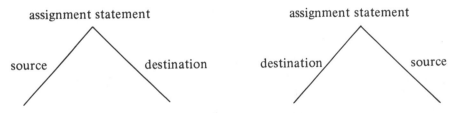

Fig. 5.4. Alternative but equivalent trees.

Preliminary to our study of syntax, therefore, will be a discussion about trees. It will be necessary to look at ways of constructing and manipulating trees, ways of selecting subtrees, etc. In the end it will transpire that trees are of more general use than has been described above for they will be used also in the description of the semantics.

In the VDL the semantics of programming languages will be defined by describing the changes in state which should take place in an abstract machine as a particular program is being executed; in effect, an interpreter for the programming language must be written. The state of the machine will be represented by a tree of the kind previously mentioned.

We begin therefore by looking at trees, or objects as they are called in the VDL. Objects come in two forms, elementary objects and composite objects. The elementary objects appear at the leaves of the trees, the trees themselves are the composite objects. In fact, the elementary objects will represent the variables, numbers, constants, etc. which appear in programs.

5.3.1 The set of objects

We presuppose some non-empty set of *elementary objects, EO*; the elements of this set are usually represented by *eo* possibly decorated - with subscripts, dashes, etc.; thus eo, eo_1, eo_2 and so on.

A *composite object* consists of zero or more named immediate components, the components themselves being objects which are either elementary or composite. The naming of the immediate components is performed by distinct simple selectors; it is assumed that there is a countably infinite number of these. The composite object with zero immediate components is called the *null object* and is represented by Ω.

Example 5.1

Figure 5.5 illustrates a composite object E representing the arithmetic expression $a + b * c$. The elementary objects are the identifiers a, b and c together with the operators $+$ and $*$. The simple selectors are *l-op*, *r-op*, and *op* referring to the left operand, right operand and operator, respectively.

If s is a selector and χ an object then $s(\chi)$ selects the immediate s-component of χ. There are some special cases to consider in this context:

       ·if χ is elementary then $s(\chi) = \Omega$
       ·if χ contains no immediate s-component then again $s(\chi) = \Omega$

Example 5.2

Using the object E depicted in figure 5.5

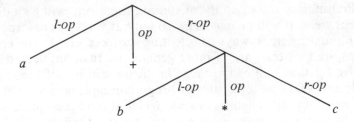

Fig. 5.5. Composite object corresponding to $a+b*c$.

(a) *l-op* (E) selects the elementary object a
(b) *r-op* (E) selects the composite object representing the expression $b*c$.

In general it makes sense to introduce a notation which allows simple selectors to be applied repeatedly. Thus if $s_1,s_2,...,s_n$ are selectors we write

$$s_1 \circ s_2 \circ ... \circ s_n (\chi)$$

to mean $s_1(s_2(...(s_n(\chi))...)$. We then refer to $s_1 \circ s_2 \circ ... \circ s_n$ as a composite selector – it is composed of simple selectors. There are now two kinds of selector.

With this notation we can now represent entire complex objects by means of a sequence of selector:elementary object pairs of the form $<s:eo>$, s being the selector and *eo* the elementary object which *s* selects.

Example 5.3
Using the example of figure 5.5 again the composite object can be represented by the set

$$\{ <l\text{-}op:a>, <op:+>, <l\text{-}op\circ r\text{-}op:b>, <op\circ r\text{-}op:*>,$$
$$<r\text{-}op\circ r\text{-}op:c> \}$$

It is convenient to have an operator which now takes a sequence of $<$selector:elementary object$>$ pairs and from these forms the appropriate composite object. The construction operation μ_0 does this. Thus

$$\mu_0(<l\text{-}op:a>, <op:+>, ... , <r\text{-}op\circ r\text{-}op:c>)$$

produces the composite object of figure 5.5. In general, in fact, μ_0 can accept a sequence of selector–object pairs of the form

$$<s_1:A_1>, <s_2:A_2>, ... , <s_n:A_n>$$

114

where the various s_i are distinct and form the composite object whose s_i-component is A_i. This allows, for example,

$$\mu_0(<l\text{-}op{:}a>, <op{:}{+}>, <r\text{-}op{:}\ \mu_0(<l\text{-}op{:}b>, <op{:}{*}>, \\ <r\text{-}op{:}c>)>)$$

However, the set of <selector:elementary object> pairs is somewhat special since it provides a linear representation of a composite object. This set is called the *characteristic set* of an object and uniquely describes that object.

To put elementary objects on a similar footing to composite objects it is convenient to introduce the *identity selector I*. It has the properties

· $I(A) = A$ for any object A, elementary or composite
· $I{\circ}\chi = \chi{\circ}I = \chi$ for any selector χ.

Given any set of <selector:elementary object> pairs these will not necessarily be the characteristic set of an object, even if the selectors are all distinct. For the set

$$\{ <s_2{:}a>, <s_1{\circ}s_2 : b> \}$$

could never be the characteristic set of any object. It would be convenient to have a simple condition which, if satisfied, would mean that a set was the characteristic set of some object. This condition requires the idea of dependency between selectors.

Definition
Let χ_1 and χ_2 be two selectors. We say that χ_1 and χ_2 are *dependent* if there is a selector τ such that either $\chi_1 = \tau{\circ}\chi_2$ or $\chi_2 = \tau{\circ}\chi_1$. In words, one of the selectors must be the tail of the other. We then define the predicate $\text{dep}(\chi_1, \chi_2)$ to be true provided there exists a τ such that

$$(\chi_1 = \tau \circ \chi_2) \vee (\chi_2 = \tau \circ \chi_1)$$

Example 5.4.
s_2 and $s_1{\circ}s_2$ are dependent but s_1 and $s_1{\circ}s_2$ are not dependent. Also s_1 is dependent on itself.

The necessary condition for a set S of <selector:elementary object> pairs to form the characteristic set of some object can now be stated: no two selectors appearing as the first elements of each pair may be dependent on each other. This condition is called the *characteristic condition* for the set S.

5.3.2 The μ-operator
It is possible to view objects in a particular way. The various selectors

define the structure of an object and the elementary objects can be regarded as the content of the object.

Using this view of objects the μ-operator is used primarily for altering the structure of objects. It can be used for inserting, removing or altering parts of an already existing object. Consider

$$\mu(A; <\chi:B>)$$

where A and B are objects and χ is a selector. The effect of this use of μ will depend on the original composition of A:

- if A contains no χ-component, i.e. if $\chi(A)=\Omega$, then a χ-component whose object is B is added to A
- if A does contain a χ-component this is removed and replaced by B
- if $B=\Omega$ the χ-component of A is removed.

An obvious extension to this notation is to allow several alterations to an object by means of a single application. Thus

$$\mu(A; <\chi_1:B_1>, <\chi_2:B_2>, \dots, <\chi_n:B_n>)$$

can be defined inductively as just

$$\mu(\mu(A; <\chi_1:B_1>); <\chi_2:B_2>, \dots, <\chi_n:B_n>)$$

The definition of $\mu(A; <\chi_1:B_1>)$ has already been given. If the assumption is made that $\mu(A;)$ is just A, this notation can be used for any number of $<$selector:object$>$ pairs.

Some examples illustrate the power of the μ-operator.

Example 5.5
Suppose the object A is represented by the tree

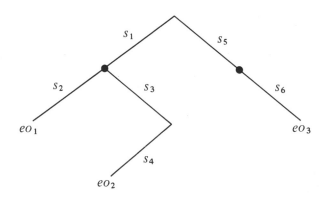

To delete eo_2 and thereby produce object A', the following application of μ is used:

$$\mu(A;<s_4 \circ s_3 \circ s_1 : \Omega>)$$

To now add eo_4 and eo_5 to A' to produce an object whose tree is

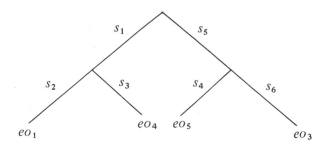

apply μ in the following manner:

$$\mu(A';<s_3 \circ s_1 : eo_4>, <s_4 \circ s_5 : eo_5>)$$

Note that both the above alterations could have been achieved by means of a single application of μ, namely

$$\mu(A;<s_3 \circ s_1 : eo_4>, <s_4 \circ s_5 : eo_5>)$$

In the previous case the $<$selector:object$>$ pairs were listed explicitly in the form $<\chi_1 : B_1>, \ldots, <\chi_n : B_n>$. A similar notation allows the use of a finite set of $<$selector:object$>$ pairs which have a particular property. More specifically

$$\mu(A; \{ <\chi:B> \mid p(\chi, B) \})$$

makes use of $\{ <\chi:B> \mid p(\chi, B) \}$, a set of pairs $<\chi:B>$ with the property $p(\chi, B)$. We adopt the convention that $\mu(A; \{ \}) = A$. In general, a union of such sets can be supplied to μ. The above notation is well defined only if the order in which the various alterations to A are made is irrelevant. If the order can affect the final outcome the result is said to be undefined.

Various other extensions of the notations involving the μ-operator are also possible, for example

$\cdot \mu_0(<\chi_1 : B_1>, <\chi_2 : B_2>, \ldots, <\chi_n : B_n>)$ can be defined to be $\mu(\Omega; <\chi_1 : B_1>, \ldots, <\chi_n : B_n>)$
$\cdot \mu_0(\{ <\chi:B> \mid p(\chi,B) \})$ can be defined as $\mu(\Omega; \{ <\chi:B> \mid p(\chi,B) \})$

$\cdot \delta(A; \chi_1, \chi_2, \dots, \chi_n)$ causes the χ_i, $1 \leqslant i \leqslant n$, components of A to be deleted by defining this to mean
$$\mu(A; <\chi_1 : \Omega>, <\chi_2 : \Omega>, \dots, <\chi_n : \Omega>)$$
$\cdot \delta(A; \{ \chi \mid p(\chi) \})$ allows a set of χ-components all with property p to be deleted from A by equating the above with
$$\mu(A; \{ <\chi : \Omega> \mid p(\chi) \})$$

With these definitions we now have at our disposal the means of altering objects, creating them and, in general, manipulating them in a variety of ways.

5.3.3 Predicates

When the abstract syntax notation of the VDL is introduced, predicates will be widely used. Take assignment statements, for example. There will be a predicate which will be true provided assignments are syntactically legal. For this to be so both the source (the right part) and the destination (the left part) must also be legal. The definition of the predicate for assignments is given therefore in terms of predicates for sources and destinations. For other constructions the situation is also similar; their predicates are defined in terms of predicates applied to components. The process of defining predicates in this way is reminiscent of the recursive descent process.

There are certain standard ways which will be used to describe more complicated predicates in terms of simpler predicates. In the sequel we use $P_1, P_2, \dots$ to represent predicates and $\hat{P}_1, \hat{P}_2, \dots$ to represent the set of objects satisfying $P_1, P_2, \dots$ respectively. Thus for each i

$$\hat{P}_i = \{ x \mid P_i(x) \}$$

Let $P_1, P_2, \dots, P_n$ be predicates. A new predicate P may be defined by

$$P = P_1 \vee P_2 \vee \dots \vee P_n$$

i.e. P is the disjunction of the n predicates, and so

$$P(x) = P_1(x) \vee P_2(x) \vee \dots \vee P_n(x)$$

It is then possible to write

$$\hat{P} = \hat{P}_1 \cup \hat{P}_2 \cup \dots \cup \hat{P}_n$$

i.e. P is the set-theoretic union of the various sets $\hat{P}_i$.

The next piece of notation allows more complicated objects to be defined in terms of simpler objects. If $P_1, P_2, \dots, P_n$ are n predicates and $s_1, s_2, \dots, s_n$ are n distinct selectors then a new predicate P can be defined as follows: $P(A)$ will be true provided there exist objects $A_1, A_2, \dots, A_n$ with the property that

$$A = \mu_0 (<s_1:A_1>,..., <s_n:A_n>)$$

and each $P_i(A_i)$ is true, i.e. $A_i \in \hat{P}_i$. In this situation we write

$$P = (<s_1:P_1>,..., <s_n:P_n>)$$

The notation introduced above provides only for a fixed finite number of selectors: no provision is made for an unknown (or infinite number). Another method of building new predicates allows this possibility. We want to be able to construct objects of the form

$$A = \mu_0 (<s_1:A_1>,..., <s_n:A_n>)$$

where n is unknown and each selector s_i satisfies a particular property in the form of a predicate Q. If each A_i satisfies P_1 we can build a new predicate P which describes the objects whose immediate components are of the form $<s:x>$ where s satisfies Q and x satisfies P_1, by writing

$$P = (\{ <s:P_1> \| Q(s) \})$$

The two definition methods can be combined to permit

$$P = (<s_1:P_1>,..., <s_n:P_n>, \\ \{ <s:P_{n+1}> \| Q_1(s) \},..., \{ <s:P_{n+m}> \| Q_m(s) \})$$

The obvious meaning is intended.
    Finally

$$(P_0; <s_1:P_1>, <s_2:P_2>,..., <s_n:P_n>)$$

is satisfied by all objects x of the form

$$\mu(x_0; <s_1:x_1>, <s_2:x_2>,..., <s_n:x_n>)$$

where each x_i satisfies the predicate P_i $(0 \leq i \leq n)$.
    Thus we know how to build more complicated predicates from simple predicates. Moreover given a complex predicate its truth can be established by checking the truth of the simpler predicates. Eventually, of course, predicates will be applied to elementary objects; in these cases it will be clear whether or not $eo \in \hat{P}$ for any given P.
    The rules for the construction of predicates can be recursive:

$$P = (<s_1:P_1>, <s_2:P>)$$

This would represent a kind of list of objects all satisfying the predicate P_1; s_1 would select the head of the list and s_2 the tail.

5.3.4 Lists of objects
In certain situations it is necessary to have a definite order associated with the various components of an object. For example, the instructions in a program occur in a particular sequence and, in general, this sequence is significant. In the VDL ordered objects are represented by lists.

Lists make use of the distinct selectors *elem* (1), *elem* (2),..., *elem*(n and are objects of the form

$$\mu_0(<elem(1):y_1>, <elem(2):y_2>,..., <elem(n):y_n>)$$

Thus there are a finite number of non-null immediate components of each list. A convenient representation of lists is:

$<>$ represents the null list
$<y_1,y_2,..., y_n>$ represents the list from which *elem* (i) selects
y_i $(1 \leqslant i \leqslant n)$

It is assumed that for each i, $y_1 \neq \Omega$.

It is now a simple matter to introduce a predicate called *P*-list. This would be satisfied by all lists of objects in which each object satisfies the predicate *P*. To be more explicit *P-list*(A) would be true provided that either

$$A = <>$$

or

$$A = <A_1, A_2,..., A_n> \text{ where each } A_i \in \hat{P}.$$

In a similar fashion the predicate *P-set*(A) would be true provided that either A is the empty set or

$$A = \{ A_1, A_2,..., A_n \} \quad \text{and each } A_i \in \hat{P}.$$

To aid the proper manipulation of lists we introduce some of the traditional list-manipulating functions and show how these can be defined. For this purpose it is convenient to have a predicate *is-list* to tell whether or not an object is a list. This predicate when applied to the object L yields true provided that either

$$L = <>$$

or there exist non-null $A_1, A_2,...,A_n$ such that

$$L = \mu_0(<elem(1):A_1>,..., <elem(n):A_n>)$$

Given a list L we write *elem* (i, L) for *elem* $(i)(L)$. Then we can define various functions using a self-explanatory LISP-like notation:

length $(L) = $ *is-list* $(L) \rightarrow$
　　$(L = <> \rightarrow 0, T \rightarrow$ the unique i such that
　　$(elem\ (i,L) \neq \Omega) \land (elem\ (i+1,L) = \Omega))$
head $(L) = $ *is-list* $(L) \land (L \neq <>) \rightarrow elem(1,L)$
tail $(L) = $ *is-list* $(L) \land (L \neq <>) \rightarrow$
　　$(length\ (L) = 1 \rightarrow <>$

$$length\ (L) > 1 \rightarrow \mu_0(\ \{\ <elem(i):\ elem(i{+}1,L)>\ \|$$
$$1 \leqslant i \leqslant length(L)\text{-}1\ \}\ ))$$

Two lists L_1 and L_2 can be concatenated or joined as follows

$$join\,(L_1,L_2) = is\text{-}list(L_1)\ \wedge\ is\text{-}list(L_2) \rightarrow$$
$$\mu(L_1;\{\ <elem(length(L_1){+}i):\ elem(i,L_2)>\ |$$
$$1 \leqslant i \leqslant length\,(L_2)\ \}\ )$$

Several lists can be concatenated in an obvious way; the operation is associative.

5.3.5 Abstract syntax
In this sub-section we look at the abstract syntax of PL/I, VDL style. The concrete syntax has already been described in the course of our discussion about the PL/I Standard. In essence it was the same in the two methods of definition.

Recall the notation

$$P{=}(<s_1:P_1>,\ <s_2:P_2>,\ ...)$$

used for defining the predicate P in terms of further predicates $P_1,P_2,...$ Objects x which satisfy P are of the form $\mu_0\ (<s_1:A_1>,$ $<s_2:A_2>,...)$, where each A_i is selected by s_i and $A_i \in \hat{P}_i$. Also we have

$$P = (\ \{\ <s:P_1>\ \|\ Q(s)\ \}\ )$$

and the objects satisfying P are composed of objects of the form $<s:x_i>$ where s is satisfied by $Q(s)$ and x_i by P_1.

In the abstract syntax of PL/I the rules are made more readable by using the prefix s- to start selectors and the prefix is- to start predicates. Take the rule which expresses a PL/I program as a set of procedures each of which is regarded as an identifier with an associated body. Thus

$$is\text{-}program{=}(\ \{\ <id:is\text{-}body>\ \|\ is\text{-}id(id)\ \}\ )$$

Further relevant definitions (slightly simplified) are then

$$is\text{-}body = (is\text{-}block;<s\text{-}param\text{-}list:is\text{-}id\text{-}list>)$$
$$is\text{-}block = (<s\text{-}decl\text{-}part:is\text{-}decl\text{-}part>,$$
$$<s\text{-}st\text{-}list:is\text{-}st\text{-}list>)$$
$$is\text{-}decl\text{-}part = (\ \{\ <id:\ is\text{-}decl>\ \|\ is\text{-}id(id)\ \}\ )$$
$$is\text{-}decl = is\text{-}proper\text{-}var\ \vee\ is\text{-}entry\ \vee\ ...$$

and so on. There is no point in itemising all the rules of the abstract syntax. But to give the flavour we give some further (simplified) examples:

Statements

$$is\text{-}st = (<s\text{-}label\text{-}list:\ is\text{-}id\text{-}list>,$$
$$<s\text{-}proper\text{-}st:\ is\text{-}proper\text{-}st>)$$
$$is\text{-}proper\text{-}st = is\text{-}call\ \lor\ is\text{-}block\ \lor\ is\text{-}assign\text{-}st$$
$$is\text{-}call\text{-}st = (<s\text{-}id:\ is\text{-}id>,$$
$$<s\text{-}arg\text{-}list:\ is\text{-}expr\text{-}list>)$$
$$is\text{-}assign\text{-}st = (<s\text{-}lp:\ is\text{-}ref>,$$
$$<s\text{-}rp:\ is\text{-}expr>)$$

Expressions

$$is\text{-}expr = is\text{-}infix\text{-}expr\ \lor\ is\text{-}prefix\text{-}expr\ \lor\ ...$$
$$is\text{-}infix\text{-}expr = (<s\text{-}opr:\ is\text{-}infix\text{-}opr>,$$
$$<s\text{-}op\text{-}1:\ is\text{-}expr>,$$
$$<s\text{-}op\text{-}2:\ is\text{-}expr>)$$
$$is\text{-}prefix\text{-}expr = (<s\text{-}opr:\ is\text{-}prefix\text{-}opr>,$$
$$<s\text{-}op:\ is\text{-}expr>)$$

A complete definition of a programming language will require the existence and careful specification of programs for translating concrete programs into their abstract counterparts. In the VDL this is done in two stages, by a parse stage and a translation stage. If *text* denotes a concrete program

$$translate \circ parse(text)$$

will transform *text* into an abstract program if this is possible. The connection between the parser and the translator is a tree *t* which is essentially the parse tree *t* imposed on *text* by the concrete syntax. Thus *parse* (*text*) produces *t* which is then processed by *translate*.

To avoid the complication of having to specify a parser an alternative approach is taken. If *t* is the parse tree a function *generate* when applied to *t* will give a concrete program. The definition of *generate* can be made recursively and involves concatenating concrete representation of the various elements in *t*. Having defined *generate* the parse function can be defined as the inverse of the *generate* function. Thus

$$parse(text) = \text{the unique parse tree } t \text{ with the property}$$
$$\text{that } text = generate(t)\ \land\ is\text{-}c\text{-}program(t)$$

Note that the uniqueness specification implies that the grammar is unambiguous and that a parser can be designed; the *is-c-program* predicate ensures that the parse tree is indeed legal – its definition is given using the concrete syntax.

The translator forms abstract programs from parse trees. This it does by selecting out the relevant aspects of the parse tree using selectors and combining these into abstract programs using the $\mu_0\text{-},\mu$-operators.

122

The translator is built using a recursive descent kind of approach. Thus there is a translator routine for dealing with assignments, one for dealing with conditionals, another for procedure calls, and so on. These are called by a routine for translating statements which in turn is called by routine for translating statement-lists, blocks, procedures and so on. As in the PL/I Standard factoring of attributes in declarations is resolved at this stage and in the abstract syntax there is a standard complete form of declaration. But unlike the PL/I Standard, the interpreter in the VDL definition does not make assumptions about checks performed earlier by the translator.

5.3.6 The abstract machine

We must now look at how the notation and ideas we have developed can be used to describe semantics. To recap, the meaning of a program is described in terms of the sequence of changes to the state of an abstract machine. Thus a computation takes the form of a sequence of states

$$\xi_0, \xi_1, \xi_2, \ldots$$

where each

$$\xi_{i+1} = \Lambda(\xi_i)$$

and Λ is the *state transition function*. The definition of the function Λ takes the form of a definition of an interpreter. In fact Λ is only a partial function since there are states for which no successor state exists, i.e. no definition of Λ is given. Programs causing this are erroneous (assuming of course that the halt state is omitted from the discussion).

As before, the abstract machine is idealised in some senses and is not concerned with tedious limitations such as restricted store size, restrictions on the magnitude and accuracy of numbers, etc. But the nature of the states of the machine will depend to some extent on the nature of the language being defined. Basically the state must simulate the environment in which an interpreter has to run.

Now the VDL can be used in describing the meaning of different kinds of languages but we shall, in keeping with our previous discussion on the PL/I Standard, look at an abstract machine which might be used for defining PL/I. In this we follow Lucas & Walk (1969). Other alternatives are possible and for further reading see the relevant references.

PL/I is a block-structured language. In many respects the activation of begin blocks and procedures are similar from an implementation point of view. Accordingly some of the mechanism of a PL/I interpreter will be devoted to dealing with block entry and exit. The usual way of implementing this is to use a stack whose various elements characterise each successive block activation. In the abstract machine certain immediate components of a state will characterise the current block. Another immediate component will be a dump, essentially a stack, containing those aspects of a state which characterise the immediately preceding block together with its dump.

Each block activation will be characterised by the following immediate components:

(a) an environment, selected from a state ξ by the selector *s-e* and satisfying the predicate *is-e*; this takes the form of a set of <selector:object> pairs representing the set of currently available identifiers and their locations in store

(b) epilogue information, selected by *s-ei* and satisfying *is-ei*; this contains information about what has to be done on leaving the current block, e.g. the local variables to be freed, the parallel tasks which are attached to the block

(c) a text part, selected by *s-tx* and satisfying *is-tx*; this holds the text part (that part of the abstract syntax tree) corresponding to the executable statements of the block

(d) a statement counter, selected by *s-sc* and satisfying *is-integer* keeps track of the next statement in the text part to be executed

(e) a control part, selected by *s-c* and satisfying *is-c*; this is basically a tree representation of the primitive instructions to be performed by the abstract machine

(f) a dump part, selected by *s-d* and satisfying *is-d*; this represents the history of currently active blocks in the form of a stack.

The state components mentioned above characterise each block activation but they are not the only components of a machine state. The other components can be likened to the store of the computer, a kind of symbol table, and so on. They are more global in nature and as such are called the global components of a state; in contrast, the others are called the local components.

Before looking at some of the global components in more detail recall that the environment component associates with each identifier in scope at a particular point in a program a unique name (or address). With this in mind, some of the global components of a state are

(a) a storage part, selected by *s-s* and satisfying *is-stg*; this corresponds to the main store of a computer and is used for allocating space to variables, arrays, etc. declared in user programs

(b) a denotation directory, selected by *s-dn* and satisfying *is-dn*; this contains (in contrast to (c) below) the evaluated attributes of identifiers, e.g. the sizes of arrays that have been declared, and the lengths of character strings that have been passed as parameters

(c) an attribute directory, selected by *s-at* and satisfying *is-at*; this contains non-evaluated information associated with the declaration of an identifier; thus the variables used in expressing dynamic bounds, the lengths of strings, etc. are retained here

(d) a unique name generator, selected by *s-un* and satisfying *is-integer*; this is used to create space by keeping a note of the address of the next free location in store.

Note the necessary distinction between components (b) and (c) above. The distinction must exist for two reasons:

· evaluation of attributes can cause certain vital information to be lost, e.g. whether a particular quantity was derived from a constant or a variable; this could yield information which is vital in, for example, passing strings as parameters

· expressions involved in declarations need not be evaluated at the time a declaration is encountered but instead when space is allocated (cf. control variables in PL/I); these two events, the declaration and the evaluation of attributes, may even happen in different environments, and in these circumstances it becomes necessary to remember the environment in which an identifier was declared.

The previous discussion can be conveniently summarised in the following set of definitions. Note that the dump component is defined recursively; the Ω-state of the dump corresponds to an activation of the initial block.

$$
\begin{aligned}
is\text{-}state = \quad (&<s\text{-}s : is\text{-}stg>, \\
&<s\text{-}un : is\text{-}integer>, \\
&<s\text{-}dn : is\text{-}dn>, \\
&<s\text{-}at : is\text{-}at>, \dots \\
&<s\text{-}e : is\text{-}e>, \\
&<s\text{-}ei : is\text{-}ei>, \\
&<s\text{-}tx : is\text{-}tx>, \\
&<s\text{-}sc : is\text{-}integer>, \\
&<s\text{-}c : is\text{-}c>, \\
&<s\text{-}d : is\text{-}d>)
\end{aligned}
$$

$$is\text{-}d = \quad (<s\text{-}e: is\text{-}e>,$$
$$<s\text{-}ei: is\text{-}ei>,$$
$$<s\text{-}tx: is\text{-}tx>,$$
$$<s\text{-}sc: is\text{-}integer>,$$
$$<s\text{-}c: is\text{-}c>,$$
$$<s\text{-}d: is\text{-}d>) \lor is\text{-}\Omega$$
$$is\text{-}e = \quad (\{ <id: is\text{-}n> \,\|\, is\text{-}id(id) \})$$
$$is\text{-}tx = \quad is\text{-}st\text{-}list \lor is\text{-}\Omega$$
$$is\text{-}dn = \quad (\{ <n: den> \,\|\, is\text{-}n(n) \})$$
$$is\text{-}at = \quad (\{ <n: (<s\text{-}attr: is\text{-}decl>, <s\text{-}e: is\text{-}e>) \,\|\, is\text{-}n(n) \})$$

Only some of the global components of a state have been described above. Hence the ellipsis after the component $<s\text{-}at: is\text{-}at>$. For PL/I others must exist, but we do not deal with these in any detail. We mention briefly the generation component, for example, which keeps the information needed to access storage. This would indicate whether or not storage had been allocated, for instance.

The local state components mentioned above characterise each block activation and will change on entering and leaving each block. These changes can be described as follows:

· at block entry we typically wish to create from a state ξ a new state ξ' with new components E, EI, TX, SC, C representing environment, epilogue information, etc. respectively

$$\xi' = \mu(\xi; <s\text{-}e:E>, <s\text{-}ei:EI>, <s\text{-}tx:TX>, <s\text{-}sc:SC>,$$
$$<s\text{-}c:C>, <s\text{-}d:stack(\xi)>)$$

where

$$stack(\xi) = \mu_0(<s\text{-}e:s\text{-}e(\xi)>, <s\text{-}ei:s\text{-}ei(\xi)>, <s\text{-}tx:s\text{-}tx(\xi)>,$$
$$<s\text{-}sc:s\text{-}sc(\xi)>, <s\text{-}c:s\text{-}c(\xi)>, <s\text{-}d:s\text{-}d(\xi)>)$$

· at block exit we typically want to create a new state ξ' from an old state ξ by letting

$$D = s\text{-}d(\xi)$$

and then setting

$$\xi' = \mu(\xi; <s\text{-}e:s\text{-}e(D)>, <s\text{-}ei:s\text{-}ei(D)>, <s\text{-}tx:s\text{-}tx(D)>,$$
$$<s\text{-}sc:s\text{-}sc(D)>, <s\text{-}c:s\text{-}c(D)>, <s\text{-}d:s\text{-}d(D)>)$$

i.e. essentially unstacking from the dump.

To illustrate in a more concrete manner the operation of the dump mechanism and the changes in environment consider the following simple piece of program:

```
BEGIN;
    DECLARE A, B, C;
        ...
        BEGIN;
            DECLARE A, D;
                ...
        END;
END;
```

Assume initially a null environment and assume that before execution
of the piece of program the dump is Ω. On entering the first block the
first set of declarations appears. This leads to a dump d_1 and an environment e_1 specified by

$$d_1 = \Omega$$
$$e_1 = \mu(\Omega; <A:n_1>, <B:n_2>, <C:n_3>)$$

where n_1, n_2, etc. denote the successive names generated by the unique
name generator. Entry into the next block results in a new environment
e_2 where, if n_4 and n_5 denote appropriate names for locations,

$$e_2 = \mu(e_1; <A:n_4>, <D:n_5>)$$
$$= \mu_0(<B:n_2>, <C:n_3>, <A:n_4>, <D:n_5>)$$

Note that the selector–object pair $<A:n_1>$ now no longer exists in the
current environment but it exists only on the dump or stack. It will
become accessible only on block-exit when the dumped environment
is restored.

When discussing environments it is convenient to discuss procedures
since the two concepts are indivisibly related. Consider a program containing the following:

```
BEGIN; DECLARE A;
    P: PROCEDURE (X, Y); A = X + Y; END P;
        BEGIN; DECLARE A; A = 1; CALL P(A, A); END;
END;
```

Which version of A is altered by the call of P? Most programming
languages would cause the initially declared A to be altered though
languages which allow shallow binding would cause the inner version
of A to be altered. Here we consider the more traditional interpretation.

In ALGOL 68 terms the situation would be described by saying that
there is associated with each procedure a necessary environment which
is just the environment which exists when a procedure is declared. When
a procedure call takes place the necessary environment is installed
before the body of the procedure is activated. Installation takes the

form of performing the usual updating of the environment and dumping the previous environment so that it can be recovered on exit from the procedure.

The value of a procedure or function is thus a set of instructions together with an environment, the necessary environment. These considerations lead to something of the form

$$is\text{-}proc\text{-}den = (<s\text{-}attr: is\text{-}proc\text{-}attr>,$$
$$<s\text{-}env: is\text{-}env>)$$
$$is\text{-}funct\text{-}den = (<s\text{-}attr: is\text{-}funct\text{-}attr>,$$
$$<s\text{-}env: is\text{-}env>)$$

where

$$is\text{-}proc\text{-}attr = (<s\text{-}param\text{-}list: is\text{-}id\text{-}list>,$$
$$<s\text{-}st\text{-}list: is\text{-}st\text{-}list>)$$

and

$$is\text{-}funct\text{-}attr = (<s\text{-}param\text{-}list: is\text{-}id\text{-}list>,$$
$$<s\text{-}st\text{-}list: is\text{-}st\text{-}list>,$$
$$<s\text{-}expr: is\text{-}expr>)$$

We now show what happens when the procedure P declared above is called. On encountering the outer block the environment becomes e_1 where

$$e_1 = \mu_0(<A:n_1>, <P:n_2>)$$

The inner block results in this environment being updated by invoking

$$\mu(e_1; <A:n_3>)$$

to produce e_2, i.e.

$$\mu_0(<A:n_3>, <P:n_2>)$$

The assignment $A=1$ causes $<n_3:1>$ to be entered into the denotation table.

Now the call $P(A,A)$ occurs. The necessary environment is installed by

$$\mu(e_2; <A:n_1>, <P:n_2>)$$

to produce

$$\mu_0(<A:n_1>, <P:n_2>)$$

and the dumping of the previous environment takes place. This environment is then altered by adding suitable entries for the (implicit) declarations of X and Y to yield

$$\mu_0(<A:n_1>, <P:n_2>, <X:n_4>, <Y:n_5>)$$

(At this point dumping of the previous environment need not occur.) In the now current environment the body of procedure P will be executed. On completion of these instructions the appropriate environment can be retrieved from the dump.

We choose not to discuss in any depth the nature of the storage part of a machine state. As mentioned in the introduction to this chapter, one of the design aims of PL/I was that the user should not have to resort to machine code in order to obtain some desired effect. In particular, therefore, he should be able to access store in a variety of different ways. Yet the language should still free him from considerations of too low a level. Thus the essential properties of storage had to be encapsulated in the facilities provided in PL/I for introducing variables of different kinds, for allocating and freeing space, for sharing it, and so on. The result is complex, and a detailed analysis of this would make the discussion heavily oriented towards PL/I. Yet the VDL can be used for a wide variety of languages. We shall therefore keep the discussion on this topic rather limited though it is by no means a straightforward part of a language definition. For further reading on this matter see Lucas & Walk (1969).

The flow of control of a program, i.e. the sequence of actions performed when executing a block, is governed by three components of that block: the text, the statement counter and the control parts. Of these, the text part remains unchanged but both the statement counter and the control part alter as execution progresses.

The text part contains the executable statements for a block in the form of a list. At the start of execution of that block the statement counter is set to zero. Upon completion of the interpretation of each statement the counter is increased by one. This simple scheme must, of course, be modified to take account of statements which themselves contain groups or lists of statements, e.g. certain kinds of if-statements. In these circumstances the statement counters are effectively stacked upon entry to such a group and unstacked on exit.

On termination of a block (perhaps caused by a go to or a return statement) certain actions must be performed. The epilogue information component of a state contains the information associated with these.

The control part of a state takes the form of a control tree holding sets of instructions which the abstract machine must execute. At any particular time the candidates for being the next instruction to be executed are those instructions which appear as the leaves of the control tree. These represent the translation of the current statement in the text part. In figure 5.6, for example, any of $instr_3$, $instr_4$, $instr_6$, or

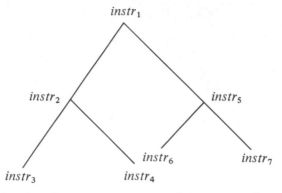

Fig. 5.6. Possible control state of abstract machine.

$instr_7$, could be executed next; these might represent, for example, the evaluation of four operands in an arithmetic expression. Execution of one of these statements causes the next state of the abstract machine to appear. In this way execution of statements causes a sequence of state changes which then describes the meaning of a program.

5.3.7 The interpreter

At the start of the interpretation phase the abstract machine is initialised in the following way:

- the storage part is initialised to some initial storage component stg_0
- the unique name counter is initialised to zero
- the statement counter is initialised to zero
- the control part contains just one instruction, the instruction for interpreting a program namely **int-program** $(t_0, call_0)$ where t_0 is the abstract program to be interpreted and $call_0$ is the procedure to be initially activated
- all other components are initialised to Ω.

The machine then updates the environment, the attribute directory and the denotation directory with information about the external procedures which constitute the abstract program t_0. Then, before proper interpretation commences, a prepass allocates storage for static variables and modifies the denotation directory entry for procedures by putting unique names in the declarations of static and controlled variables, files and external entries; it must also initialise other components such as the generation component.

Thereafter interpretation progresses. The control component is altered and replaced by sets of instructions which in turn alter the other

130

components of a state. When and if interpretation terminates the control component of the state of the abstract machine will be empty.

The actions of interpreting a program have, because of the nature of the initial instruction, been reduced essentially to the task of calling a single VDL procedure. Consequently we look at the part of the interpreter that describes what happens when a procedure is called. We look first at several other simpler situations to give the flavour of the abstract machine instructions.

Instructions of the abstract machine take the form

$$\textbf{in } (a_1, a_2, ..., a_n) =$$
$$\begin{aligned} p_1 &\rightarrow group_1 \\ p_2 &\rightarrow group_2 \\ &... \\ p_m &\rightarrow group_m \end{aligned}$$

Here,

- **in** denotes the instruction name and is built from bold words composed of small letters, digits and hyphens
- $a_1, a_2, ..., a_n$ denote the parameters, objects passed to the instruction
- $p_1, p_2, ..., p_m$ denote predicates, the truth of p_i implying that $group_i$ may be selected for execution; p_1 is examined, then p_2, etc. and the first predicate which is true produces the group to be executed
- each $group_i$ is a set of instructions.

An instruction of the form

$$\textbf{in } (a_1, a_2, ..., a_n) =$$
$$T \rightarrow group$$

is, for simplicity, replaced by

$$\textbf{in } (a_1, a_2, ..., a_n) =$$
$$group$$

The groups of instructions themselves take the form

$$\begin{aligned} s\text{-}sc_1 &: \quad m\text{-}expr_1 \\ s\text{-}sc_2 &: \quad m\text{-}expr_2 \\ &... \\ s\text{-}sc_r &: \quad m\text{-}expr_r \end{aligned}$$

The $s\text{-}sc_k$ ($1 \leqslant k \leqslant r$) are simple selectors and these components of the current state are replaced by the objects $m\text{-}expr_k$. Each $m\text{-}expr_k$ represents a macro-expression which generally indicates the replacing of a node of the control tree by a different node or by a subtree. Consequently a notation for subtrees takes the form

131

root node;
$$\{subtree_1, subtree_2,...,subtree_5\}$$

or, equivalently,

root node;
$$subtree_1,$$
$$subtree_2,$$
$$...$$
$$subtree_5$$

With this introduction we can now look at some examples of instructions used in the PL/I interpreter. ξ will denote the current state of the abstract machine.

1. If **D** denotes $s\text{-}d(\xi)$, the dump component of the current state,

    unstack=
     s-e: $s\text{-}e(\mathbf{D})$
     s-ei: $s\text{-}ei(\mathbf{D})$
     s-d: $s\text{-}d(\mathbf{D})$
     s-tx: $s\text{-}tx(\mathbf{D})$
     s-sc: $s\text{-}sc(\mathbf{D})$
     s-c: $s\text{-}c(\mathbf{D})$

2. A simplified version of the instructions to be performed on block exit is

    epilogue =
     unstack;
      free-local

Note that the instructions will be executed not in the order implied above but in the reverse order; for the leaf of the control tree will contain the instruction **free-local** (**unstack** will not be at a leaf).

3. The **free-local** instruction is, in a simplified form, **free-local=**

    null;
     $\{\mathbf{free}\ (b) \mid b \in s\text{-}ei(\xi)\}$

4. To place a variable in the epilogue information, so that it can be freed later at block exit

    note-ei (b) =
     $s\text{-}ei$: $s\text{-}ei(\xi) \cup \{b\}$

5. To interpret a statement list

int-st-list=
$$s\text{-}sc\,(\xi) < length\,(s\text{-}tx\,(\xi)) \to$$
$$\text{int-st-list;}$$
$$\text{int-st}\,(s\text{-}proper\text{-}st \circ elem\,(s\text{-}sc\,(\xi)+1,\, s\text{-}tx\,(\xi));$$
$$\text{update-sc}$$
$$T \to \textbf{null}$$

The sequential ordering outlined above will be interrupted, of course, by jumps

6. To update the statement counter

    update-sc=
    $$s\text{-}sc : s\text{-}sc\,(\xi)+1$$

7. To interpret a statement

    int-st(*st*)=
    $$is\text{-}call\text{-}st\,(st) \to \textbf{int-call-st}\ (st)$$
    $$is\text{-}block\text{-}st\,(st) \to \textbf{int-block}(st)$$
    $$is\text{-}assign\text{-}st\,(st) \to \textbf{int-assign-st}(st)$$
    $$...$$

There will be one test here for each kind of statement permitted in the language.

In the instructions we have looked at it is possible to decipher aspects of macro-expansion. Basically instructions are replaced by other sets of instructions.

The abstract machine of the VDL permits another set of instructions, instructions which produce results to be passed back up the control tree to other instructions. These functions, as they are called, are similar in concept and design to the earlier instructions but the groups of instructions now take the form

$$\text{PASS:}\quad m\text{-}expr_0$$
$$s\text{-}sc_1:\quad m\text{-}expr_1$$
$$s\text{-}sc_2:\quad m\text{-}expr_2$$
$$...$$
$$s\text{-}sc_r:\quad m\text{-}expr_r$$

The PASS component is then the result of the function. On completion of the execution of the instruction the result is inserted at the point of the function call. In fact, the groups for the previous macro-instructions could be regarded as groups of the same kind with a component

$$\text{PASS:}\ \Omega$$

inserted at the start of the group.

133

Below we give some examples of the functions of the PL/I abstract machine

1. **pass**(x)=
    PASS:x

2. The unique name generator will produce successively the addresses $n_0, n_1, n_2,...$ Thus

    un-name=
    PASS:$n_{s\text{-}un\,(\xi)}$
    $s\text{-}un$: $s\text{-}un\,(\xi)+1$

3. To evaluate an expression *expr* in an environment *e*

    eval-expr(*expr,e*)=
    $is\text{-}infix\text{-}expr(expr) \rightarrow$
        eval-infix-expr(*op-1,op-2,s-opr(expr)*);
            op-1 : **eval-expr**(*s-op-1 (expr),e*),
            op-2 : **eval-expr**(*s-op-2 (expr),e*)
    $is\text{-}prefix\text{-}expr(expr) \rightarrow$
        eval-prefix-expr(*op,s-opr(expr)*);
            op:**eval-expr**(*s-op(expr),e*)
    $is\text{-}ref\text{-}expr(expr) \rightarrow$
        eval-ref(*expr,e*)

    ...

    There will be one condition for each kind of expression permitted by the abstract syntax of the language.

Having introduced the two kinds of instructions we now look at the method of defining a PL/I procedure call and in doing this we conclude our look at the VDL. (The procedure calls are somewhat simpler than full PL/I permits.)

    int-call(*body,e,arg-list*) =
        s-e :*e*
        s-ei: { }
        s-d :*stack*(ξ)
        s-tx:*s-st-list*(*body*)
        s-sc:0
        s-c :**int-proc-body**(*body,arg-list*)

The above makes use of the stack function which is defined as follows

    stack(ξ) =
        $\mu_0(<s\text{-}e\ :s\text{-}e(\xi)>,$
            $<s\text{-}ei:s\text{-}ei(\xi)>,$

$$\langle s\text{-}d : s\text{-}d(\xi)\rangle,$$
$$\langle s\text{-}tx : s\text{-}tx(\xi)\rangle,$$
$$\langle s\text{-}sc : s\text{-}sc(\xi)\rangle,$$
$$\langle s\text{-}c : s\text{-}c(\xi)\rangle)$$

Further interpreter instructions are (bold letters such as **E** select the appropriate components of the current state)

int-proc-body($body, arg\text{-}list$) =
    epilogue;
        int-st-list;
            update-dn($s\text{-}decl\text{-}part(body)$);
                install-arg-list($arg\text{-}list, s\text{-}param\text{-}list(body)$,
                              $s\text{-}decl\text{-}part(body)$);
                update-at($s\text{-}decl\text{-}part(body)$);
                    update-e($s\text{-}decl\text{-}part(body)$)

update-e(dp) =
    null;
        { **update-id**(id, n); n: **un-name** | $is\text{-}decl \circ id(dp)$ }

update-id(id, n) =
    s-e:$\mu(\mathbf{E}; \langle id : n\rangle)$

update-at(dp) =
    s-at:$\mu(\mathbf{AT};$ { $\langle id(\mathbf{E}):\mu_0(\langle s\text{-}attr:\delta(id(dp);s\text{-}den)\rangle,$
                $\langle s\text{-}e : \mathbf{E}\rangle)\rangle$ | $is\text{-}decl \circ id(dp)$ })

Recall that δ denotes the delete function introduced when the definition of μ was being extended.

install-arg-list($arg\text{-}list, idl, dp$) =
    $length(arg\text{-}list) = length(idl) \rightarrow$
        null;
            { **install-arg**($arg_i, decl_i, n_i$) | $1 \leq i \leq length(idl)$ }
    $\mathbf{T} \rightarrow$ **error**
where: $arg_i = elem(i, arg\text{-}list)$
      $id_i\ = elem(i, idl)$
      $decl_i = id_i(dp)$
      $n_i\ \ = id_i(\mathbf{E})$

install-arg($arg, decl, n$) =
    $test\text{-}arg(arg, decl)$ & $is\text{-}\text{PARAM} \circ s\text{-}scope(decl) \rightarrow$
        s-dn: $\mu(\mathbf{DN}; \langle n : s\text{-}den(arg)\rangle)$
        s-ei :$\mathbf{EI} \cup dummy\text{-}den(arg)$
    $\mathbf{T} \rightarrow$ **error**

Here *test-arg* checks that the parameters match properly. Denotations of dummy variables are inserted into $s\text{-}ei(\xi)$ for later freeing. The function *dummy-den* used above is defined as

135

$$dummy\text{-}den\,(arg) =$$
$$is\text{-}DUMMY \circ s\text{-}type\,(arg) \to \{\,s\text{-}den\,(arg)\,\}$$
$$T \to \{\,\}$$

Finally we note three other instructions

update-dn$(dp) =$
    null;
        $\{\,$**update-decl-dn**$(id(E),den);$
                $den:$ **eval-den**$(id,id(dp)) \mid is\text{-}decl \circ id(dp)\ \&$
                            $is\text{-}PARAM \circ s\text{-}scope \circ id(dp)\}$

update-decl-dn$(n,den) =$
    s-dn$: \mu(DN; <n:den>)$

eval-den$(id,decl) =$
    $is\text{-}STATIC \circ s\text{-}stg\text{-}cl(decl) \lor is\text{-}CTL \circ s\text{-}stg\text{-}cl(decl) \lor$
    $is\text{-}file\,(decl) \to$
        PASS: $s\text{-}den\,(decl)$
    $is\text{-}AUTO \circ s\text{-}stg\text{-}cl(decl)\ \&\ is\text{-}INT \circ s\text{-}scope\,(decl) \to$
        pass $(b);$
            note-ei $(b);$
                allocate $(b,eda);$
                    $b:$ **un-name**,
                    $eda:$ **eval-da**$(s\text{-}da(decl),E)$
    $is\text{-}entry\,(decl)\ \&\ is\text{-}INT \circ s\text{-}scope\,(decl) \to$
        PASS: $\mu_0(<s\text{-}body:s\text{-}den(decl)>, <s\text{-}e:E>)$
    $is\text{-}entry\,(decl)\ \&\ is\text{-}EXT \circ s\text{-}scope\,(decl) \to$
        PASS: $s\text{-}den\,(decl)(DN)$
    $is\text{-}based\,(decl) \to$ **null**
    $T \to$ **error**

There will be further entries here depending on the type of the declaration.

Observe that at certain stages of the interpreting process the interpretater is performing checks, e.g. that the number and types of actual parameters passed to a procedure match the number and type of the formal parameters.

5.4 Final remarks

In this chapter we have examined the definition methods of the PL/I Standard and the Vienna Definition Language and thus we have seen two contrasting and yet similar approaches to operational semantics. Much can be said in favour and much can be said against these kind of methods. Rather than examine the arguments here we leave the discussion till the concluding chapter since at that time the operational approach can be compared with other methods of definition.

References on the work described in this chapter can be found in the relevant part of the references at the end of the book. Many of the origins of the methods can be found in the earlier references to the work on LISP.

The programming language PASCAL stemmed from some investigations into possible developments resulting from the inclusion of data structuring facilities in an ALGOL 60-like language. The language was designed by N. Wirth around 1970 but it benefited from some of the ideas of C.A.R. Hoare who, at that time, was also working on data-structuring facilities in programming languages.

The original definition of PASCAL was itself presented in an ALGOL 60 style. Thus the context-free syntax was given formally in (slightly modified) BNF notation; the semantics were given using mainly informal English prose, but also some definition by substitution, and each individual construct was described separately. As with its earlier predecessor ALGOL 60, there were some areas of doubt about the meaning of various constructs and this led to further attempts to produce a complete specification. Certain aspects of this further work will be the main concern of this chapter.

For the moment, however, we note one aspect of the original definition, the semantic description of the **repeat ... until** loop. The statement

> **repeat** S **until** B

where S is some statement and B some Boolean was defined to be equivalent to

> **begin** S;
>> **if not** B
>>> **then repeat** S **until** B
>
> **end**

Note that this is recursive. Although definition by substitution occurred in the ALGOL 60 Report, at no stage was a construct defined recursively in the above manner.

In 1973 Hoare and Wirth attempted a formal definition of the semantics of PASCAL. The formality shed light on various areas of uncertainty and this led to a kind of revision and extension of the original language. The story of the development of PASCAL did not end at this point for there were still areas of doubt in the revised PASCAL definition. For example, there were questions concerning types: when should two types, such as the type of formal and actual parameters, be regarded as equivalent? Many of the remaining doubts could be removed by providing a more rigorous and ambitious syntactic specification which includes context-sensitive features.

In this chapter then, we begin by looking at attribute grammars and discussing and examining some of their theoretical properties. We then demonstrate how these can be used in defining the syntactic aspects of PASCAL. Finally, we look at the work of Hoare and Wirth on formal semantics.

6.1 The attribute idea

6.1.1 Motivation

We have seen that context-free grammars are often used to define the syntax of programming languages. The basic structure of any syntactically correct program can then be represented by an appropriate parse or derivation tree. It is natural to imagine that this tree, and consequently the grammar itself, might be used in describing certain aspects of the original program. We shall illustrate some of the possibilities by example.

Consider a very simple grammar for arithmetic expressions expressed in BNF notation.

$$
\begin{aligned}
&\text{<expression>}::=\text{<term>}|\text{<expression>}+\text{<term>}\\
&\text{<term>} \quad ::=\text{<factor>}|\text{<term>}*\text{<factor>}\\
&\text{<factor>} \quad ::=x\,|\,y\,|\,z\,|\,(\text{<expression>})
\end{aligned}
$$

A parse tree for the expression

$$(x+y)*z$$

is presented in figure 6.1.

When such an expression is to be evaluated each of x, y and z will possess a value. Assume these are respectively 3, 4 and 12. Execution will proceed by evaluating $x+y$ to produce 7 and multiplying this by 12 to give a final result of 84. Thus, 3 is the value associated with the node x, 4 with the node y, 12 with the node z, 7 with the subtree representing $x+y$, and 84 with the subtree representing $(x+y)*z$.

The process of evaluation can be described by saying a value has been associated with each node of the tree, i.e. each terminal or non-terminal associated with expressions. Evaluation takes the form of values being passed up the tree from the terminal nodes to produce a result at the

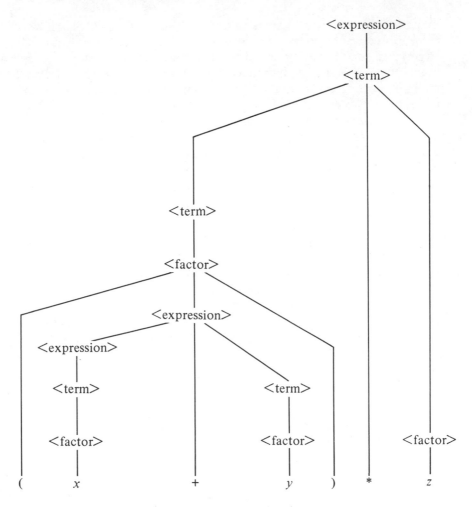

Fig. 6.1. Parse tree for $(x+y)*z$.

root of the tree. The rules that define the way in which values are processed as they move up the tree are just the semantic rules or rules which define the value produced by an expression.

A value as described above is an example of a more general property called an *attribute*. Since these travel up the tree they are referred to as *synthesised attribute values*. In discussing the definition of ALGOL W it was seen that arithmetic and logical expressions and subexpressions have modes and priorities associated with them. These could also be cited as examples of other properties which could be associated with the terminals and non-terminals for expressions (arithmetic or otherwise). The ALGOL W syntax examined in section 4.1 mentioned these attributes explicitly. Indeed, one of the many tasks a compiler must perform is to move attributes (such as the type and priority) up the parse tree so that certain decisions can be made, e.g. about the precise identity of each operator, the type of result produced by an arithmetic expression, the type changes to be made, and so on.

To illustrate another possibility consider the following piece of syntax taken from the ALGOL 60 Report:

<type list>::=<simple variable>|<simple variable>, <type list>
<type>   ::=**real** | **integer** | **Boolean**
<local or own type>::=<type> | **own** <type>
<type declaration>::=<local or own type><type list>

Part of the parse tree resulting from the declaration

    integer *a,b*

is given in figure 6.2.

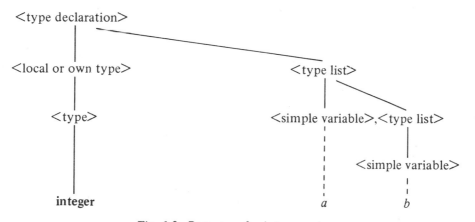

Fig. 6.2. Parse tree for **integer** *a, b*

It would seem natural to associate a type with the various nodes (and therefore terminals and non-terminals) in the tree. This type can be regarded as another example of an attribute. Given that <type declaration> has the attribute 'integer' – obtained by a process of synthesis performed on the left-hand branch of the tree – this attribute is then passed down the right-hand subtree to the node corresponding to <type list>. It then passes further down to all the other nodes lower in the tree. Attributes which travel down in this way are called *inherited attributes.*

We have seen then that there are properties or qualities called attributes which can be associated with terminals and non-terminals. There are two kinds of attributes, synthesised and inherited. The synthesised attributes travel up the parse tree. They represent aspects of terminals and/or non-terminals that are independent of the environment in which they occur within a program. As we have seen, examples of these might be just values, modes and priorities of expressions. Inherited attributes, on the other hand, tend to represent aspects of terminals and/or non-terminals which are context-sensitive in nature. It is customary to use inherited attributes to describe, for example, aspects of block structure.

We hope to be able to use attributes to formally define certain aspects of programming languages. Consequently we shall formalise the ideas outlined above in the concept of an *attribute grammar.* Such grammars are obtained from context-free grammars by associating with each terminal and non-terminal a particular set of attributes and giving rules which describe how attributes combine and are passed up or down parse trees.

Before embarking on this let us look at a common use of attributes. The following program merely reads two real numbers and prints their sum

```
begin real x,y,z;
      read((x,y));
      z := x+y;
      print(z)
end
```

One possible (skeleton) tree for this is given in figure 6.3.

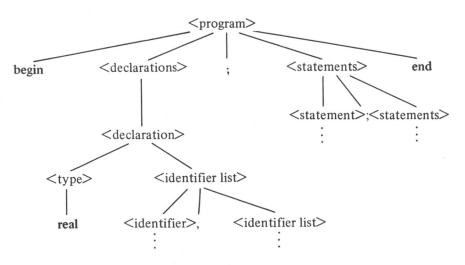

Fig. 6.3. Parse tree for program.

142

This program will be executed in an environment which 'understands' the meaning of *read* and *print* together with other standard identifiers, operators, modes, etc. This environment, which can also be thought of as a symbol table, will be the object of our immediate interest. When execution of the program starts the environment will be augmented with the information about x, y and z. The various calculations and statements are then performed in this new environment. The information in this environment, which includes type or mode information, is necessary for the proper evaluation of the program; for this determines that the addition to be performed is the addition of two reals and not the addition of two integers or the concatenation of two character strings, for example.

If we represent the environment as an attribute then it passes down through the declaration part of the tree being augmented in the process. It must then be passed back up and then passed down the statements part of the tree as an inherited attribute representing the context in which the various statements have to be interpreted and executed.

In conclusion, then, certain attributes have to be sucked up some branches of the parse tree and other attributes have to be blown down other branches. The various processes must combine in such a way that the proper meaning and effect is described.

6.1.2 Attribute grammars

In keeping with the notation used in defining a context-free grammar we define an attribute grammar G to be a quadruple (V_T, V_N, S, P) consisting of

- a finite set V_T of terminals
- a finite set V_N of non-terminals
- a special sentence symbol $S \in V_N$ which, we assume, cannot appear in the right part of any production
- a set of productions P.

With each $X \in V = V_T \cup V_N$ we associate two disjoint and finite sets of attributes:

- $I(X)$ denotes the inherited attributes of X
- $S(X)$ denotes the synthesised attributes of X.

For convenience we write $A(X) = I(X) \cup S(X)$ for the set of attributes of the terminal or non-terminal X.

The restriction on the occurrences of the start symbol S implies that the underlying context-free grammar cannot be completely general. Consequently it is sometimes said to be a *reduced* context-free grammar.

Noting this allows some restrictions to be naturally placed on the sets of attributes

    (a) $I(S) = \emptyset$, the empty set
    (b) $I(X) = \emptyset$ for each $X \in V_T$.

Let $p \in P$ be a production written in the form

$$p : X_0 \rightarrow X_1 X_2 \ldots X_{n_p}$$

where $n_p \geq 0$, $X_0 \in V_N$ and each $X_j \in V$ for $1 \leq j \leq n_p$. Associated with each X_j on the right-hand side of p will be a set of attributes. Accordingly a production p is said to have *attribute occurrence* (a,k) provided that $a \in A(X_k)$. If an attribute is to be regarded as a data type then an attribute occurrence is to be regarded as a variable which takes on values of that type, i.e. the attribute values.

With these introductory remarks it is now possible to describe how synthesised attributes and inherited attributes are passed up and down the parse tree.

    · Let s represent a synthesised attribute. For each occurrence $(s,0)$ of s in the left part of production p there is a *semantic function* $f_{(s,0)}^{(p)}$ which yields the value of the attribute occurrence $(s,0)$ as a function of other attribute occurrences in p. This describes the process of moving synthesised attribute values one level up the parse tree.

    · Let i represent an inherited attribute. For each occurrence (i,k) of i in the right part of production p there is a semantic function $f_{(i,k)}^{(p)}$ which gives the value of the attribute occurrence (i,k) as a function of the other attribute occurrences in p. Such functions exist for each value of $k = 1,2,\ldots,n_p$. This describes the process of moving attribute values one level down the parse tree.

This completes the definition of attribute grammar. But some discussion about various aspects of this definition might be beneficial.

It might seem natural to insist that terminal symbols have no synthesised attributes. But this is not so. The syntax analysis phase of compilation is generally preceded by a lexical phase which groups together sequences of characters which naturally form entities or words. Thus it would group together all the characters that constitute an integer denotation, a real denotation, etc., store these in a table or file perhaps, and replace these by some suitable fixed-size token. Similarly bold words such as **begin**, identifiers, multicharacter symbols such as the becomes symbol, :=, or the less-than-or-equal-to symbol <= are all replaced by single tokens which then act as terminals in subsequent phases of the compilation process. The lexical scan can then be said to impart synthesised attribute values to these tokens. In the case of a real denotation these might be a type, a position in a table or file where the actual number that appeared in the program is now held, or a size indicating single or multiple precision, and so on.

There are various methods of representing attributes and their occurrences and of distinguishing between synthesised and inherited attributes. One common method is to express attribute occurrences in some distinguished printing font, e.g. in capital or bold letters, and to place ↑ before synthesised and ↓ before inherited attribute occurrences. It is then convenient to write attribute occurrences, always the same set, immediately after each occurrence in the grammar of the terminal or non-terminal they describe. Note then that $\downarrow A$ and $\uparrow A$ represent occurrences of different attributes. The arrows thus indicate the direction of travel of the attribute values.

Of course, the necessary steps must be taken to ensure that there is no danger of confusing attributes with terminals or non-terminals of the programming language or indeed with the metalanguage. Otherwise unfortunate ambiguities would result. One common approach to the avoidance of such ambiguities is to write each occurrence of a terminal or non-terminal in the right part of a production on a separate line and follow this with its list of attributes. Thus

$$<A> \downarrow ENV_1 \rightarrow <B> \uparrow C \uparrow ENV_2 \downarrow ENV_3$$
$$a \uparrow ENV_4$$

The semantic functions described above give rules for the evaluation of certain attribute values. In practice, these functions are usually fairly simple and can be expressed in a very natural way. Attributes A and B can be defined by writing after the relevant production something akin to

where $A = ..., B = ...$

If no confusion can be caused, if the ordering of the attributes is fixed and if the meaning is clear, it is sometimes convenient to replace each occurrence of A and B in the production by the expression which defines their value. Thus instead of writing

$$<A> \downarrow ENV_1 \rightarrow <B> \uparrow C \uparrow ENV_2 \downarrow ENV_3$$
$$a \uparrow ENV_4$$
$$\textbf{where } \downarrow ENV_3 = \downarrow ENV_1$$

it is simpler to write

$$<A> \downarrow ENV_1 \rightarrow <B> \uparrow C \uparrow ENV_2 \downarrow ENV_1$$
$$a \uparrow ENV_4$$

It is clear that, in the previous notation, $\downarrow ENV_3$ is an inherited attribute occurrence of $<B>$ and must be defined. The appearance of $\downarrow ENV_1$ in the second rule can be taken to act as the necessary definition.

One other important means of describing semantic actions or rules is the use of *action symbols*. These appear in the grammar itself and describe what has to be done when a particular construct has been recognised; consequently the relevant actions will occupy a position immediately following the grammatical definition of the construct. The resulting grammar is then something more than an attribute grammar since it now has action symbols. It is usually referred to as an *attribute translation grammar*. The actions will usually operate on some attributes and must be described in some previously defined programming language or using some well-understood mechanism.

To illustrate their use, consider the following simplified attribute translation grammar for describing a small set of arithmetic expressions. The actions appear in curly brackets. ADD and MULT operate on the first two operands and place the sum and product respectively in the third operand. LOOKUP (*name, value*) places in *value* the contents of the location referred to by *name*.

$$<\text{expression}> \uparrow value \rightarrow <\text{expression}> \uparrow value_1$$
$$+$$
$$<\text{term}> \uparrow value_2$$
$$\{ ADD(value_1, value_2, value) \}$$
$$<\text{expression}> \uparrow value \rightarrow <\text{term}> \uparrow value$$
$$<\text{term}> \qquad \uparrow value \rightarrow <\text{term}> \uparrow value_1$$
$$*$$
$$<\text{factor}> \uparrow value_2$$
$$\{ MULT(value_1, value_2, value) \}$$
$$<\text{term}> \qquad \uparrow value \rightarrow <\text{factor}> \uparrow value$$
$$<\text{factor}> \uparrow value \rightarrow ($$
$$<\text{expression}> \uparrow value$$
$$)$$
$$<\text{factor}> \uparrow value \rightarrow <\text{identifier}> \uparrow name$$
$$\{ LOOKUP(name, value) \}$$

In this grammar we have used some of the conventions outlined earlier. Thus

- ↑*value* is a synthesised attribute
- the same attribute occurrence can appear on both sides of one rule, e.g. ↑*value* appears on the two sides of the rule for <factor>, thereby indicating that the left-hand occurrence receives a value which is just that of the right-hand occurrence.

As it happens no further semantic rules are necessary. The grammar then defines not only the syntax of these arithmetic expressions but also the meaning in the sense that it describes how the value of an arithmetic expression is to be calculated.

In conclusion let us note that there are substantial dangers in confusing the various symbols now being used in the production and other rules of the language. Not only are there terminals and non-terminals together with the symbols (,), <, > or whatever for expressing productions but now there are attribute symbols, action symbols, perhaps rules for describing the semantic rules, etc.

6.1.3 Algorithms and theoretical results

There are problems associated with the semantic evaluation of the various attributes for a given parse tree. In the first place it must be possible to find some order of evaluation which will result in all attribute occurrences being given their correct values. If such an order does not exist, the attribute occurrences can never receive values and, in fact, are undefined or circularly defined. When such an order does exist the attributes as described by the semantic rules are said to be *well-defined*. The necessary algorithms exist for testing for circularity.

In discussing the order of evaluation of the attribute values it is natural from a compiling point of view to hope that the attributes of a parse tree will be evaluated in a left-to-right order. For then the attributes can be determined as the source program is being read by the compiler. To be positive about what we mean by a left-to-right scan let

$$p: X_0 \rightarrow X_1 X_2 \dots X_{n_p}$$

be a production of the language corresponding to some node of a parse tree. Then we mean one execution of the following algorithm, expressed in an ALGOL 68 kind of notation:

proc *process node* = (**node** X_0) **void**:
begin for k **from** 1 **to** n_p
    do if $X_k \in V_N$
        then update inherited attributes
            of X_k from semantic rules of p;
            process node (X_k)

                    fi
            od;
            update synthesised attributes of X_0 from the
            semantic rules of p
     end

In effect this recursive procedure amounts to a traversal of the parse
tree in which inherited attributes are evaluated on the way down the
tree and synthesised attributes are evaluated on the way up the tree.

Unfortunately it is not always possible to evaluate all the attributes
in such a simple-minded way, even when circularity has been dismissed.
But this possibility is so attractive that it is worthwhile outlining when
it is possible. Before enunciating the relevant theorem we introduce
some terminology.

Definition
Using the notation employed in defining attribute grammars the *dependency set* $D_{(a,k)}^{(p)}$ is defined to be the set of attribute occurrences whose
values must be known so that the attribute occurrence (a,k) can be
evaluated using the semantic rule $f_{(a,k)}^{(p)}$.

With this definition we can now enunciate the relevant theorem.
The statement of the theorem is merely a statement that the appropriate
dependency sets are known when required. Its truth follows from the
algorithm given earlier outlining the meaning of a left-to-right scan.

Theorem 6.1
Given an attribute grammar with the synthesised and inherited attributes of X being represented by $S(X)$ and $I(X)$ respectively, the attributes can be evaluated in a single left-to-right scan provided that the
following condition is satisfied. For each production p where

$$p: X_0 \rightarrow X_1 X_2 \ldots X_{n_p}$$

the dependency sets are such that

(a) $D_{(s,0)}^{(p)} \cap S(X_0) = \emptyset$
        for all synthesised attributes $s \in S(X_0)$
(b) for each $k = 1,2,\ldots,n_p$

$$D_{(i,k)}^{(p)} \cap \{ S(X_0) \cup \bigcup_{t=k}^{n_p} [I(X_t) \cup S(X_t)] \} = \emptyset$$

        for each inherited attribute $i \in I(X_k)$.

One possible kind of circularity of attributes can be described as *local* circularity. This arises when the semantic rules of a single production, regardless of any other productions in the grammar, imply circularity. If we exclude such productions from our attribute grammar the theorem stated above can be reformulated as

Theorem 6.2
The attributes of any derivation tree of an attribute grammar can be evaluated in a single pass if and only if, for each production p,

$$D^{(p)}_{(i,k)} \cap \overset{n_p}{\underset{t=k}{\cup}} S(X_t) = \emptyset$$

is satisfied for each $k = 1, 2, ..., n_p$ and each attribute $i \in I(X_k)$.

Having established the conditions under which a single scan is sufficient, what can be said about other situations in which these conditions are not satisfied? There are various possibilities:

- the attributes are circularly defined and no number of scans will suffice
- some fixed number of scans is required
- the number of scans required is not fixed but depends on the particular program.

There is an algorithm for determining which of these possibilities arises. As a prelude to the algorithm let us introduce some variables. Let

- *scan no* represent the cardinality of the current scan
- *curratt*(X) represent the attributes of X which may be evaluated during the current scan
- *evalatt*(X) represent the attributes of X evaluated during previous scans
- $A_m(X)$ represent those attributes of X which are calculated on the mth scan; clearly $A_m(X) \subseteq A(X)$.

The initialisation phase of the algorithm is straightforward, namely

> *scan no* := 0;
> **for all** $X \in V_T$ **do** *evalatt* $(X) := A(X)$ **od**;
> **for all** $X \in V_N$ **do** *evalatt* $(X) := \emptyset$ **co** empty set **co od**

For the next part we introduce a notation to describe those attributes which do not occur on the left of an occurrence (a, k) in a particular production p. To be more precise let

$$NL^{(p)}_{(a, 0)} = S(X_0) \text{ for all } (a, 0) \in S(X_0)$$

149

and

$$NL^{(p)}_{(a,\,k)} = S(X_0) \cup \bigcup_{t=k}^{n_p} A(X_t)$$

for all $k=1,2,...,n_p$ and all $(a,k)\in I(X_k)$.

On each left-to-right scan the following is performed

    scan no := *scan no* + 1;
    for all $X \in V$ **do** *curratt*(X) := $A(X)$ - *evalatt*(X) **od**;
    co now remove certain items from each *curratt*(X) **co**
    for all $p \in P$
    do for k **from** 1 **to** n_p
        do co let X_{pk} represent kth symbol in right
            part of production p **co**
            for all inherited attributes $a \in$ *curratt*(X_{pk}) and
                all synthesised attributes $a \in$ *curratt*(X_{po})
            do bool *cond* := **true**;

                for all $(b,t) \in D^{(p)}_{(a,k)}$ **while** *cond*

                  do   **if** $(b,t) \in NL^{(p)}_{(a,k)}$
                      co i.e. if (b,t) occurs on left of
                          occurrence (a,k) in p **co**
                      then *cond* := *cond* $\wedge$ ($b \in$ *evalatt*(X_{pt}))
                      fi;
                      cond := *cond* $\wedge$ ($b \in$ *evalatt*(X_{pt}) $\cup$
                            curratt(X_{pt}))
                od;
                if not *cond* **then** remove a from
                    curratt(X_{pk}) or *curratt*(X_{po}) as required **fi**
            od
        od
    od

Having completed a scan in this way the following assignments can be made

    for all $X \in V_N$ **do**
    do $A_{scan\ no}(X)$:= *curratt*(X);
        evalatt(X) := *evalatt*(X) $\cup$ *curratt*(X)
    od

Repeated scans will thus result in the various $A_m(X)$ being given their appropriate values.

At the end of each scan there are various possibilities:

(a) for each $X \in V_N$

$$evalatt(X) = A(X);$$

then all the attributes can be evaluated and no more scans are required; no attribute was thus eliminated from any $curratt(X)$

(b) some attribute was removed from a $curratt(X)$ and

$$curratt(X) = \emptyset \text{ for all } X \in V_N;$$

the attributes that remain cannot be determined in any limited number of left-to-right scans

(c) some attribute was removed from a $curratt(X)$ and yet

$$curratt(X) \neq \emptyset \text{ for some } X \in V_N;$$

under these circumstances another scan over the grammar is required.

These three are the only cases that can arise; note that case (b) covers, in particular, the situation in which the attributes are circularly defined. Yet some commentary is necessary for it was remarked earlier that in some peculiar cases the number of scans may depend on some features peculiar to the particular program being processed – such a feature may be the level to which blocks are nested.

Theorem 6.3
If the attribute grammar satisfies the condition

$$D_{(a,k)}^{(p)} \subset I(X_0) \cup \bigcup_{t=1}^{n_p} S(X_t)$$

for each production $p \in P$ and each

(a) $k=0$ and $a \in S(X_0)$

together with

(b) $k=1,2,...,n_p$ and $a \in I(X_k)$

the algorithm gives the minimum number of scans necessary for the evaluation of all the attributes of an arbitrary derivation tree.

If the condition is not satisfied the algorithm gives a maximum number of scans necessary.

6.2 Attributes and language definition

6.2.1 Introductory remarks

From the point of view of language definition there are various factors to recommend the use of attribute grammars:

- the basic ideas and notation are relatively simple
- there is a clear distinction between synthesised and inherited attributes
- both the context-free and the context-sensitive aspects of a programming language can be defined
- the underlying context-free grammar is quite visible
- the semantic rules refer to a single production and do not straddle several productions; this makes for ease of understanding
- the semantic rules are structured according to the syntax
- there is an algorithm for detecting circularity
- there is an algorithm for detecting language features requiring several passes
- the idea of a pass of a compiler is given some theoretical basis, and there is an algorithm for finding the number of passes required.

In practice, it is convenient to use attribute grammars for defining the context-free and the context-sensitive parts of programming languages. In theory, they can also be used for defining semantics; for an attribute representing meaning or object code can be associated with the various constructs, and therefore terminals and non-terminals, of the language. However, this meaning or object code will usually have to be expressed in some other programming language and the problem of describing semantics is thereby transferred to the other language. Attribute translation grammars with embedded action symbols are more suitable for describing translations of this kind.

This method of describing programming languages, perhaps in the form of attribute translation grammars, tends to be favoured by compiler writers since it tends to suit their needs. That it suits the needs of others is not so apparent. The various theorems give a theoretical basis to the meaning of pass or scan as used in compiler writing. The various available algorithms will permit the attributes that can be evaluated on each individual pass to be listed.

It is possible to write programs which will accept descriptions of attribute grammars and perform the necessary lexical analysis, context-free analysis, context-sensitive analysis, attribute propagation, etc. Thus the compilation process can be automated to a considerable extent. The use of attribute translation grammars allows the production of object code and thus compiler-compilers result.

At this juncture of course it is natural to question the interplay between the underlying context-free grammar and the attribute evaluation. From a compiler writer's point of view it is desirable that it should be possible to parse any programs without backtracking. For then the attributes can be evaluated as the source program is being parsed. In this connection it can be shown that attribute evaluation and syntax analysis can proceed in parallel if, for example,

(*a*) the underlying context-free grammar is $LL(k)$ and the attributes satisfy the conditions of theorem 6.1

(*b*) the underlying context-free grammar is $LR(k)$ and the attributes satisfy the condition

$$D_{(s,0)}^{(p)} \cap S(X_0) = \emptyset$$

for all productions $p \in P$ and all $s \in S(X_0)$.

6.2.2 *Application to PASCAL*

The ideas of section 6.1 will now be applied to a partial definition of PASCAL. This definition will include the context-free and the context-sensitive aspects of the language.

A complete formal definition of the syntax using attribute grammars should begin with a list of the various terminals and non-terminals used in the grammar together with their attributes. However, here it will be assumed this can be done for the attributes can be derived by merely inspecting the grammar. Attributes such as ↓ENV (for environment) and ↑TYPE (for type) will be used and it is intended that

- the meaning of each attribute is clear; where this is not so an explanation is given
- the direction of the initial arrow distinguishes between synthesised and inherited attributes
- instructions for indicating semantic functions are given in the form of rules enclosed within square brackets; these will be imbedded in the part of a syntax rule to which they apply
- auxiliary notes occur before the syntax rules they apply to.

The syntax begins by looking at expressions, then at statements, and finally at declarations. Basically a BNF form of definition will be given but this is augmented with appropriate attribute information. Each occurrence of a particular terminal or non-terminal (such as <expression>) will always be followed by the same list of attributes. What follows is not a complete syntax of PASCAL but is sufficient to illustrate how a complete attribute-directed definition of the syntax could be obtained; it is based on the work in Watt (1979).

Expressions

<expression> ↓ENV ↑TYPE ::=
        <simple expression> ↓ENV ↑TYPE|
        <simple expression> ↓ENV ↑TYPE1
        <relational operator> ↑OP
        <simple expression> ↓ENV ↑TYPE2
        [rule: operator ↑OP applied to
                ↑TYPE1 and ↑TYPE2 produces ↑TYPE]

<simple expression> ↓ENV ↑TYPE ::=
      <term> ↓ENV ↑TYPE |
      <simple expression> ↓ENV ↑TYPE1
        <adding operator> ↑OP
        <term> ↓ENV ↑TYPE2
        [rule: operator ↑OP operating on ↑TYPE1
            and ↑TYPE2 produces ↑TYPE] |
      <adding operator> ↑OP
        <term> ↓ENV ↑TYPE1
        [rule: ↑OP applied to ↑TYPE1 produces ↑TYPE]

<term> ↓ENV ↑TYPE ::=
      <factor> ↓ENV ↑TYPE |
      <term> ↓ENV ↑TYPE1
        <multiplying operator> ↑OP
        <factor> ↓ENV ↑TYPE2
        [rule: ↑OP applied to ↑TYPE1 and ↑TYPE2
            produces ↑TYPE]

<factor> ↓ENV ↑TYPE ::=
      <variable> ↓ENV ↑TYPE |
      <unsigned constant> ↓ENV ↑TYPE |
      <function designator> ↓ENV ↑TYPE |
      <set> ↓ENV ↑TYPE |
      (<expression> ↓ENV ↑TYPE) |
      not <factor> ↓ENV ↑TYPE

Statements
The syntax of statements makes use of attributes ↑STMLABELS and
↓LABELENV. These should be regarded as sets of labels, the former
being the labels used to mark statements and the latter being the labels
declared; in syntactically correct programs ↑STMLABELS should be a

154

subset of ↓LABELENV. Since these are sets, set notation is used; in particular ↑ { } represents the empty set of statement labels. The attribute ↑ENV contains information about all declarations other than declarations of labels.

<statement> ↓ENV ↓LABELENV ↑STMLABELS ::=
    <unlabelled statement> ↓ENV ↓LABELENV
       ↑STMLABELS |
    <label> ↑LABEL
      :<unlabelled statement> ↓ENV ↓LABELENV
       ↑STMLABELS1
      [rule: ↑STMLABELS= ↑LABEL ∪
       ↑STMLABELS1 and ↑LABEL does not belong
       to ↑STMLABELS1]

<unlabelled statement> ↓ENV ↓LABELENV ↑STMLABELS˙
    <simple statement> ↓ENV ↓LABELENV ↑STMLABEL⸴
    <structured statement> ↓ENV ↓LABELENV
       ↑STMLABELS

<simple statement> ↓ENV ↓LABELENV ↑{ } ::=
    <assignment statement> ↓ENV |
    <procedure statement> ↓ENV |
    <go to statement> ↓LABELENV |
    <empty statement>

<structured statement> ↓ENV ↓LABELENV ↑STMLABELS
    <compound statement> ↓ENV ↓LABELENV
       ↑STMLABELS |
    <conditional statement> ↓ENV ↓LABELENV
       ↑STMLABELS |
    <repetitive statement> ↓ENV ↓LABELENV
       ↑STMLABELS |
    <with statement> ↓ENV ↓LABELENV ↑STMLABELS

Assignment statements
The definition of assignment statements makes use of the phrase 'assignment compatible'. Informally the types on the left- and right-hand sides of an assignment are assignment compatible if

    · they are identical, or
    · the left is of type real and the right is of type integer, or
    · the type of the right mode is a subrange of the type of the
      left mode.

This definition can be expressed formally using set notation or using predicates similar to those used in the ALGOL 68 Report (Chapter 7).

<assignment statement> ↓ENV ::=
   <variable> ↓ENV ↑TYPE1 :=
     <expression> ↓ENV ↑TYPE2 |
   <function identifier> ↓ENV ↑TYPE1 :=
     <expression> ↓ENV ↑TYPE2
[rule: ↑TYPE1 and ↑TYPE2 must be assignment compatible]

Procedure statements

In the definition of procedure statements use is made of the attributes ↑MODE and ↑PLAN. ↑MODE is used to indicate the type of a procedure and will include the types of all parameters in the form of an ordered list or plan together with the type of the result.

Note that one of the obscure areas of PASCAL is the exact relationship in terms of types between formal and actual parameters. Accordingly the definition below makes use of a vague verb 'contained in' at the appropriate part of the syntax.

<procedure statement> ↓ENV ::=
   <procedure identifier> ↓ENV ↑MODE
     [rule: ↑MODE indicates a procedure with no
        parameters] |
   <procedure identifier> ↓ENV ↑MODE
     (<actual parameter> ↓ENV ↓PLAN1
     {,<actual parameter> ↓ENV ↓PLANi })
     [rule: if all ↓PLANi are concatenated they should
        produce an overall ↓PLAN which is contained
        in ↑MODE]

<procedure identifier> ↓ENV ↑MODE ::=
   <identifier> ↑NAME
   [rule: look up ↑NAME in ↑ENV to produce ↑MODE]

<actual parameter> ↓ENV ↓PARAM ::=
   <expression> ↓ENV ↑TYPE |
   <variable>　　 ↓ENV ↑TYPE |
   <procedure identifier> ↓ENV ↑MODE |
   <function identifier> ↓ENV ↑MODE
[rule: ↑TYPE or ↑MODE is contained in ↓PARAM]

Conditional statements

Conditional statements come in two forms, the if statement and the

156

case statement. The syntactic ambiguity caused by the appearance of

if ... **then if** ... **then** ... **else** ...

is resolved by associating the **else** with the nearest preceding **then**.

<conditional statement> ↓ENV ↓LABELENV ↑STMLABELS
::=
    <if statement> ↓ENV ↓LABELENV ↑STMLABELS |
    <case statement> ↓ENV ↓LABELENV ↑STMLABELS

<if statement> ↓ENV ↓LABELENV ↑STMLABELS ::=
    if <expression> ↓ENV ↑TYPE
        then <statement> ↓ENV ↓LABELENV
            ↑STMLABELS
    [rule: ↑TYPE = Boolean] |
    if <expression> ↓ENV ↑TYPE
        then <statement> ↓ENV ↓LABELENV
            ↑STMLABELS1
        else <statement> ↓ENV ↓LABELENV
            ↑STMLABELS2
    [rules: ↑TYPE = Boolean,
            ↑STMLABELS = ↑STMLABELS1 ∪
                ↑STMLABELS2,
            ↑STMLABELS1 ∩ ↑STMLABELS2 = ∅]

Go to statements

<go to statement> ↓LABELENV ::=
    go to <label> ↓LABELENV

<label> ↓LABELENV ::=
    <unsigned integer> ↑LABEL
    [rule: ↑LABEL is in ↓LABELENV]

Repetitive statements

<repetitive statement> ↓ENV ↓LABELENV ↑STMLABELS ::=
    <while statement> ↓ENV ↓LABELENV
        ↑STMLABELS |
    <repeat statement> ↓ENV ↓LABELENV
        ↑STMLABELS |
    <for statement> ↓ENV ↓LABELENV
        ↑STMLABELS |

157

<while statement> ↓ENV ↓LABELENV ↑STMLABELS ::=
    while <expression> ↓ENV ↑TYPE
        do <statement> ↓ENV ↓LABELENV ↑STMLABELS
        [rule: ↑TYPE = Boolean]

With statement

<with statement> ↓ENV ↓LABELENV ↑STMLABELS ::=
    with <record variable list> ↓ENV ↑INNERENV
        do <statement> ↓INNERENV ↓LABELENV
        ↑STMLABELS

<record variable list> ↓ENV ↑INNERENV ::=
    <record variable> ↓ENV ↑INNERENV
    [rule: ↑INNERENV is obtained from ↓ENV by
        replacing all components of the record
        specified by <record variable> by the field
        selectors only] |
    <record variable list> ↓ENV ↑INNERENVA
    ,<record variable> ↓INNERENVA ↑INNERENV
    [rule: ↑INNERENV is obtained from ↓INNERENVA
        by replacing all components of the record
        specified by <record variable> by the field
        selectors only]

Blocks and programs

<block> ↓GLOBALS ↓FORMPARS ↓GLOBLABELS ::=
    <label declaration part> ↑LOCLABELS
    <constant definition part> ↓GLOBALS ↓FORMPARS
        ↑NEWLOCALS1
    <type definition part> ↓GLOBALS ↓NEWLOCALS1
        ↑NEWLOCALS2
    <variable declaration part> ↓GLOBALS ↓NEWLOCALS2
        ↑NEWLOCALS3
    <procedure and function declaration part> ↓GLOBALS
        ↓NEWLOCALS3 ↑NEWLOCALS ↑LABELENV
    <statement part> ↓ENV ↓LABELENV ↑STMLABELS
    [rules: (*a*)   ↓ENV is formed from ↑NEWLOCALS by adding
        those identifiers of ↓GLOBALS not already
        present in ↓NEWLOCALS;
        (*b*)   ↓LABELENV is obtained from ↓LOCLABELS by

adding those items in ↓GLOBLABELS but not in
↓LOCLABELS;
  (*c*) ↑STMLABELS is a subset of ↓LABELENV;
ideally both should be identical]

<label declaration part> ↑LABELS ::=
    <empty> ↑LABELS
       [rule: ↑LABELS = ↑ { } , the empty set] |
    label <label> ↑LABEL1 { , <label> ↑LABELi } ;
       [rule: ↑LABELS is union of all ↑LABELi;
          these must be disjoint]

<constant definition part> ↓GLOBALS ↓LOCALS ↑NEWLOCALS ::=
    <empty> ↑NEWLOCALS
    [rule: ↑NEWLOCALS = ↓LOCALS] |
    const <constant definition> ↓GLOBALS ↓LOCALS
    ↑NEWLOCALS1
       { , <constant definition> ↓GLOBALS ↓LOCALS
       ↑NEWLOCALSi }
    [rule: ↑NEWLOCALS is obtained from ↓LOCALS by adding
    all the ↑NEWLOCALSi; the latter must all be distinct
    from themselves and from elements of ↓LOCALS]

<statement part> ↓ENV ↓LABELENV ↑STMLABELS ::=
    <compound statement> ↓ENV ↓LABELENV ↑STMLABELS

<compound statement> ↓ENV ↓LABELENV ↑STMLABELS ::=
    begin <statement> ↓ENV ↓LABELENV ↑STMLABELS1
      { ; statement ↓ENV ↓LABELENV ↑STMLABELSi }
    end
    [rule: ↑STMLABELS is union of all ↑STMLABELSi and these
    must be mutually disjoint]

<program> ::=
    <program heading> ↑NAME
      <block> ↓STANDARDENV ↓ { } ↓ { } .

6.3 Axiomatic semantics

In this section we shall look at the formal approach of Hoare and
Wirth to the problem of describing semantics. It will be assumed that
the syntax of the programming language has already been defined. Not
only will the context-free aspects of the syntax have been defined but

in some appropriate way the context-sensitive aspects will have been specified; thus the relationship between the use and declaration of variables, the priority of operators, the appropriate use of types and modes will all be clear. Consequently this section will blend somewhat conveniently with the previous section which concentrated on precisely those aspects of a formal definition of PASCAL whose existence we now choose to assume.

This *axiomatic* approach, as it is called, was first suggested by Hoare. Its origins are in mathematical logic and much of the notation and terminology of that subject has been carried across. PASCAL was the first programming language to which this method of defining semantics was applied.

6.3.1 Program verification

The axiomatic method is especially suited to the needs of the theorist interested in proving (or verifying) the correctness of the programs he writes. In program verification it is customary to begin with some initial predicate or logical formula which describes certain aspects of and the relationships between the various pieces of input data. It is also customary to have an output or final predicate which specifies certain aspects of the intended output. In the case of a simple program to calculate and print $n!$ where n is supplied as data

- the input predicate might be: n integral, $n \geqslant 0$
- the output predicate might be: z printed, $z = n!$

The program prover has then to show by a mathematical proof that the value of z that is evaluated by the program will actually be $n!$

This is no place to begin a detailed exposition of the various methods of proving the correctness of programs. But we look at two relatively simple examples to illustrate the general ideas. We begin with a simple program to interchange the values of two integer variables. We then look at a program to calculate $n!$ In both cases we ignore, for simplicity, the possibility of read and print statements. We merely make use of variables of appropriate kinds:

- $n, x, x_1, x_2, \ldots$ are input variables; these hold the data for the program and have read-only access; they cannot be altered by statements but replace read statements
- $z, z_1, z_2, \ldots$ are output variables; these hold the results of calculations and have write-only access; they essentially replace the print or write statements
- $y, y_1, y_2, \ldots$ are program variables and are used as temporary or auxiliary variables for holding intermediate results; these

160

are equivalent to the usual variables used in programming languages.

Finally we surround predicates with curly brackets { and } . It will transpire that a predicate is allowed to appear

- at the beginning of a program, and then it is the initial predicate which will be phrased in terms of the input variables
- at the end of a program, and then it is the final predicate which will be phrased in terms of both the input and the output variables, or
- between any two phrases in a program, and in these circumstances the predicate can contain mention of the input and/or program variables.

A predicate of **true** will imply that there is no interrelationship between variables, and any values for the variables suffice.

With these conventions we can now write, in an ALGOL-like notation, the program which essentially interchanges the values of two variables:

$$\{\textbf{true}\}$$

$$
\begin{array}{ll}
A: & (y_1, y_2) := (x_1, x_2); \\
B: & y_1 := y_1 + y_2; \\
C: & y_2 := y_1 - y_2; \\
D: & y_1 := y_1 - y_2; \\
E: & (z_1, z_2) := (y_1, y_2) \\
F: & \{ z_1 = x_2 \wedge z_2 = x_1 \}
\end{array}
$$

The labels are used merely to ease the task of referring to different parts of the program; the initial assignment involves evaluating both x_1 and x_2 (essentially the data) and, on completion of this, assigning the results to y_1 and y_2 respectively, etc.

A proof of the correctness of this program can be developed as follows. We start with the final predicate and ask: for this to be true at F what predicate must be true at label E? Obtaining this answer is relatively straightforward:

$$y_1 = x_2 \wedge y_2 = x_1$$

Again for this to be true at E what predicate must be true at D? Answer:

$$(y_1 - y_2 = x_2) \wedge (y_2 = x_1)$$

Continuing backwards in this fashion produces predicates between all the statements. On reaching label A the predicate that is being dragged backwards through the predicate is just **true** and this of course is the initial predicate. The situation can be depicted by inserting all the predicates. Hence

$\{\textbf{true}\}$
$(y_1,y_2) := (x_1,x_2);$
  $\{y_1 = x_1 \wedge y_2 = x_2\}$
$y_1 := y_1 + y_2;$
  $\{y_1 - y_2 = x_1 \wedge y_2 = x_2\}$
$y_2 := y_1 - y_2;$
  $\{y_2 = x_1 \wedge y_1 - y_2 = x_2\}$
$y_1 := y_1 - y_2;$
  $\{y_2 = x_1 \wedge y_1 = x_2\}$
$(z_1,z_2) := (y_1,y_2)$
  $\{z_2 = x_1 \wedge z_1 = x_2\}$

It should be regarded as something of a coincidence that the input predicate turns out to be the same as the predicate obtained by dragging the output predicate back through the program. In general this will not be so; the two predicates will be different. In these circumstances it is then necessary to show that the truth of the input predicate implies the truth of the other predicate.

The method of proving the correctness of this program involved using the statements to transform the assertions. The assertions were, in fact, changed by a process of back substitution. Given a statement of the form

$\{\text{first predicate}\}$
$y_1 := \text{expression}$
$\{\text{second predicate}\}$

then in all cases the { first predicate } could be obtained from the { second predicate } by replacing all occurrences of y_1 in { second predicate } by 'expression'. The obvious generalisations apply. Consequently the technique is often referred to as just *back substitution*.

Now take the factorial example. The program might take the form (again labels are used to refer to positions within the program; in particular, C is the position just before the test)

$\qquad \{n \geq 0\}$
$A: \quad (y_1,y_2) := (0,1);$
$B: \quad \textbf{while } C : y_1 \neq n \textbf{ do } (y_1,y_2) := (y_1 + 1, y_2 \times (y_1 + 1)) \textbf{ od};$
$D: \quad z := y_2$
$E: \quad \{z = n!\}$

We can again proceed from the end of the program and deduce that at label D the predicate $y_2 = n!$ must be satisfied. But how do we cope with the loop? It was mentioned earlier that predicates are used to describe the relationship between the variables in a program. This remains true even for loops. Consequently we must deduce a predicate, called the *loop invariant*, which captures the relationship between the variables on each circuit of the loop. Tracing the above program suggests that the following predicate will be satisfied at label C:

$$y_2 = y_1! \wedge y_1 \leq n$$

The proof of correctness of the program then involves showing that

- on first entering the loop this predicate is true on reaching C
- if the predicate is true at C then on returning to C after one circuit of the loop the predicate is again true
- on leaving the loop the predicate at E is satisfied.

The method of proof involved here is clearly inductive in nature. Consequently it is referred to as the method of *inductive assertions*.

Each stage of the above proof can now be performed in a manner which is similar to that employed earlier for the program to interchange the values of the two variables. The program with all its assertions inserted is then

$$\{n \geq 0\}$$
$A:$ $(y_1, y_2) := (0,1);$
$B:$ **while** $C:$ { $y_2 = y_1! \wedge y_1 \leq n$ } $y_1 \neq n$
       do $(y_1, y_2) := (y_1 + 1, y_2 \times (y_1 + 1))$ **od**;
       $\{y_2 = n!\}$
$D:$ $z := y_2$
$E:$ $\{z = n!\}$

Take path ABC:

- back substitution from C to B to A means that at label A we have to show that the truth of the input predicate $n \geq 0$ must imply the truth of

$$1 = 0! \wedge 0 \leq n$$

This is clearly correct.

Take path CC which involves a circuit of the loop:

- back substitution again implies that, on the assumption that $y_1 \neq n$, then the truth of

$$y_2 = y_1! \wedge y_1 \leq n$$

implies the truth of

$$y_2 \times (y_1 + 1) = (y_1 + 1)! \wedge y_1 + 1 \leq n$$

Again this is clearly true.

Finally take path CDE:

> · on the assumption that $y_1 = n$ it is necessary to show that the truth of
>
> $$y_2 = y_1! \wedge y_1 \leq n$$
>
> implies the truth of
>
> $$y_2 = n!$$

Again this is straightforward.

In this way then the truth of the correctness of the factorial program can be established. In fact, we have shown only that if the program terminates the result obtained will be correct. We have not shown or proved that the program terminates. In the jargon we have established *partial correctness* but not *total correctness*. A proof of total correctness can be provided but we shall not dwell on the details. Roughly, each time round the loop there is a quantity (in this case $n - y_1$) which keeps on decreasing but never becomes negative. Consequently the loop can be traversed only a finite number of times and so eventually the program will terminate. A proof of termination together with the previous proof of partial correctness provides a proof of total correctness.

Now let us consider the general problem. Suppose that each S_i $(1 \leq i \leq r)$ represents a statement and

$$S_1 ; S_2 ; \ldots ; S_r$$

represents a program which has to be shown to be (partially) correct with respect to an input predicate P_0 and an output predicate P_r. Then essentially predicates P_i $(1 \leq i \leq r - 1)$ have to be found and these have to be such that if P_i is true and statement S_{i+1} is executed then P_{i+1} will be true on termination of S_{i+1} for each i, $0 \leq i \leq r - 1$. If this can be achieved then the (partial) correctness of the program follows.

In this discussion we have assumed that each S_i represents a statement of the programming language. These may be simple assignment statements or even conditionals, loops, function calls, etc. An S_i might even be a compound statement or block and so contain other statements. In these circumstances the appropriate P_i and P_{i+1} can themselves be regarded as a kind of initial and final predicate or assertion of S_i; the whole process must then be repeated. In this way, proofs of programs expressed in typical programming languages can be developed.

So far we have paid little attention to the very real possibility that a program might not terminate. In what follows we shall have to be rather careful in dealing with such situations.

The discussion of this section has been conducted in a rather *ad hoc* and informal atmosphere. We shall now attempt to make the discussion more rigorous and formal. We shall look at the possibility of supplying axioms or rules which formally describe the manner in which the different kinds of statements transform predicates. Collectively these rules are often referred to as the proof rules for the various constructions in the programming language.

6.3.2 *Notation and terminology*

We begin by introducing some appropriate notation

- $P,Q,R,P_1,\ldots$ will be used for logical variables, expressions or symbols, i.e. for predicates
- $S, S_1, S_2,\ldots$ will be used to represent statements or sequences of statements of our programming language.

A notation which expresses the essence of what is required in program proving, i.e. the interplay or relationship between statements and predicates, is the *inductive expression*. This is of the form

$$\{P\} \quad S \quad \{Q\}$$

It is a shorthand for

if the predicate P is true before S is executed and if the execution of S terminates then predicate Q will be true.

Note that no commitment to termination of S is included. It is customary to refer to P as the *precondition* and to Q as the *postcondition* of the inductive expression. For consistency, the curly brackets are used to surround the predicates. (Some authors use these brackets to surround the statements.)

One of the proof rules will of course deal with assignment statements. This provides a formalisation of the back substitution rule. To be more precise there is a rule

$$\{P\} \quad x := y \quad \{Q\}$$

where P is obtained from Q by replacing all occurrences of x in Q by y.

The assignment rule above is of little use. It is not even sufficient to provide a formal proof of the correctness of the program to interchange the values of two variables. In verifying the correctness of programs various kinds of inductive expressions will generally have to be combined. For example, from

$$\{P\}\, S_1\, \{Q\} \quad \text{and} \quad \{Q\}\, S_2\, \{R\}$$

it is reasonable to deduce

$$\{P\}\, S_1\, ; S_2\, \{R\}$$

This (concatenation) rule can be expressed in the form of a *rule of inference* as

$$\frac{\{P\}\, S_1\, \{Q\} \wedge \{Q\}\, S_2\, \{R\}}{\{P\}\, S_1\, ; S_2\, \{R\}}$$

Thus the truth of the *antecedent* (i.e. in arithmetical terminology, the numerator) implies the truth of the *consequent* (the denominator).

With just the assignment rule (generalised in the obvious way to accommodate multiple assignment) and the concatenation rule it is possible to give a formal proof, based on the proof rules alone, of the interchange program. Thus

1. $\{\textbf{true}\}\ (y_1, y_2) := (x_1, x_2)\ \{y_1 = x_1 \wedge y_2 = x_2\}$
   by the assignment rule
2. $\{y_1 = x_1 \wedge y_2 = x_2\}\ y_1 := y_1 + y_2\ \{y_1 - y_2 = x_1 \wedge y_2 = x_2\}$
   by the assignment rule
3. $\{y_1 - y_2 = x_1 \wedge y_2 = x_2\}\ y_2 := y_1 - y_2\ \{y_2 = x_1 \wedge y_1 - y_2 = x_2\}$
   by the assignment rule
4. $\{y_2 = x_1 \wedge y_1 - y_2 = x_2\}\ y_1 := y_1 - y_2\ \{y_2 = x_1 \wedge y_1 = x_2\}$
   by the assignment rule
5. $\{y_2 = x_1 \wedge y_1 = x_2\}\ (z_1, z_2) := (y_1, y_2)\ \{z_2 = x_1 \wedge z_1 = x_2\}$
   by the assignment rule
6. $\{\textbf{true}\}$
   $(y_1, y_2) := (x_1, x_2)\ ; y_1 := y_1 + y_2$
   $\{y_1 - y_2 = x_1 \wedge y_2 = x_2\}$
   by the concatenation rule applied to 1 and 2 above
7. $\{\textbf{true}\}$
   $(y_1, y_2) := (x_1, x_2)\ ; y_1 := y_1 + y_2\ ; y_2 := y_1 - y_2$
   $\{y_2 = x_1 \wedge y_1 - y_2 = x_2\}$
   by concatenation rule applied to 6 and 3
8. $\{\textbf{true}\}$
   $(y_1, y_2) := (x_1, x_2)\ ; y_1 := y_1 + y_2\ ; y_2 := y_1 - y_2\ ; y_1 := y_1 - y_2$
   $\{y_2 = x_1 \wedge y_1 = x_2\}$
   by concatenation rule applied to 7 and 4
9. $\{\textbf{true}\}$
   $(y_1, y_2) := (x_1, x_2)\ ; y_1 := y_1 + y_2\ ; y_2 := y_1 - y_2;$
   $y_1 := y_1 - y_2\ ; (z_1, z_2) := (y_1, y_2)$
   $\{z_2 = x_1 \wedge z_1 = x_2\}$
   by concatenation rule applied to 8 and 5.

This kind of proof is of course too long and tedious to be undertaken each time a program has to be verified. Informal methods of proof, like those given in section 6.3.1, are a more realistic possibility. This situation is quite analogous to the corresponding situation in mathematics. Although axioms underlie many aspects of mathematics these axioms are not usually cited every time the axioms are invoked. But if necessary they could be. In program verification informal proofs of correctness are the norm. But the axioms provide the formal framework on which the informal proofs are based and on which formal proofs can be based if necessary.

It is something of a coincidence that the above proof materialises so simply and so neatly. In general it is necessary to use the two *consequence rules*. If $\supset$ denotes 'logical implies' these can be written as

$$\frac{P \supset Q \text{ and } \{Q\} \ S \ \{R\}}{\{P\} \ S \ \{R\}} \quad \text{and} \quad \frac{\{P\} \ S \ \{Q\} \text{ and } Q \supset R}{\{P\} \ S \ \{R\}}$$

To give an example of another proof rule consider the PASCAL **while** statement. Its rule is:

$$\frac{\{P \wedge B\} \ S \ \{P\}}{\{P\} \ \textbf{while } B \textbf{ do } S \quad \{P \wedge \neg B\}}$$

Again this means that to prove the truth of the consequent it is sufficient to prove the truth of the antecedent. Here the predicate P is just the loop invariant. On completing the loop (if in fact it does terminate) then the condition B is false and so $\neg B$ can be part of the postcondition.

The notation for rules of inference has been lifted from mathematical logic. There are two basic forms of these rules, the first being

$$\frac{P_1, P_2, ..., P_n}{P}$$

This expresses the fact that from the truth of the predicates P_1, P_2, ..., P_n the truth of P can be deduced or inferred. The second form of inference rule is

$$\frac{P_1, P_2, ..., P_n \vdash P_{n+1}}{P}$$

This expresses the fact that, if from the truth of P_1, P_2, ..., P_n the truth of P_{n+1} can be proved, then the truth of P follows.

Finally we introduce a notation for obtaining one predicate from another simply by replacing one set of variables by another. In assignments and in function or procedure calls this kind of situation often arises. Thus if P is a predicate, P_y^x denotes the predicate obtained from P by replacing all occurrences of the variable x by y. A simple generalisation permits

$$P \begin{array}{l} x_1, x_2, ..., x_n \\ \\ y_1, y_2, ..., y_n \end{array}$$

to denote the predicate obtained from P by replacing simultaneously the set of variables $x_1, ..., x_n$ by the set $y_1, ..., y_n$; the various x_i, $1 \leqslant i \leqslant n$, must be distinct.

In axiomatic semantics it is customary (because it is most convenient) to have general postconditions rather than general preconditions. This tends to support the view that programming is a goal-directed activity. The proof rule is then a statement of the most general precondition which, if satisfied, will ensure that when the statement in question has been executed, and if it terminates, the postcondition will be satisfied. This condition is sometimes referred to as the weakest liberal precondition. If this precondition is not satisfied then the postcondition cannot possibly be satisfied. Thus the proof rules characterise in a precise manner the way in which each basic construct of the programming language transforms its precondition. In this way the effect of any statement, or any combination of statements and thus any program, can be described. The proof rules are therefore a means of describing the semantics of the programming language.

6.3.3 Application to PASCAL
We now examine how the axiomatic approach can be used to define aspects of the semantics of PASCAL. Throughout the discussion that follows it will be assumed that there are no side-effects – the evaluation of expressions, parameters, functions, etc. should not access global variables, etc. The reader should pay particular attention to the restrictions of this kind which tend to pervade this kind of definition process.

A complete axiomatic definition of semantics necessitates that all the various aspects of these semantics have been properly defined. All the properties of integers and, in the case of PASCAL, scalar types, pointers, files, etc., must be clearly and completely defined. In keeping with the spirit of the axiomatic method these properties could themselves be defined in an axiomatic manner.

The axioms for integers would specify the existence of 0 and 1, the associative and commutative laws of addition and multiplication, the distributive laws, and so on and so forth. There will also be comparison operators such as equals, not equals, less than, etc. In many respects the relevant axioms are similar to the usual laws of arithmetic. But there is one major difference. In computers only integers of a certain limited magnitude can be manipulated. The usual rules of arithmetic apply provided that the limit is not exceeded.

Real numbers provide an even more serious difficulty. Since reals are held only approximately in computers the usual associative and distributive laws do not hold; moreover the magnitude of reals is again limited. So care should be taken in manipulating them within predicates.

Other axioms will include axioms about the characters that are permitted, their ordering, etc., axioms about Booleans, scalars, arrays, records or structures, etc. In all cases the axioms describe in an abstract way the rules of algebra which can be applied in manipulating predicates. The problem of specifying the semantics of these basic quantities is solved by specifying the appropriate set of axioms. The consistency, completeness, etc. of these axioms is, of course, crucial.

Whenever declarations occur in the programming language identifiers are introduced and given a type. That type then means that the identifier can be manipulated according to the axioms associated with objects of that type, as described above.

Let us now examine the axiomatic semantics of some PASCAL statements.

Assignment statement

$$\{P_y^{\ x}\} \quad x := y \quad \{P\}$$

Note: it is assumed that the necessary type checking has been performed and that it is sensible to replace all occurrences of x by y in P.

Conditional statements

    · **if** ... **then** ... statement

$$\frac{\{P \wedge B\} \ S \ \{Q\} \ \text{and} \ P \wedge \neg B \supset Q}{\{P\} \ \textbf{if} \ B \ \textbf{then} \ S \quad \{Q\}}$$

    · **if** ... **then** ... **else** ... statement

$$\frac{\{P \wedge B\} \ S_1 \ \{Q\} \quad \text{and} \quad \{P \wedge \neg B\} \ S_2 \ \{Q\}}{\{P\} \quad \textbf{if} \ B \ \textbf{then} \ S_1 \ \textbf{else} \ S_2 \quad \{Q\}}$$

    · **case** statement

$$\frac{\{P \wedge (x=k_i)\} \ S_i \ \{Q\} \quad \text{for } i=1,2 \ ..., n}{\{(x \in [k_1, k_2, ..., k_n]) \wedge P\} \ \textbf{case} \ x \ \textbf{of} \ k_1 : S_1 \ ;...; k_n : S_n \ \textbf{end} \ \{Q\}}$$

Note: for the purposes of the rule for case statements

$k_m, k_n, ..., k_t : S$ should be regarded as an abbreviation for $k_m : S; k_n : S; ...; k_t : S$.

Repetitive statements
  · **while** statement

$$\frac{\{P \wedge B\} \ S \ \{P\}}{\{P\} \ \textbf{while} \ B \ \textbf{do} \ S \ \{P \wedge \neg B\}}$$

· **repeat** statement

$$\frac{\{P\} \ S \ \{Q\} \ \text{and} \ Q \wedge \neg B \supset P}{\{P\} \ \textbf{repeat} \ S \ \textbf{until} \ B \ \{Q \wedge B\}}$$

· **for** statement

$$\frac{\{a \leqslant x \leqslant b \wedge P([a..x))\} \ S \ \{P([a..x])\}}{\{P([\ ])\} \ \textbf{for} \ x := a \ \textbf{to} \ b \ \textbf{do} \ S \ \{P([a...b])\}}$$

$$\frac{\{a \leqslant x \leqslant b \wedge P((x..b])\} \ S \ \{P([x..b])\}}{\{P([\ ])\} \ \textbf{for} \ x := b \ \textbf{downto} \ a \ \textbf{do} \ S \ \{P([a..b])\}}$$

Note: $[p..q] = \{ i : p \leqslant i \leqslant q \}$
  $[p..q) = \{ i : p \leqslant i < q \}$
  $(p..q] = \{ i : p < i \leqslant q \}$
  $[\ ] \quad = \quad$ empty interval

Assumption: in the **for** statement S must not alter the values of x, a or b.

· **with** statement

$$\frac{\{P \ {}^{r.s_1 \ ... \ r.s_m}_{s_1...s_m}\} \ S \ \{Q \ {}^{r.s_1 \ ... \ r.s_m}_{s_1 \ ... \ s_m}\}}{\{P\} \ \textbf{with} \ r \ \textbf{do} \ S \ \{Q\}}$$

Note: for the purposes of this rule
  with $r_1, r_2, ..., r_n$ **do** S
  should be interpreted as
  with r_1 **with** r_2 ... **with** r_n **do** S
Assumption: r should not contain any variables that might be altered by S.

Compound statements

$$\frac{\{P_{i-1}\} \ S_i \ \{P_i\} \quad \text{for} \ i = 1, 2, ..., n}{\{P_0\} \ \textbf{begin} \ S_1 \ ; ... ; S_n \ \textbf{end} \ \{P_n\}}$$

Jumps

$$\frac{\{Q\}\,\textbf{go to }l\,\{\textbf{false}\}\vdash\{P\}S_1\{Q\},\{Q\}\,\textbf{go to }l\,\{\textbf{false}\}\vdash\{Q\}S_2\{R\}}{\{P\}\ S_1\ ;l:S_2\ \{R\}}$$

Assumption: it is assumed that l is the only label within the block in which it is used.

Procedure statement

$$\{P\begin{array}{c}v_1,v_2,\dots,v_m,g_1,g_2,\dots,g_n\\[4pt]f_1(\bar{v},\bar{g}),f_2(\bar{v},\bar{g}),\dots,f_m(\bar{v},\bar{g}),h_1(\bar{v},\bar{g}),\dots,h_n(\bar{v},\bar{g})\end{array}\}\,p(\bar{v})\ \{P\}$$

Notes: (a) The vector $\bar{v}$ represents the set of actual parameters of p and $\{\,v_1,v_2,\dots,v_m\,\}$ is the subset of these corresponding to formal parameters which were specified as variables.

  (b) Similarly $\bar{g}$ represents the set of all variables declared globally to p and accessed by it. $\{\,g_1,\dots,g_n\,\}$ represents the subset of $\bar{g}$ which may be altered by p.

  (c) The functions f_i $(1\leqslant i\leqslant m)$ and g_j $(1\leqslant j\leqslant n)$ indicate how the initial values of $\bar{v}$ and $\bar{g}$ map onto the final values on completion of execution of $p\,(\bar{v})$. Thus for each $1\leqslant i\leqslant m$ and each $1\leqslant j\leqslant n$ the assignment

$$v_i := f_i(\bar{v},\bar{g})\text{ and }g_j := h_j(\bar{v},\bar{g})$$

  are, in effect, executed simultaneously.

  (d) No member of $\{\,v_1,\dots,v_m,g_1,\dots,g_n\,\}$ can be or can contain a variable accessed by another. If this rule is violated the meaning is undefined.

Examples of standard procedures
  · the procedure *put*

$$\{\,eof(x)\wedge P^{x\mathrm{L}}_{x_\mathrm{L}\ \&\ <x\uparrow>}\}\ put\,(x)\ \{P\wedge eof(x)\}$$

Notes: (a) For *put* to be defined the end-of-file procedure *eof* should produce true. It remains true after execution of *put*.

  (b) The effect is to append to the file x the value referred to by the buffer variable $x\uparrow$. Thus the assignment

$$x := x\ \&\ <x\uparrow>$$

effectively occurs. Moreover $x\uparrow$ becomes undefined.

(c) x_L denotes that part of file x to the left of the current printing position.

(d)   Only x_L (not x, $x\uparrow$, etc.) should appear in P.

· the procedure *rewrite*

$$\{P^x_{<>}\}\quad rewrite\ (x)\quad \{P\}$$

Notes: (a) $<>$ denotes the empty file.

(b)   The effect is as if the assignment

$$x : = <>$$

had occurred.

(c)   Only x (and not x_L, $x\uparrow$, etc.) should occur in P.

6.3.4   *Commentary on the axiomatic approach*

As we have seen the axiomatic approach is not an entirely satisfactory method of describing the semantics of PASCAL. At various stages it is necessary to remark that the rules which are given are valid only if assumptions (such as no side-effects) exist. The situation can be viewed in at least two ways: either there is something wrong with the method of definition or there is something wrong with the programming language. The axiomatic technique for defining semantics tends to favour the program prover. But PASCAL was not designed with ease of program verification in mind. Hence there is a kind of conflict.

Modern thinking on the design of programming languages suggests that languages should encourage the construction of reliable programs; one aspect of this is the ease with which programs can be verified. The programming language EUCLID, for example, is based on PASCAL and its definition is given in terms of proof rules of the kind discussed for PASCAL. But then the proof rules alone define the semantics of EUCLID; exceptional cases, restrictions, etc. do not exist and have no place.

With an approach to language definition based on program verification many new ideas about the design of programming languages and even about the construction of programs start to emerge. From the programming point of view programmers should attempt to construct program segments which are easy to verify. As such they should be relatively short and simple and they should be well structured; proofs of the correctness of well-structured programs are easier to provide than proofs of correctness of unstructured programs. The overriding considerations are clarity and simplicity, efficiency is unimportant. In the initial conception of his program, the programmer should avoid the use of

- side-effects and other similar activities, e.g. altering the control variable or the bounds, if they are present, in a loop
- **go to**, since its use tends to betray a lack of understanding of structure
- pointers, since these are to data structures what **go to**'s are to statements; their use permits unstructured data
- aliasing, whereby alterations to one variable can affect other variables
- machine code segments, since the programmer can then interfere with other variables and therefore other proofs of correctness

and so on. The language should therefore provide facilities which encourage the above practices; it should also provide suitable structuring facilities including

- a proper set of program constructs and data types or modes
- procedures and functions
- mode or type declarations and operator declarations to allow the introduction of operators to act on the new modes
- module facilities to allow encapsulation of abstract data types

An implementation should further provide adequate separate compilation and linkage facilities, and perhaps a means of checking the validity of proofs of correctness.

It can be argued that restrictions such as the explicit forbidding of side-effects, alterations to control variables within loops and, altering the upper bounds of loops, introduce a certain irregularity into programming languages and their definition and they complicate the implementation since compile-time checks must be performed to ensure that the rules are obeyed. But if an axiomatic approach to language definition is adopted this is just not so; in fact the reverse is true. Moreover, the various restrictions are prohibiting what might well be regarded as poor programming practice (though there are exceptions).

The attitude that efficiency should be regarded as unimportant in the initial conception of a program merits some comment. If some program manipulation system can automatically perform transformations on the source text to remove inefficiency much can be gained. In effect, various kinds of optimisation can be performed, e.g. the removal of recursion, removing constant expressions from within loops. It is, of course, crucial that the transformations that are performed are guaranteed to be correct. Then the program produced by the transformation system can be guaranteed to be more efficient, yet still correct, though perhaps less clear or apparently less well structured. But there is still liable to be a sacrifice in efficiency for a gain in reliability.

The proof rules associated with axiomatic semantics can provide assistance to the programmer in the construction and the design of his programs. Current thinking about programming suggests that programs can be constructed by concentrating first on the eventual correctness proof of the program. Having realised this the proof rules of the axiomatic definition of the language suggest constructions which can then achieve the desired effect. In this way the construction of reliable programs goes hand-in-hand with their correctness proof. Such methods of program construction are called semi-formal and hint at machine aid in the development of programs. For further reading on this topic see Dijkstra (1976).

In the preceding sections we have only scratched the surface of the work and the consequences of an axiomatic approach to describing semantics. The same ideas can be developed to deal with languages for parallel processing, expression-oriented languages such as ALGOL 68, and so on. In fact, the methods can even be extended, and in the process they become much more complex, to provide an axiomatisation of side-effects, aliasing, etc.; the previous arguments are scarcely weakened.

The inductive expressions and the proof rules we examined ignored the problems associated with ensuring that the execution of a program terminates. As such, the axioms are axioms for partial correctness. Another development in axiomatic semantics is the provision of axioms which guarantee both termination and correctness. There are axioms for total correctness. These axioms are, in many cases, similar to the axioms for partial correctness but extra detail is added to ensure that loops, for example, terminate. If total correctness is equated with showing both correctness (partial) and termination, partial correctness is equated with showing that the program cannot produce the wrong result.

There is some debate about whether the axioms for partial or total correctness give the more accurate description of the semantics of a programming language. The former axioms provide meaning for a wider class of programs since they include the programs which never terminate. On the other hand, they provide no proof, or the means of acquiring such a proof, of termination. The opposite arguments can be levelled at axioms for total correctness.

THE REVISED ALGOL 68 REPORT

The programming language ALGOL 68 was designed by Working Group 2.1 of the International Federation for Information Processing, the same group who were responsible for ALGOL 60, though the individual members were by this time different. ALGOL 68 was the official successor of ALGOL 60. It appeared initially in 1968.

The document which defined the new language was novel in two respects: an entirely new language was defined and a new method of defining programming languages appeared. Between 1968 and 1975 work proceeded on producing a revised version of the language. In the intervening years implementators had been working on attempts to produce compilers, and their experience both in wrestling with the original document and in writing compilers indicated that some changes could profitably be introduced.

The document which finally emerged represented even more of an advance both in terms of language design and in terms of definition methods. But its origins were still apparent. Most of the ideas of the earlier document were still present or had been superseded by better ideas or by a better presentation of the old ideas. Accordingly we shall, in what follows, look rather carefully at the Revised Report and references to ALGOL 68 will imply reference to the revised language, not the original language.

7.1 Introductory remarks

Essentially the language is defined in terms of four aspects – representations, standard environment, syntax and semantics. In the usual way, the syntax provides a definition of the allowable strings of characters and the semantics gives a meaning to such strings. The standard environment gives the set of standard procedures and functions, etc. whose existence can be assumed by the programmer; but due to the nature of ALGOL 68 this includes all the standard operators, identifiers, modes, etc. The representation section is concerned with the way in which the various symbols of the language appear on paper or in machine-readable form.

If the Report had to consist only of the four aspects described above, it would have been even more difficult to follow. The authors therefore permitted pragmatic remarks to be included in the Report enclosed by { and } ; these include explanatory remarks, illustrative examples, and discussions of various kinds, but strictly speaking they do not form part of the formal Report.

Before turning to look at the four aspects of the ALGOL 68 document it seems sensible to begin by looking at the aims and principles of design which the ALGOL 68 authors saw fit to set out in an introductory section at the start of their Report.

The ALGOL 68 designers saw their task as the following: to produce a programming language which would serve the needs of the computing community in different countries, would help in communicating and executing algorithms and would help in teaching about algorithms and programming. The language would be suitable for expressing algorithms from a wide variety of application areas including those of a numeric and non-numeric nature. The language that would eventually be produced would be defined completely and clearly. Moreover,

- the number of primitive concepts would be minimised but these should be applied in an orthogonal manner
- most syntactical and other errors should be caught at compile-time
- programs in ALGOL 68 should be capable of being executed efficiently on the computers of the day without the compilers having to resort to sophisticated optimisation techniques.

Also, the syntax of the language should encourage separate compilation. Some remarks about these aims now follow.

The primitive concepts on which ALGOL 68 is based include the concepts of mode, value, declaration, expression and routine. In comparison with earlier languages such as ALGOL 60 these concepts are more fully developed

- values are associated not only with arithmetic expressions but with, for example, expressions of all kinds, with serial clauses, closed clauses and units, together with arrays, structures, routines and so on
- modes include not just **integer, real,** and so on, but an infinity of possibilities including structures of all kinds, arrays of objects of all kinds, united modes, recursive modes, etc.
- declarations of objects of any mode are permitted; included also are mode declarations and priority and operator declarations to encourage the hierarchical construction of programs

- expressions involving objects of any allowable modes are permitted provided suitable operators exist as standard operators or are declared by the programmer
- with regard to multiple values, it is possible not just to subscript but to select subsets of arrays including rows or columns; the notions of subscripting and selecting subsets can be combined in arbitrary ways and applied to the different dimensions of arrays
- routines can be introduced and associated with functions and procedures in a manner similar to that employed in ALGOL 60; but routines can be introduced and associated with operator symbols so that, for example, multiplication can be defined for use with matrices; routines can also be assigned to suitable variables and, in general, can be manipulated like other objects.

From these remarks it is natural that type checking (associated with modes and declarations) should be carried to its obvious logical conclusion. Security and the ability to catch many errors at compile-time thus become a feature of ALGOL 68 programs. It is natural that the ALGOL 68 syntax should reflect this preoccupation with types or modes. Yet, on the other hand, the syntax is also designed in such a way that ALGOL 68 programs can be parsed without knowing the modes of the constituent identifiers; it also permits the independent compilation of segments of programs which can then be incorporated into other programs at a later stage.

The principle of orthogonality dictates that these concepts should always be applicable in their full generality (subject to suitability of modes, correct and valid declarations, etc.). The rules which govern the separate concepts remain unaltered when concepts are combined i.e. when the syntax and semantic rules are composed, there are no separate rules to govern the intersection of concepts. The rules which stipulate the manner in which arithmetic expressions, for example, are written and evaluated are also valid for expressions involving character strings, say; there are no restrictions imposed merely because character strings are being manipulated.

Further evidence of orthogonality is given in the earlier description of indexing. Both subscripting and selection of subsets can be applied arbitrarily on separate dimensions to select parts of arrays. There are no unnatural restrictions.

Recall that in ALGOL 60 the dangling **else** problem gave rise to a subdivision of statements to overcome a syntactic ambiguity. Thus there was the rule that **if** cannot follow **then**, and so on. Such restrictions do not occur in ALGOL 68 – again because of the orthogonal approach to its design. Thus if we ignore modes and scope rules and use *serial clause* to denote any sequence of statements possibly terminated by an expression the conditional clause has the syntax

if *serial clause* **then** *serial clause* **else** *serial clause* **fi**

The serial clauses are all perfectly general, there are no restrictions about what kind of statements can occur within them. Moreover, this one construct covers both conditional statements and conditional expressions (in ALGOL 68 a statement is essentially a special kind of expression). In a similar way certain kinds of loop clauses have a syntax

while *serial clause* **do** *serial clause* **od**

Again there are no unnatural restrictions.

ALGOL 68, then, does not have sets of peculiar rules and irregularities. The principle of orthogonal design was introduced to remove these. With such a philosophy the designers of ALGOL 68 then intended that their language would be easy to learn, to teach, to remember and to implement.

The desire for efficiency is partially satisfied by the fact that all modes or types are known at compile-time and consequently run-time checks are unnecessary. Efficiency considerations lead also to special features in the language to permit loop optimisation (lower limit, upper limit, increment and control identifier all produce integer constants), to avoid the copying of large arrays, etc.

To allow programs to run on machines with restricted character sets and to encourage portability of programs the basic symbols of ALGOL 68 can be expressed in terms of a minimal set of characters. Further characters can be used if they are available.

We look now at the definition of ALGOL 68 itself and look in turn at each of the four aspects of its definition: representations, standard environment, syntax and semantics.

7.2 Representations

The section on representations in the ALGOL 68 Report is concerned with the way in which programs are written on paper or are presented to a computer. To avoid any confusion between the metalanguage used in defining the syntax of ALGOL 68 and ALGOL 68 itself the production rules of the language do not contain any terminals in the sense of ALGOL 60, ALGOL W, etc. There is no mention in the syntax rules of **begin**, := or even ; . Instead something akin to the begin symbol, becomes symbol, go on symbol, etc. appears.

To be more precise about this matter the syntax rules tend to con-

178

tain 'begin token', 'becomes token', 'go on token', etc. A token is merely a symbol possibly preceded by comments or pragmatic remarks. So each of

> **pr** switch on listing **pr begin**
> # assignment statement # :=
>
> ;

is a legitimate token.

The precise hardware representation of the various symbols is not given in the Report, but representations are listed and it is stated that a minimal character set is sufficient to express them; thus it is not stated how bold words should appear, only one representation of the 'at most symbol' is given (namely ≤), etc.

Shortly after the ALGOL 68 Report had appeared, IFIP WG2.1, the committee responsible for the language, put forward certain proposals for standardising the hardware representation of programs expressed in the language. They subsequently viewed this document together with the Report itself as a complete definition of ALGOL 68.

The hardware representation document was desirable from various points of view including the provision of a then complete definition, portability considerations, the use of standard programs for indenting and laying out ALGOL 68 programs, etc. The standard hardware representation was chosen to minimise both the character set and the parsing problems, to be practical, to provide a congenial method of expressing ALGOL 68 programs, to conform to the Report and to be teachable. Three standard methods of distinguishing bold words were permitted, i.e. three standard stropping regimes:

(a) bold words in upper case with identifiers appearing in lower case
(b) bold words preceded by period and followed by some suitable delimiter
(c) bold words regarded as reserved words (this would limit then the allowable identifiers).

Example 7.1
To illustrate the three approaches

(i) *BEGIN INT n; read(n); print(n↑2) END*
(ii) *.BEGIN .INT N; READ(N); PRINT(N↑2) .END*
(iii) *BEGIN INT N; READ(N); PRINT(N↑2) END*

The hardware representation went further and discussed actual characters and various other matters. Included were the following

179

· portability was enhanced, since a program expressed in one character code could be expressed in another merely by transliterating individual characters
· it was possible to change from one stropping regime to another by including in an ALGOL 68 program appropriate pragmatic remarks (messages to the compiler which would in no way affect the meaning of a program).

7.3 The standard environment

Recall that one of the design aims of ALGOL 68 was to allow independent compilation, i.e. to permit a programmer to incorporate into his programs certain prepared procedures or pieces of program, provided, of course, that certain mode information about these prepared objects was made available. Accordingly the syntax of the Report makes no specific reference to the set of functions, etc. which a programmer can assume are present.

In writing programs in other languages it is customary to assume the existence of *sin, cos, read, print,* etc. In ALGOL 68 the story is no different but the situation is formalised. The set of standard objects whose existence can be assumed by the programmer – this now includes procedures, constants, modes, operators, their priorities and even variables – is collected together to form a *standard environment.*

The standard environment is defined within the Report as a sequence of declarations. For the most part these declarations are written in ALGOL 68 itself but sometimes pseudo-comments are used when ALGOL 68 is unsuitable. To illustrate we give some examples:

· the procedure *char in string* is used for detecting the existence of a character in a given string; its declaration is

> **proc** *char in string* = (**char** *c,* **ref int** *i,* **string** *s*) **bool**:
> (**bool** *found* := **false**;
> **for** *k* **from lwb** *s* **to upb** *s* **while** ¬ *found*
> **do** (*c* = *s* [*k*] | *i* := *k*; *found* := **true**) **od**;
> *found*)

· the dyadic operator **lwb** detects the lower bound in the *n*th dimension of an array; this cannot be defined in ALGOL 68 itself since the mode of the parameter can be specified (it must include all possible arrays); its declaration in the standard environment is

> **op lwb** = (**int** *n,* **rows** *a*) **int**:
> c the lower bound in the *n*th bound pair of the descriptor

180

of the value of a, if that bound pair exists **c**

- having defined the operator $<$ to operate between two integral operands using a pseudo-comment all the other comparisons between integers can be defined in terms of this operator
- having defined monadic and dyadic minus between integers most other arithmetic operators acting on integers can be defined
- the entire section on transput – the ALGOL 68 term for input and output – is defined mainly in terms of ALGOL 68 itself; all the transput procedures for dealing with formatted, unformatted and binary transput are all present.

The definition of all the operators cannot be given in terms of previously defined operations. There must be some operators whose existence is assumed. These are

- the less-than operator acting on two integers or on two reals
- subtraction between two integers
- subtraction, multiplication and division between reals.

The Report further acknowledges the possibility of overflow and the fact that real arithmetic will be performed only approximately. It uses the phrase 'in the sense of numerical analysis' to describe the idea of approximation. Yet the Report does insist that 'less than' between two integers or reals cannot cause overflow. Thus a compiler writer cannot perform a straightforward subtraction.

The large number of similar declarations of various kinds caused the ALGOL 68 designers to introduce a macro-facility for describing the declarations. For example,

op P = (L real a, L int b) L real : a P L real (b)

represents several declarations:

- **P** can be replaced consistently throughout the declaration by one of –, +, × or /
- **L** can be omitted altogether or it can be replaced consistently by one of *long, short, long long, short short,* etc.

Basically the above declaration describes arithmetic between a real number and an integer (of equal size) in terms of arithmetic between two reals – the latter is already defined in the Report.

The standard environment is itself divided into various preludes, postludes and tasks. To be more precise, a complete program is viewed in the following way:

```
(c standard-prelude c; c library-prelude c; c system-prelude c;
par begin c system-task - 1 c, c system-task - 2 c,
     (c particular-prelude for user program 1 c;
     (user program 1 : begin ... end);
     c particular-postlude for user program 1 c),
     (c particular-prelude for user program 2 c;
     (user program 2: ...
end)
```

At the outermost level is the standard prelude which contains most of the usual declarations common to and accessible by any of the tasks within the parallel clause **par begin ... end**. The parallel clause contains all the tasks which can be thought of as being executed in parallel; it includes systems tasks of various kinds together with a set of user programs. The user programs themselves certainly possess particular preludes which contain those items in the standard environment which are private to the program and cannot be accessed by other users. Included here are declarations of the standard transput files *standin* and *standout* together with instructions for opening them. There are declarations of the variables associated with random-number generators and these are suitability initialised. Predefined libraries or sections of program can be incorporated immediately following the particular prelude of a user program. A particular postlude will contain the declaration of the label *stop* and includes instructions to lock the standard transput files.

Note that the skeleton scheme given above explains the extent to which different programs can access the same objects. The necessary protection is provided by the ALGOL 68 scope rules.

Although the standard environment was expressed in ALGOL 68, itself, it was necessary to introduce some subsidiary notation to indicate that certain declarations were introduced only for explanatory reasons and were not for the use of ALGOL 68 programmers. For example there were

- input procedures for converting strings of characters to integers and to reals
- the mode **file** which was explicitly declared as a structure and yet it could not be broken open by selection in an ALGOL 68 program
- the operator **straightout** which took multi-dimensional arrays and straightened them for printing by producing a one-dimensional array holding the elements row after row.

Essentially there was a problem in giving items their correct visibility (although items were in scopes they could not be accessed directly by the programmer). Subsequently the IFIP WG2.1 produced a document which defined a module and separate compilation scheme for ALGOL 68. It allowed separate compilation and predefined libraries, and it allowed visibility to be limited. Had this existed earlier it would, no doubt, have been used to provide a neater definition of the ALGOL 68 standard environment.

7.4 The syntax of ALGOL 68

The method used to describe the ALGOL 68 syntax is based on BNF notation but many of its aspects have origins in the T-notation of ALGOL W. The syntax is relatively complex since it contains many of the context-sensitive restrictions and defines all aspects of a program which a compiler can be guaranteed to check.

The syntax contains mode information in a manner similar to that employed in the definition of ALGOL W. But ALGOL 68 allows an infinite number of possible modes, not a finite number, and so the earlier ideas of ALGOL W have to be modified. The syntax contains information about coercions, i.e. automatic mode changes, but again the infinity of modes means that the triplet rules, etc. of ALGOL W become inappropriate. It contains also the rules which state that an identifier, mode, operator, etc., can be used only if it has been properly declared.

Many aspects of the syntax can be viewed as attributes and the syntax explains essentially how these are to be passed up or down a syntax tree. Consequently, aspects of the syntax can be viewed as inherited or synthesised attributes.

Rather than look at the complete syntax immediately we begin from a skeleton syntax similar in conception to the BNF notation as used in the definition of ALGOL 60. From this base, different aspects can be gradually introduced until finally the complete syntax can be revealed in all its power. To the skeleton syntax will be added, successively, mode information, coercions and finally the process of checking that identifiers, etc. have been used and declared properly.

Recall that one of the aims of the ALGOL 68 designers was to permit mode-independent parsing of programs. Consequently, from the initial skeleton grammar, which excludes modes and so on, it should be possible to parse ALGOL 68 programs.

7.4.1 Skeleton syntax

In the skeleton syntax that follows both lower-case letters and capital letters will be used. The distinction between these will turn out to be important but at this early stage it can be ignored.

The terminals of the grammar will be sequences of lower-case letters ending in 'symbol' or in 'token', other sequences of capital or lower-case letters will be non-terminals. The following further notational conventions apply:

· 'is defined to be' appears as either '::' or as ':'
· 'or' appears as ';'
· 'followed by' appears as ','
· and the end of a rule appears as '.'

Again the distinction between the double and single colon for 'is defined to be' can remain blurred for the moment.

Note that there is now no possible confusion between the language being defined and the various symbols used in expressing the syntax rules. For now the terminals appear as symbols or tokens and these are expressed as sequences of small letters. Moreover, the non-terminals cannot cause confusion.

To illustrate the rules note the following:

character denotation : quote symbol, string item, quote symbol.

Thus a character denotation is defined to be a quote symbol followed by a string item (essentially a character or a pair of quotes) and a further quote symbol. In BNF parlance

<character denotation> ::= "<string item>"

Another rule of the skeleton grammar would be:

UNIT :: assignation; identity relation; routine text;
          jump; skip; TERTIARY.

Here a UNIT is defined to be either an assignation or an identity relation or ... or a TERTIARY. In BNF notation this would have been written as

<unit> ::= <assignation> | <identity relation> |...|<tertiary>

To permit discussion of mode-independent parsing aspects of the syntax of ALGOL 68 some further syntax rules are given. See figure 7.1 for the definition of UNIT, TERTIARY, SECONDARY and PRIMARY and figure 7.2 for further rules defining assignation, identity relation, etc.

For the reader who is not familiar with the ALGOL 68 vocabulary of terms, examples of constructions are given in Example 7.1

184

UNIT :: assignation; identity relation; routine text;
jump; skip; TERTIARY.

TERTIARY :: formula; nihil; SECONDARY.

SECONDARY :: generator; selection; PRIMARY.

PRIMARY :: slice; call; cast; denoter; format text;
identifier; ENCLOSED clause.

Fig. 7.1. Syntactic definition of UNIT, etc.

assignation : destination, becomes token, source.

destination : TERTIARY.

source : UNIT.

identity relation : TERTIARY1, identity relator, TERTIARY2.

identity relator : is token; is not token.

slice : PRIMARY, indexer bracket.

selection : identifier, of token, SECONDARY.

call : PRIMARY, parameter pack.

Fig. 7.2. Syntactic definition of assignation, etc.

Example 7.1

Assume suitable declarations of the various identifiers used below. Then

(i) $a := b \times c$ is an assignation, a being the destination, $b \times c$ being a formula or expression and the source, and := being the becomes token

(ii) $p :=: q$ is an identity relation; it compares two items and asks if they represent different ways of accessing the same variable

(iii) $x[i,j]$ is a slice, access to all or part of an array; it is therefore a PRIMARY – the square brackets and their contents constitute an indexer

(iv) *age* **of** *boy* is a selection

(v) *print*(4) and *sin*(pi/5) are calls, the brackets and their contents being the parameter pack.

Using a grammar containing the above rules (and similar other rules) mode-independent parsing of ALGOL 68 programs can be performed. Take $a+b[i]$ for example. Should this be parsed as

$$(a + b)[i] \quad \text{or as} \quad a + (b[i]) \ ?$$

185

Of course the latter would be expected but do the syntax rules ensure this by allowing this parse and prohibiting the other? The syntax rule for a slice allows a PRIMARY and so an identifier to be subscripted but it does not allow a formula (or a TERTIARY) such as $a + b$ to be subscripted. Thus the required parsing can take place regardless of the modes of the constituent items; note that the knowledge of the modes might prohibit even the parse $a + (b\,[i]\,)$, for b may have been declared as a Boolean constant!

Example 7.2
Further examples illustrating mode-independent parsing are given below,

> (i) $a := b := c$ must be parsed as $a := (b := c)$ since the destination of an assignation must be a TERTIARY and not, as the parse $(a := b) := c$ would imply, a UNIT
> (ii) $a := : b := c$ is illegal since it cannot be legitimately parsed
> (iii) a **of** $b\,[i]$ must be parsed as a **of** $(b\,[i]\,)$.

7.4.2 Production rules of the language
Strictly speaking, the production rules which define ALGOL 68 appear without capital letters and without resorting to the use of :: for 'is defined to be'. Thus production rules use small letters and use : for 'is defined to be'. Some illustrative examples can be given:

> boolean denotation : true token; false token.
> identity relator : is token; is not token.

Sequences of small letters thus describe the equivalent of the BNF terminals and non-terminals but the technical terms used are different.

Any sequence of small letters (possibly containing opening and closing round brackets or spaces) is called a *protonotion*. The spaces have no significance but improve readability and the brackets are introduced to avoid possible syntactic ambiguity – see subsection 7.4.4. Certain of these protonotions are of particular interest, those corresponding to the terminals and non-terminals. The protonotions ending in 'symbol' are called *symbols* and these are basically the terminals of the grammar. The protonotions for which there are syntax rules are called *notions* and these correspond to the non-terminals.

A production rule of the language therefore has a notion as the left-hand side. The right-hand side can be described by saying that it consists of a sequence of *alternatives* separated by semi-colons. The alternatives themselves consist of *members* separated by commas.

Example 7.3
The right part of

>   times ten to the power choice : times ten to the power symbol;
>   letter e symbol.

contains two alternatives each of which has just one member.

It has been seen that certain of the syntax rules of the ALGOL 68 Report contain not just small letters but also capital letters (e.g. UNIT appeared earlier). The capitals play a role which is similar in concept to the role played by the T-notation in the definition of ALGOL W, but much more complete, more formal and more integrated into the definition of the language. Thus capitals will often convey mode information but they are used also to perform certain other tasks. Consider

>   plain denotation : PLAIN denotation; void denotation.

From this rule it is possible to derive production rules of the language by replacing PLAIN by any one of the ALGOL 68 plain modes, e.g. boolean, character, etc. The allowable alternatives for PLAIN are described by another grammar, a grammar for another language called the metalanguage.

A typical rule of the metalanguage is

>   PLAIN :: INTREAL; boolean; character.

i.e. PLAIN is defined to be either a member of INTREAL, boolean or character. For this grammar there are of course non-terminals, terminals, productions, etc., and so a new set of terminology is applicable:

> · the rules of the language are metaproduction rules
> · a metanotion is a sequence of capital letters for which there is a metaproduction rule
> · the terminals of the grammar are protonotions.

Unlike other grammars there is no unique sentence symbol. In fact, parts of the grammar are quite disjoint and it is possible to isolate several smaller grammars. There are sections defining modes, sections for phrases and coercions, sections for nests (used for relating applied and defining occurrences), sections for formulae, etc. Consequently there is no true equivalent of a sentence of a grammar. But in lieu of such a definition, a *terminal metaproduction* of a metanotion N is defined to be a protonotion derived from N.

To illustrate some of the ideas discussed above consider

>   PLAIN :: INTREAL; boolean; character.
>   INTREAL :: SIZETY integral; SIZETY real.
>   SIZETY :: long LONGSETY; short SHORTSETY; EMPTY.
>   LONGSETY :: long LONGSETY; EMPTY.

SHORTSETY :: short SHORTSETY; EMPTY.
EMPTY :: .

Then 'long long integral' is a terminal metaproduction of the meta-notion INTREAL.

Return now to the task of deducing productions of the language from these subsidiary rules which include capital letters. In the rule

plain denotation : PLAIN denotation; void denotation.

the metanotion PLAIN can be replaced by any of its terminal metaproductions and a production rule of the language results. Thus replacing PLAIN by 'long long integral' gives

plain denotation : long long integral denotion; void denotation.

This then is analogous to the application of the T-notation. The analogy can be carried somewhat further in the form of the consistent substitution rule.

Certain of the syntax rules of ALGOL 68 contain several occurrences of the same metanotion. Thus

SIZE INTREAL denotation : SIZE symbol, INTREAL denotation.

When this happens consistent substitution applies, i.e. each metanotion must be replaced at each of its occurrences by the same terminal metaproduction. Thus using the earlier definition of INTREAL together with

SIZE :: long; short.

it follows that consistent substitution ensures that

long long integral denotation : long symbol, long integral denotation.

is admissible but does not allow rules such as

long long integral denotation : short symbol, ...

There are, of course, cases where consistent substitution is not necessary and subscripts can be used to indicate this. Thus in

identity relation : TERTIARY1, identity relator, TERTIARY2.

no consistent substitution is indicated.

At this stage two sets of rules have been formalised, the production rules of the language and the metaproduction rules of the metalanguage. But there is a third set of rules typified by

SIZE INTREAL denotation : SIZE symbol, INTREAL denotation.

This rule is used to generate production rules of the language by appealing to the metalanguage and employing (consistent) substitution. Rules such as the above are called *hyper-rules*. Again a new set of terminology is indicated and the terms *hypernotion* and *hyperalternative* have their expected meaning. Thus 'SIZE INTREAL denotation' is a hypernotion; the rule for 'plain denotation' indicates that 'PLAIN denotation' is a hyperalternative, etc.

Note that hyper-rules make use of a single colon. This should be as expected since strict production rules are obtained from hyper-rules by a process of substitution which does not alter the 'is defined to be' symbol. Note also that consistent substitution applies only to hyper-rules, not to metaproduction rules for instance. Indeed some of the metaproduction rules, e.g. those involving recursion, do not make sense if consistent substitution is applied – take as an example

FIELDS :: FIELD; FIELDS, FIELD.

The grammar used in the definition of ALGOL 68 is, for obvious reasons, called a two-level grammar or a van Wijngaarden grammar, after its originator.

Now we have reached the point where production rules of the language can be generated from the hyper-rules by appealing to the metaproduction rules. In essence, many of the earlier ideas of the T-notation have been expanded, developed and formalised. Due to the fact that ALGOL 68 permits an infinite number of possible modes – there are even an infinite number of modes 'long long ... long integral' – there are an infinite number of production rules of the language. In fact, the nature of the metalanguage is causing the infinity of rules; the skeleton grammar which was examined earlier in this chapter was finite in nature.

Care should be taken in choosing the different metanotions, etc. For if A and B represent legitimate metanotions so also does A concatenated with B. Ambiguities arising from this kind of confusion should not occur. Care should also be taken by people translating the ALGOL 68 Report into other natural languages since this kind of difficulty can exist in one language but not in another. Recall that ALGOL 68 was designed to serve the needs of peoples in many countries.

Certain of the hyper-rules of the ALGOL 68 syntax are of a very general kind. Given that the terminal metaproductions of NOTION are the set of non-empty sequence of small letters, note the following

NOTION option : NOTION; EMPTY.
NOTION sequence : NOTION; NOTION, NOTION sequence.
NOTION list : NOTION; NOTION, and also token, NOTION
      list.

By these declarations all kinds of options, sequences and lists were defined. For example,

plusminus option : plusminus; EMPTY.

and this is required in the syntax of numerals, for example, for exponent parts which may be optionally signed. The above rules permit even definitions of non-terminals such as 'digit cypher sequence option'. Note that a crucial aspect of these definitions is the fact that NOTION is always followed (and not preceded) by the protonotions 'option', 'sequence' and 'list'; for this prevents ambiguity arising from protonotions containing, for example, both 'list' and 'option'.

Other definitions of a similar kind define items which are liable to be enclosed in brackets, e.g. parameters of procedures, statements and so on. As an example take

NOTETY STYLE pack: STYLE begin token, NOTETY, STYLE end token.

Here

- STYLE indicates either brackets such as (and) or **begin** and **end**; consistent substitution ensures (matches) and does not match **end**
- NOTETY is defined as any possible empty sequence of characters.

At certain stages of the ALGOL 68 syntax the hypernotions in their full form become rather lengthy and so certain carefully defined abbreviations are allowed. These abbreviations are called *paranotions* and basically the set of paranotions forms the vocabulary of terms used in talking about ALGOL 68 constructs and programs. Included as paranotions are expression, constant, destination, etc. Note the explicit attention paid in the definition of the language to providing a suitable vocabulary in which to talk about aspects of the language.

To conclude this section we take the opportunity to pass certain remarks of a theoretical nature.

Example 7.4
The set

$$\{ a^n \, b^n \, c^n : n \geqslant 1 \}$$

can be described by a context-sensitive grammar, but not by a context-free grammar. An appropriate context-sensitive grammar is:

$$
\begin{array}{rcl}
S & \rightarrow & T \\
T & \rightarrow & aTBC \\
T & \rightarrow & abC \\
CB & \rightarrow & AB \\
AB & \rightarrow & AC \\
AC & \rightarrow & BC \\
bB & \rightarrow & bb \\
C & \rightarrow & c
\end{array}
$$

It is not immediately obvious that this grammar does as required. The same set can be described in a more natural manner using two-level grammars. Let the metanotion N be used for counting:

> $N ::$ one; one N.

Then elements of the set $\{ a^n \ b^n \ c^n : n \geqslant 1 \}$ are sentences of the two-level grammar given below defining S.

> $A ::$ letter a symbol; letter b symbol; letter c symbol.
> one $N\,A : A, N\,A$.
> $S : N$ letter a symbol, N letter b symbol, N letter c symbol.

The uniform replacement rule ensures that the same number of occurrences a, b and c appears in each sentence.

In more general terms the formalism of the van Wijngaarden grammar often ensures that a language can be described in a very natural way. Even context-free languages can often be better described by two-level grammars in the sense that they are more natural, i.e. it is easier to determine the language they describe.

The metarules of a two-level grammar can themselves be isolated and treated as a separate grammar. The (Chomsky-like) classification of this metagrammar will be significant. If it is merely a finite choice grammar then the power of the two-level grammar has not been significantly exploited but has merely been used as a notational convenience. For an equivalent context-free grammar, though longer than its two-level equivalent, would have the same expressive power. But if the metagrammar is context-free the story is different. The two-level grammar then generates a potentially infinite number of production rules and is equivalent in expressive power to a type-0 grammar. Moreover the general van Wijngaarden grammar is so general that the problem of deciding which production rule should be applied after a particular rule is unsolvable. From the compiler writers' point of view, therefore, the general two-level grammar is too powerful.

7.4.3 Inserting modes into the syntax
We now start to introduce some detail into the skeleton ALGOL 68

syntax of the previous sections by adding mode information. In learning ALGOL 68 one becomes accustomed to associating modes and values with constructs, the mode being just the mode of the value delivered by that construct. The mode information is carried through the syntax of ALGOL 68 in a manner similar to that employed in the definition of ALGOL W.

Take the identity relation. It delivers a result of mode boolean and both sides must produce variables of the same mode which are then compared for equality. A more detailed, but still simplified, syntax of identity relations illustrates the mode conditions

> boolean identity relation : reference to MODE TERTIARY1,
> identity relator, reference to MODE TERTIARY2.

The existence of 'reference to' and consistent substitution combine to ensure that variables of equivalent modes appear on both sides of the identity relator.

As another example consider the (still simplified) syntax rule for an assignation:

> REF to MODE assignation : REF to MODE destination,
> becomes token, MODE source.

This conveys various pieces of information about the nature of assignations. The destination must deliver a variable of mode REF to MODE and the right-hand side must deliver an item of mode MODE. Consistent substitution ensures that certain mode restrictions are enforced. But, on closer inspection, the mode restrictions are too strong since assignations such as (assume x is of mode **ref real**)

> $x := 1$

seem to be illegal. But this is not so since a source is defined by

> MODE1 source : MODE2 unit.

But now this is too general since it permits

> $x := "a"$

Further information must be incorporated into the syntax to ensure that the correct degree of freedom is permitted. The further information that has to be added is the inclusion of coercions (automatic mode changes). This is done in two stages:

> · by introducing a set of permissible coercions
> · by associating a strength with each syntactic position.

The strength is a measure of the amount of mode change that can take

192

place in a particular part of a program, e.g. to operands in formulae, to parameters, to sources or destinations of assignments. Let us look at these matters in more detail.

The various coercions that can be applied in an ALGOL 68 program are listed below together with some examples to illustrate their use:

· widening alters, for example, an integer to an appropriate real number or a real number to a corresponding complex number. Thus in

real $x := 0$

the 0 is widened to a corresponding real (denoted by 0.0) which can then be assigned to the variable x. Similarly in

compl $z := pi$

the real pi is widened to an appropriate complex number namely pi **i** 0 which is then assigned to z.

· rowing alters, for example, integers, reals, etc. into arrays of the appropriate kind. In

$[1:1]$ **int** $array := 3$

the 3 is transformed into an array with a single element, namely 3.

· voiding occurs when assignations (or indeed any units) are used as statements. No voiding of $n := 1$ occurs when this is used within an expression as in

$(n := 1) \times 4 + 5$

but it does occur in

$...; n := 1; ...$

· uniting allows an object to be assigned to a variable which can accept objects of one of several modes. Thus it occurs on the right in

union (int, char) $x := 4$

· deproceduring is the compile-time process which corresponds to activating a parameterless procedure to deliver its result. In

real $x := random \times 10 + 1$

$random,$ whose original mode is **proc real**, is deprocedured to produce a real result.

• dereferencing is the compile-time process of taking the value of a variable given the variable itself. Thus if n is an integer variable an expression such as $n + 1$ causes n to be dereferenced, and 1 added to the value obtained.

These then are the six coercions. The mode of a construct before a coercion occurs is called the *a priori* mode, the mode after coercion is called the *a posteriori* mode. In the last example therefore the *a priori* mode of n was **ref int**, its *a posteriori* mode was **int**.

Now the coercions listed here are not always applicable. The different positions in ALGOL 68 programs are given a strength and this strength determines the coercions which can be applied to any object appearing there. There are five different strengths designated as strong, firm, meek, weak and soft. In

• soft positions, only deproceduring can be applied
• weak positions, deproceduring and a limited form of dereferencing called weak dereferencing (a final **ref** cannot be removed) can occur in either order
• meek positions, deproceduring and dereferencing can occur in either order
• firm positions, the coercions that can be applied are similar to the coercions that can be applied in meek positions but uniting can also occur
• strong positions, any of the coercions can be applied.

How are all these considerations incorporated into the syntax of ALGOL 68? The strength is included in a very direct manner. Thus part of the syntax for assignations (still simplified) reads

REF to MODE destination : soft REF to MODE TERTIARY.
MODE1 source : strong MODE2 unit.

The presence of 'soft' therefore indicates that only deproceduring can occur in the destination part of an assignation. But in the source any of the coercions can be applied if necessary.

Other pieces of the syntax show that, for example,

• a subscript occupies a meek position – for there is a rule

subscript : meek integral unit.

• the SECONDARY in a selection occupies a weak position, for

REFETY MODE1 selection : MODE1... selector ..., of token, weak ....

194

· an operand occupies a firm position, for

MODE operand : firm MODE ...

To show how coercions themselves are incorporated into the syntax consider the simple assignation:

$x := n$

where x, n are of mode **ref real, ref int**, respectively. Informally, the n must be dereferenced and the resulting value widened before the variable x can receive the value obtained from the source.

Take this situation one step at a time and write down at each stage of the coercion process the last coercion applied, the mode that this produces and the nature of the source. Initially n is a

(a) reference to integral applied identifier.

After the first coercion we obtain a

(b) dereferenced-to-integral applied identifier

and after the second coercion a

(c) widened-to-real applied identifier.

The final result is then described as a

(d) strong real applied identifier coercee

by placing the strength of syntactic position at the start and the word 'coercee' at the end.

The syntax works in the reverse order by moving from (d) to (c) to (b) and eventually to (a). An applied identifier is an example of a FORM and one of the rules of the ALGOL 68 Report reads

strong MOID FORM coercee : STRONG MOID FORM.

STRONG can be replaced by 'widened to' and MOID by 'real' to take us from (d) to (c) above. The rule

widened to real FORM : MEEK integral FORM

takes us to stage (b) on replacing MEEK by 'dereferenced to'. Finally there is a rule

· dereferenced to integral FORM : MEEK referenced to integral FORM.

and (in effect) MEEK can merely be removed from this to give the required result.

In a similar kind of way all the coercions can be incorporated into the ALGOL 68 syntax using this mechanism. No essentially new ideas are needed. The above description has been somewhat simplified but all the main ideas are present.

Before leaving this section on modes it is perhaps worth noting that there is a sense in which the MODE of a construct can be regarded as an attribute. The syntax can be viewed as a description of how mode information can be passed up the syntax tree as a synthesised attribute.

7.4.4 Introducing predicates into the syntax

A predicate is a kind of Boolean – essentially it delivers either true or false – and it is used in the syntax essentially to enforce the context-sensitive conditions. (But it does serve other purposes.) Thus an assignation

$$x := 1$$

is legal only if x has been properly declared. This context-sensitive condition appears in the syntax of an assignation in the form of a predicate whose truth implies that a suitable declaration of x exists but whose falseness would imply that no such declaration exists and the program would therefore be (syntactically) illegal.

In a similar way a declaration such as

int x

is legal only if another declaration of x does not occur locally. Again a suitable predicate will be true for a legal declaration and false for an illegal declaration.

The mechanism by which legal programs and true predicates interrelate is rather curious. The syntax arranges that true predicates disappear but false predicates do not disappear. Consequently legal programs are described as a sequence of tokens and ultimately symbols. But illegal programs are not so formed since there will be at least one predicate which cannot be made to disappear.

All predicates are introduced by either 'where' or 'unless'. The simplest predicates are 'where true', 'where false', 'unless true', 'unless false'. There are then rules

       where true : EMPTY.
       unless false : EMPTY.

and

        EMPTY ::.

No such definitions exist for 'where false' or 'unless true', and so these cannot be made to disappear; they result from illegal programs.

196

In many respects predicates are combined as in Boolean algebra and can be separated by 'and' and 'or' with the expected meaning. Thus

> where THING1 and THING2 :
> > where THING1, where THING2.
> where THING1 or THING2 :
> > where THING1; where THING2.
> unless THING1 and THING2 :
> > unless THING1; unless THING2.
> unless THING1 or THING2 :
> > unless THING1, unless THING2.

There is a primitive set of predicates which perform such tasks as checking if two strings of characters are identical, checking if one string is contained within another, and so on. The predicate comparing for identity has a definition which starts:

> WHETHER (NOTETY1) is (NOTETY2): ...

WHETHER can be replaced by 'where' or 'unless'. NOTETY1 and NOTETY can be any sequence of letters, even a sequence which might contain the letters 'is'. To avoid ambiguity in interpreting this rule the brackets are used to delimit essentially the two operands of the predicate.

More complex predicates are later defined in terms of the simple predicates and these check if two modes are equivalent, check if one mode can be coerced to another in a particular syntactic position, etc. It is now possible to illustrate in more detail part of the syntax of assignations by noting that

> MODE1 source : strong MODE2 unit,
> > where MODE1 deflexes to MODE2.

The predicate 'deflexes to' then contains the information which prohibits, if x is of mode **ref real**,

> $x := $ "a"

but allows

> $x := 1.4$

For 'where real deflexes to character' cannot be made to disappear yet 'where real deflexes to real' does disappear.

The process of checking whether items have been previously or appropriately declared requires that the syntax has something analogous to a symbol table which reflects block structure and can be examined at the appropriate time. The metanotion NEST corresponds to the symbol table and is passed through the syntax basically as an inherited attribute. Block entry and exit together with declarations and procedure or operator calls cause the NEST to be altered. Statements cause the NEST to be examined so that the context-sensitive conditions can be checked.

When an ALGOL 68 program is being executed it is assumed that there is a standard environment which can be viewed as containing the declarations of all the standard modes, operators, procedures, etc. This environment, or environ as the Report calls it, will be augmented or updated as a result of declarations in a program and a new environ will result. The process of augmenting is described by saying that the new environ consists of the old environ together with a locale which contains the declarations of the new block. In the syntax environs appear as NESTs and locales as LAYERs. The appropriate metanotions have rules:

> NEST :: LAYER; NEST LAYER.
> LAYER :: new DECSETY LABSETY.

Each occurrence of 'new' starts a fresh locale. Within that locale there is the sequence of items analogous to declarations in the corresponding part of the program; declarations must appear before labels and hence the relative ordering of DECSETY and LABSETY. The DECSETY LABSETY represents a possibly null sequence of DECs followed by LABs. The rules

> LAB :: label TAG.
> DEC :: MODE TAG; priority PRIO TAD; MOID TALLY TAB;
> DUO TAD; MONO TAM.

indicate that in a locale each object is accompanied by its relevant attributes or qualities. Thus

> ·labels (as depicted by some TAG) have the quality 'label'
> ·identifiers (included under TAG) have a mode (MODE)
> · operators appearing in priority declarations (included under TAD) have the quality 'priority' and a representation of one of the digits 1, 2, ..., 9 (PRIO)
> · modes (TAB) have a description of their meaning in terms of other simpler or known modes
> · dyadic operators (TAD) have the modes of their operands and the mode of their result

·monadic operators (TAM) have the mode of their operand and the mode of their result.

The situation can be described by saying that a locale consists of 'new' followed by a sequence of elements of the form QUALITY TAX where QUALITY encompasses all the attributes and TAX encompasses all forms of identifiers, operator symbols, mode symbols etc. A sequence of zero or more items of the form QUALITY TAX is encompassed in the metanotion PROPSETY.

How then are these ideas incorporated into the syntax to enforce the context-sensitive conditions? Take first the case of the assignation

$$x := 1$$

This use of x is called an applied occurrence of x (as opposed to a defining occurrence when x would appear in a declaration as the item being declared). There is then a rule

QUALITY NEST applied INDICATOR with TAX :
   where QUALITY TAX identified in NEST, TAX token.

and, in this, INDICATOR can be replaced by 'identifier'. Thus the legality of the use of an identifier depends on whether the appropriate QUALITY TAX can be identified in the current NEST. The predicate 'identified in' merely searches out through the various LAYERs looking for an appropriate QUALITY TAX. If a successful search is performed the predicate disappears, otherwise it does not.

Take now the case where an identifier appears in a declaration and is declared. For this to be legal there must be no other declaration of that identifier in the same locale. The piece of syntax which enforces this reads

QUALITY NEST new PROPSETY1 QUALITY TAX
   PROPSETY2
   defining INDICATOR with TAX:
      where QUALITY TAX independent PROPSETY1
      PROPSETY2, TAX token.

In this hyper-rule note that

NEST new PROPSETY1 QUALITY TAX PROPSETY2

is a NEST whose most recent LAYER is

new PROPSETY1 QUALITY TAX PROPSETY2.

For the declaration to be legal the predicate 'independent' is used. Again, if the declaration is legal

199

where QUALITY TAX independent PROPSETY1 PROPSETY2

disappears, otherwise it does not. Basically the predicate ensures that no declaration of the identifier appears either before (PROPSETY1) or after it (PROPSETY2) in that locale.

Finally we can now give the complete syntax of assignations

REF to MODE NEST assignation : REF to MODE NEST
destination, becomes token, MODE NEST source.
REF to MODE NEST destination :
soft REF to MODE NEST TERTIARY.
MODE1 NEST source : strong MODE2 NEST unit,
where MODE1 deflexes to MODE2.

Before ending this section on NESTs note that the syntax makes no assumptions whatever about the standard environment. The syntax merely uses NEST and LAYER. Consequently it permits the inclusion and use of libraries of declarations, etc.

7.4.5 Some examples

Before leaving the syntax of ALGOL 68 we look at two examples which illustrate many of the ideas we have been discussing together with some others. We look at the syntax of loop clauses and the syntax of formulae or expressions.

The interesting aspect of the syntax of loops is the manner in which the particular NESTs or environs are created. Informally there are four potentially different environs depicted in figure 7.3. In the syntax NEST1, NEST2, NEST3 and NEST4 will correspond to the respective environs.

The complete rule for a loop clause reads

strong void NEST1 loop clause:
NEST1 STYLE for part defining new integral TAG2,
NEST1 STYLE intervals,
NEST1 STYLE repeating part with integral TAG2.

Combined with the further rule

NEST1 STYLE repeating part with DEC2:
NEST1 new DEC2 STYLE while do part;
NEST1 new DEC2 STYLE do part.

this implies that the environ associated with the while do part (or just the do part if the while part is omitted) is NEST1 combined with the new locale consisting of integral TAG2. This then gives NEST2.

To see the creation of NEST3 within the syntax it is necessary to

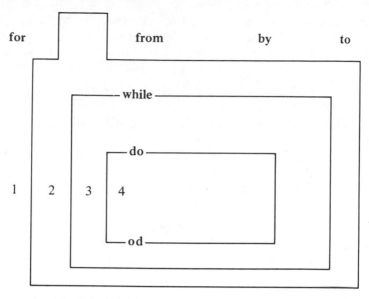

Fig. 7.3. Environs associated with loop clauses.

assume the existence of a while part. Then

> NEST2 STYLE while do part:
>> NEST2 STYLE while part defining LAYER3,
>> NEST2 LAYER3 STYLE do part.

LAYER3 is thus constructed from declarations appearing between the while part and do part and these together with the environ corresponding to NEST2 are passed down to the do part and form NEST3. Finally

> NEST3 STYLE do part :
>> STYLE do token,
>> strong void NEST3 serial clause defining LAYER4,
>> STYLE od token.

indicates the manner in which NEST4 is created.

Finally we look at the syntax of formulae. This will provide yet another illustration of the use of the two-level grammar. The syntax rules must include the rules for the implied bracketing of a wide variety of expressions. Consequently it must be rather sophisticated and yet it turns out to be remarkably simple.

In keeping with the ALGOL W approach, formulae have a mode associated with them (the *a priori* mode of the result produced by the formula) and also a priority. If all extraneous brackets are removed the priority is just that if the lowest priority operator not enclosed in brackets. Thus $a + b$ is a priority 6 formula since the operator + has priority 6, $-(x \times y + 4)$ is a priority 10 formula since monadic operators such as '–' have effectively priority 10. Within the syntax, priorities appear in several forms:

- DYADIC covers the priorities of all dyadic operators, namely 1, 2, ..., 9
- MONADIC is the priority of all monadic operators, effectively 10
- DYADIC TALLY gives a priority strictly greater than that of DYADIC
- DYADIC TALLETY gives a priority greater than or equal to that of DYADIC.

In the syntax, operators appear as procedures. Dyadic operators are represented by procedures taking two parameters and delivering a single result, monadic operators as procedures taking a single parameter and producing a single result. Thus for dyadic operators there appears

procedure with MODE1 parameter MODE2 parameter
yielding MOID NEST applied operator with TAD

and for monadic operators

procedure with MODE parameter yielding MOID NEST
applied operator with TAM

The syntax rules for formulae can now be given:

MOID NEST DYADIC formula :
MODE1 NEST DYADIC TALLETY operand,
procedure with MODE1 parameter MODE2 parameter
yielding MOID NEST applied operator with TAD,
where DYADIC TAD identified in NEST,
MODE2 NEST DYADIC TALLY operand.
MOID NEST MONADIC formula :
procedure with MODE parameter yielding MOID
NEST applied operator with TAM,
MODE NEST MONADIC operand.

In the first of these rules note that the right-hand operand must have a priority which is strictly greater than the priority of the formula itself. Thus $a - b - c$ must be parsed as $(a - b) - c$, not as $a - (b - c)$. Similarly expressions such as $a + b \times c \uparrow d$ can only be given one interpretation.

These rules, then, should be compared with the rules of ALGOL W for describing expressions. Note that the metanotions DYADIC, etc. have been used here to provide a kind of macro-facility which has led

202

to a much more compact set of rules which now encompass all kinds of expressions including both arithmetic and logical.

7.5 Semantics

The method used to describe the semantics of ALGOL 68 is just English, but used in a rather formal manner. Many of the words such as name, value, are defined in an early part of the Report and are used later in a technical sense. Many aspects of programming appear in the presentation of the semantics : symbols, quantifiers, predicates and recursive functions are all used; ideas from top-down structured programming are apparent – the absence of jumps, the use of case statements, etc.

To illustrate the flavour of the semantics sections of the Report, the following gives the semantics of identity relations. Recall that their (simplified) syntax takes the form

> identity relation : TERTIARY1, identity relator, TERTIARY2.

and that these are used in comparing two variables (not their values).

The yield W of an identity-relation I is determined as follows:

> •let N1 and N2 be the collateral yields of the TERTIARYs of I;
> Case A : The token of the identity-relator of I is an is-token :
> •W is true if { the name } N1 is the same as N2, and is false otherwise
> Case B : The token of the identity-relator of I is an is-not-token:
> •W is true if N1 is not the same as N2, and is false otherwise.

To describe the effect of a program a hypothetical computer is introduced and the meaning of a construct is described in terms of the actions this computer has to perform as a program is executed. Thus the semantics are interpreter-oriented. The hypothetical computer is, of course, idealised in the usual ways (in terms of size, etc.) and an actual implementation is regarded as a model of the hypothetical computer with physical limitations.

The ALGOL 68 Report goes to considerable lengths to distinguish between external objects and internal objects. External objects correspond to some piece of text which appears in a program. Internal objects, on the other hand, are the realisation of external objects within the hypothetical computer; they include values, locales, environs and scenes. The values are classified as plain values (such as integers, reals, Booleans and characters), names (i.e. variables), multiple values (arrays), structured values and routines. Locales and environs have already been discussed. A scene takes the form of a construct of the

203

language together with the environ in which it appears and is to be interpreted; thus a scene contains all its own context-sensitive information.

As interpretation of a program (or more precisely of a scene) proceeds, the hypothetical computer performs certain instructions or actions. These are serial or collateral actions, the former being executed or performed one after the other, the latter being merged in time. Actions can and usually involve other actions; eventually there are the primitive instructions of the hypothetical computer, the inseparable actions.

Actions performed by the computer take one of three forms : relationships can be made to hold, new names can be generated and other scenes can be elaborated. Of these, only the first requires further explanation. Relationships can either be permanent (in the sense that they are independent of a program and its execution) or they are not permanent and can be made to hold or cease to hold as a result of actions. The permanent relationships include 'to be of the same mode as', 'to be smaller than', 'to be widenable to', 'to be lengthenable to', 'to be equivalent to'. Relationships of the other kind include 'to refer to', 'to access', 'to be the yield of', 'to be newer (older, the same as) in scope' and 'to be a subname of'. For example,

- 'to refer to' is the relationship between a variable and its value
- 'to access' is the relationship between a QUALITY TAX and a value or scene and this may hold within a particular locale
- 'to be the yield of' is the relationship between a value and an action such as the elaboration or execution of a scene.

In fact, the various actions perform the expected operations. If the reader looks back at the semantics of identity relations given earlier he will see that various actions are invoked.

7.6 Concluding remarks

ALGOL 68 has been one of the most rigorously defined programming languages. Yet there are still faults (both errors and obscurities) in its definition. Unfortunately many people find the definition somewhat awe-inspiring, difficult to read and difficult to interpret. Yet there are numerous points in its favour.

The syntax now describes all those aspects of the definition which can reasonably be checked at compile-time; it includes all the context-sensitive requirements. Those aspects of the definition of ALGOL 60 which formed the static semantics are now incorporated into the syntax.

The two-level grammar has provided a very convenient notation for describing syntax. The idea of a two-level grammar together with consistent substitution tends to encourage orthogonal design and regular languages. In some respects the axes of orthogonality are the two levels of grammar.

Using the single mechanism of the van Wijngaarden grammar the designers of ALGOL 68 were able to encompass many ideas:

- the context-free grammar which provides the mode-independent parsing can easily be abstracted from the syntax by omitting modes, nests, predicates, etc.
- the formalism can be viewed as a means of passing attributes through the grammar, both synthesised and inherited attributes
- the context-sensitive aspects of a language definition have been included in the syntax
- a macro-facility as used in the definition of formulae is present
- the definition is independent of the environment in which a program runs and so permits separate compilation.

But it could have been used also for describing the semantics of ALGOL 68. Thus it could have been employed to describe not just the static aspects of the programming language but also its dynamic aspects.

To illustrate the use of this formalism for the purposes of specifying semantics we look first at some aspects of arithmetic, in particular the equality, addition and multiplication of non-negative integers.

For simplicity assume that the integers appear in unary forms as a sequence of ones. Thus 'one one one' represents the number three and so on. Formally

NUMBER :: ONES; EMPTY.
ONES :: one; ONES one.

Equality between such numbers can then be established in a relatively straightforward manner. We represent this equality by the predicate 'is':

where NUMBER1 one is NUMBER2 one:
    where NUMBER1 is NUMBER2.
where NUMBER1 is NUMBER2 :
    where NUMBER2 is NUMBER1.
where EMPTY is NUMBER one : where false.
where EMPTY is EMPTY : where true.

With these preliminary definitions we can now look at the definition of addition:

where NUMBER1 equals NUMBER2 plus NUMBER3 :
    where NUMBER1 is NUMBER2 NUMBER3.

The definition of multiplication is less straightforward and is based on the observations that

$$n = n \times 1$$
$$0 = n \times 0$$
$$n \times (m+1) = (n \times m) + n$$

Thus

where NUMBER equals NUMBER times one : where true.
where EMPTY equals NUMBER times EMPTY ; where true.
where NUMBER1 equals NUMBER2 times NUMBER3 one :
    where NUMBER1 equals NUMBER4 plus NUMBER2,
    where NUMBER4 equals NUMBER2 times NUMBER3.

These definitions then indicate how a very limited set of semantics can be specified. In fact, the definition of multiplication is based on a kind of axiomatic definition of multiplication, a definition expressed in terms of primitive recursive functions. It is well known that all the functions which computers execute can be expressed in terms of recursive functions and so can be expressed in terms of these predicates.

Using the formalism of the van Wijgaarden grammar it is possible to go much further and define the meaning of not just other arithmetic and logical functions but also the meaning of programs.

It should be relatively clear how the arithmetic and logical operations can be handled. But many aspects of semantics require a representation in some sense of the computer store, the state of the input and output files and so on. Even more there must be a presence in some sense of the program being described and the statement being currently executed. In our brief description of one way of dealing with these problems we follow Cleaveland & Uzgalis (1977).

Assume a programming language which permits one input stream and one output stream. The state of the machine store together with the input and output files, i.e. the run-time environment, can then be simulated by SNAP where

SNAP :: memory LOCS FILE FILE.
FILE :: DATA end of file.
DATA :: EMPTY; space VALUE DATA.

The first occurrence of FILE refers to the input stream and the second occurrence refers to the output stream. The metanotion LOCS refers to identifiers in scope and in the main store of the machine and includes

206

information about the mode of these identifiers and the values to which they refer. Thus

> LOCS :: LOC; LOCS, LOC.
> LOC :: loc TAG has MODE refers BOX end.

Thus the identifier TAG has been declared to be of mode MODE and might refer to a value BOX. The latter metanotion might be defined as

> BOX :: VALUE; undefined; TAG.

indicating that uninitialised variables will be given an initial value of 'undefined' and variables may have values which are other variables or TAGs.

To describe the semantics of programs using the van Wijngaarden formalism it is convenient to look again at the nature of predicates. These were essentially functions which gave a Boolean result. We extend the formalism to more general kinds of functions and look at two special functions, 'execute' and 'evaluate', for describing the semantics of statements and expressions respectively. Thus if STMT is a metanotion which represents any statement of a language and if STMTS refers to several statements

> execute STMTS with SNAPS

will be used for describing the effect of STMTS. If EXPR refers to expressions then

> evaluate EXPR from SNAP giving VALUE

will describe the effect of evaluating EXPR.

As the execution of a program progresses the history of these SNAPS, i.e. snapshots, describes the meaning of a program. Thus if STMT is a metanotion which represents any statement of the language and if STMTS refers to several statements

> execute STMT STMTS with SNAPS1 SNAP SNAPS2:
>   execute STMT with SNAPS1 SNAP,
>   execute STMTS with SNAP SNAPS2.

In effect, 'execute' behaves like an interpreter and so describes the meaning of the various statements and eventually entire programs.

With these remarks it becomes possible to illustrate briefly how all aspects of the definition of a program can be covered by the one mechanism. A program will be described as a piece of text representing the program itself together with the input stream, the output stream and the interpreter for the program. Thus

program :
    begin symbol,
        declare NEST1, NEST1 restrictions,
        NEST1 STMTS
    end symbol,
    FILE1 stream,
    FILE2 stream,
    execute STMTS with
        memory NEST1 FILE1 end of file
        SNAPSETY
        memory NEST2 FILE3 FILE2.

Note now the role played by the consistent substitution rule. Consider just NEST1 :

- the metanotion NEST1 essentially is the symbol table set up by the initial declarations
- all STMTS are to be interpreted within the environment of NEST1
- the initial snapshot of memory has locations which reflect the NEST1 environment.

Moreover note that

- the STMTS in the program are the same as the statements acted on by the interpreter
- the input stream FILE1 appears twice as does the output stream FILE2.

These remarks then are intended to give a feeling for how two-level grammars can be used to describe not only syntax but also semantics.

In this chapter we shall give an introduction to a mathematical approach to the problem of specifying in a formal manner the semantics of programming languages. The resulting topic is variously known as denotational, mathematical or functional semantics. The work on which this chapter is based was performed by D. Scott and C. Strachey at the University of Oxford, England. If a division has to be made it could be said that Scott was responsible for the mathematical ideas and Strachey was responsible for applying these ideas to the problem of describing semantics.

The motivation for the Scott–Strachey work on semantics stems from a recognition of the fact that programs and the objects they manipulate are in some sense concrete realisations or implementations of abstract mathematical objects. For instance, appropriate bit patterns are implementations of numbers and certain kinds of routine are implementations of mathematical functions. It is the very nature of these mathematical objects that provides the true meaning of programs, procedures, etc.

The denotational approach to semantics makes use of mappings which are called *semantic interpretation functions* or *semantic valuation functions*. These map constructs of a programming language into their abstract mathematical counterpart; thus numerals are mapped into numbers, procedures of appropriate kinds are mapped into mathematical functions, and so on.

In contrast to the operational approach to describing semantics the denotational approach is free of implementation detail, which is unnecessary for the understanding of meaning. As such it is perhaps of less value to the implementor but of more value to language designers and to theorists and so favoured by them; problems of program equivalence, etc. become easier to attack.

One of the criticisms often levelled at the operational approach is that it transfers the problems of specifying semantics from one language (the source language) to another language (the language of the abstract machine). In a similar way the denotational approach relies on mathematics for the solution of its problem. But unfortunately traditional mathematics (prior to about 1969) was not too well equipped to take the strain – it was not clear whether mathematical inconsistencies or mathematical paradoxes might be possible. Such possibilities would be very undesirable from the point of view of the specification of semantics.

The investigations into denotational semantics struck at the very essence of understanding computing and programming from a mathematical viewpoint and consequently led to much deep mathematical work. It is *not* our intention here to become heavily involved in the mathematical side of this topic but rather we proceed with the intention of showing the relevance of the approach and of the ideas and theory to the task of describing semantics.

The work presented in this chapter relies heavily on the publications of Scott and Strachey together with their collaborators J.E. Stoy, C. Wadsworth, P.D. Mosses, *et al.*

8.1 Introduction to basic ideas

We have said that in denotational semantics we shall provide mappings which essentially describe meaning. These mappings will map from syntactically correct constructs into suitable domains of mathematical quantities. A simple example will help in setting the scene.

In most programming languages numerals are used to represent numbers. Thus each of

$$3 \qquad 03 \qquad 003 \qquad 0003$$

represents the same mathematical entity, namely the integer three. In denotational semantics each of these numerals would be mapped onto the same mathematical object and this provides the true 'meaning' of each of the above sequences of characters.

To be more explicit, the syntax of numerals reads, in a kind of BNF notation,

$$\nu ::= 0 \,|\, 1 \,|\, \nu 0 \,|\, \nu 1$$

where $\nu \in$ Numerals. To give meaning to these numerals a mapping of the form

$$\mathcal{N}: \text{Numerals} \rightarrow \text{Integers}$$

must be provided. The definition of $\mathcal{N}$ can be based on the syntactic definition of a numeral. Thus

$$\mathcal{N}[\![0]\!] = 0$$

$$\mathcal{N}[\![1]\!] = 1$$
$$\mathcal{N}[\![v0]\!] = 2 \times \mathcal{N}[\![v]\!]$$
$$\mathcal{N}[\![v1]\!] = 2 \times \mathcal{N}[\![v]\!] + 1$$

The brackets $[\![\ ]\!]$ enclose numerals or, more generally, constructs in the source language. The italicised digits represent mathematical objects and appear only on the right of the above definitions; non-italicised digits appear as parts of numerals. It is now a simple matter to check that indeed

$$\mathcal{N}[\![3]\!] = \mathcal{N}[\![03]\!] = \mathcal{N}[\![003]\!] = \mathcal{N}[\![0003]\!] = 3$$

Functions such as $\mathcal{N}$ used above are called semantic functions, semantic valuations, interpretation functions, etc. The domain of such a function, e.g. 'Numerals' above, is a syntactic domain, i.e. a set of elements described by a non-terminal in the grammar for the language. The codomains – 'Integers' above – are semantic domains.

What we now aim to do is to extend the ideas outlined above to all aspects of programming languages. It should be clear how the ideas can be so extended to produce mappings from numerals representing real or complex numbers into their corresponding mathematical counterparts. But they can also be extended to cover expressions, statements or commands, procedures, functions and so on. This will be our concern for the rest of this chapter.

Traditionally the syntax of programming languages has been defined in a hierarchical fashion. Starting with numerals and variables, the definition usually proceeds by defining expressions, simple statements or commands, more complex statements or commands such as loops and conditionals, and finally procedures; declarations and other such items are also defined. The meaning of the various constructs will be defined in a similar way for the semantics will be based on the syntactic specification using a kind of recursive descent approach. Having described the meaning of expressions, statements and eventually programs will be discussed and their meaning explained. Consequently there will be semantic functions of the form

$$\mathcal{E} : Exp \rightarrow \ \ldots$$
$$\mathcal{C} : Cmd \rightarrow \ \ldots$$
$$\mathcal{M} : Prog \rightarrow \ \ldots$$

where *Exp*, *Cmd* and *Prog* represent the syntactic classes for expressions, commands or statements, and programs respectively; the dots indicate sets of some appropriate kind. The mapping $\mathcal{M}$ then gives the meaning of any syntactically correct program.

Commands in programming languages usually cause changes in the values of the variables used in a program. To reflect this and to describe their meaning, a machine state S will be introduced. The details of precisely what constitutes a machine state will be discussed later but it must include at least the values of all variables. In a simplified situation (which ignores the possibility of jumps, etc.) the command $\mathscr{C}$ will map commands into functions which describe state changes:

$$\mathscr{C} : [Cmd \rightarrow [S \rightarrow S]\,]$$

A denotational approach to language definition must therefore make clear several sets of quantities:

- the syntactic domains
- the semantic domains
- the syntax rules
- the definitions of the various semantic functions.

The last quantity will, of course, include a statement of the functionality of each semantic function, i.e. its domain and codomain. In all this work it will be vitally important to be quite clear about the precise nature of the domains and codomains for they can become rather complex.

8.2 The lambda calculus

If programming language constructs have to be mapped into mathematical objects it is important to ensure that all the mathematical objects are defined in a clear and unambiguous fashion. It will therefore be necessary to have a means of specifying, in particular, functions and how they are to be evaluated.

In discussing the programming language LISP we had occasion to discuss the λ-notation, a means of expressing functions without having to give them any particular name. We shall use this notation for describing functions and indeed other objects but it must be formalised and precise rules must be given for the evaluation of functions. The formalised system is called the λ-calculus and itself is a kind of language (which requires careful and accurate specification).

In the λ-calculus no clear distinction is made between functions and their arguments since functions themselves can be passed as arguments or parameters to other functions. Thus instead of using the traditional mathematical notation $f(x)$ for function application we merely write fx. Given abc then we associate to the left and regard the above as an abbreviation for $((ab)c)$.

The expressions of the λ-calculus are defined by the grammar

```
<expression> :: =    <variable>
                   | <expression> <expression>
                   | λ<variable> . <expression>
                   | (<expression>)
```

It is assumed that there are plenty of variables, and for convenience we represent these by lower-case letters.

Expressions of the form <expression> <expression> are called *applications* – they include function application in the form of expressions such as

$(\lambda x. x)a$

Expressions of the form λ <variable> . <expression> are called *abstractions* since these constitute the λ-calculus equivalent of functions.

The above syntactic rules are by themselves inadequate – they are, for example, syntactically ambiguous. The further rules necessary to ensure unambiguous interpretation are

· association occurs to the left
· when an abstraction $\lambda x.E$ occurs (here E represents some λ-expression) the E is understood to extend as far as possible to the right, to the first unmatched closing bracket or to the end of the expression, whichever occurs first.

These rules imply that expressions such as

$(\lambda x. \lambda y. xy)ab$

are well defined; for the above is interpreted as

$(\lambda x. (\lambda y. xy))ab$ or as $((\lambda x. (\lambda y. xy))a)b$

In this notation all the functions (or, more accurately, abstractions) have only one argument or parameter. Consequently it is not permissible to have functions of more than one parameter. But consider a function f of two variables x and y. A function g with the property that

$g(x)(y) = f(x, y)$

can be defined and is, in some sense, equivalent to f. The function g is called the *curried version* of f. The idea extends in a natural way to functions of several variables; curried functions can be used to obtain their effect.

In the earlier discussion of LISP the terms free and bound variable were introduced. A bound variable had an existence only within the construct under discussion, it was in a sense local. A free variable, on the other hand, had a meaning and existence global to a construct. The

213

same terms can be used in connection with the λ-calculus. A formal definition can be based on the syntactic definition of λ-expressions.

Definition of 'free'
Let capital letters denote arbitrary λ-expressions
 1. x occurs free in x but not in any other variable
 2. x occurs free in XY if it occurs free in X or in Y or in both
 3. x occurs free in $\lambda y.X$ if x and y are different and x occurs free in X
 4. x occurs free in (X) if it occurs free in X.

An analogous definition can be used to explain what it means to say that a variable occurs bound in a λ-expression.

Definition of 'bound'
 1. No variable occurs bound in y, for any variable y
 2. x occurs bound in XY if it occurs bound in X or in Y or in both
 3. x occurs bound in $\lambda y.X$ if x and y are the same variable or if x occurs bound in X
 4. x occurs bound in (X) if it occurs bound in X

In summary, bound variables follow occurrences of λ, and free variables are not bound variables.

Example 8.1
In the λ-expression

$$(\lambda x.\ \lambda y.xy)ab$$

both x and y occur bound, a and b occur free.

With these ideas we are now in a position to discuss function application and evaluation in the context of the λ-calculus. Given an application such as

$$(\lambda x.N)a$$

evaluation proceeds by substitution, by replacing occurrences of x by a. But there are some complications since N is, in general, any arbitrary λ-expression and might contain expressions involving a and x as bound variables. In fact, the usual programming language scope rules apply and x used as a bound variable has a meaning and existence only within the expression in which it is so used. A precise definition of substitution is required.

The following definition discusses the desired effect of replacing the

214

variable x which occurs in X by the λ-expression M. Note that alterations in the names of variables may be necessary. Again the substitution rule is based on the syntactic specification of λ-expressions.

Substitution rule
Let x be a variable and M and X λ-expressions. Then $[M/x]\,X$ is defined as follows:

1. If X is a variable, two cases occur
   (*a*) X is x; then result is M
   (*b*) X is not x; result is X
2. If X is of the form YZ then result is
   $([M/x]\,Y)\,([M/x]\,Z)$
3. If X is of the form $\lambda y.\,Y$ two cases occur
   (*a*) y is x; then result is X
   (*b*) y is not x;
        (i) if x does not occur free in Y or if y does not occur free in M then result is
           $\lambda y.\,[M/x]\,Y$
        (ii) if x does occur free in Y and y does occur free in M then the result is
           $\lambda z.\,[M/x]\,([z/y]\,Y)$
           where z is some variable not occurring free in M or Y.

Note that the renaming performed in step 3(*b*)(ii) is done to prevent trouble arising in cases such as

$$(\lambda x.\ \lambda y.xy)y$$

and

$$(\lambda x.\ \lambda a.ax)\lambda y.yay$$

For in both cases forgetting to rename would mean that essentially different variables would become confused as the one variable.

Example 8.2   The substitution rule

   (i) $(\lambda x.\ \lambda y.x)ab$ produces a
   (ii) $(\lambda x.\ \lambda y.y)ab$ produces b
   (iii) $(\lambda x.\lambda y.\lambda z.y(xyz))\,(\lambda x.\lambda y.xy)$ produces $\lambda x.\lambda y.x(xy)$

This substitution rule defines evaluation. But consider

$$(\lambda x.\lambda y.y)\,((\lambda x.xx)\,(\lambda x.xx))$$

This can be evaluated in two different ways:

· taking the λ-expression

$$(\lambda x.\lambda y.y)$$

and replacing all occurrences of x by the parameter produces

$$\lambda y.y$$

· if an attempt is first made to evaluate

$$(\lambda x.xx)\,(\lambda x.xx)$$

then performing the substitution results in the same λ-expression and so the evaluation never terminates.

Consequently two different outcomes are obtained by using different evaluation sequences. The first produces a result; the second never terminates and is said to be *irreducible*.

This experience starts to cast doubt on the wisdom of using this mathematical framework for language definition. Fortunately a number of results come to the rescue. The Church–Rosser theorem states that if two evaluations take place and if neither produces an irreducible sequence then the results are always the same. The resulting expression is then given a special name and called the *normal form* of the λ-expression.

Fortunately also there is one particular order of evaluation which is guaranteed to terminate wherever possible – this is called the normal order of evaluation. Basically, no arguments are evaluated unless they are needed. Evaluation essentially proceeds from the outside in.

The λ-calculus in its present form would appear to be very restrictive In a sense it is. But it is possible to devise λ-expressions representing integers, Booleans, conditionals, equalities of some kind, and so on. To illustrate, **true** and **false** can appear as

$$\lambda x.\lambda y.x \quad \text{and} \quad \lambda x.\lambda y.y$$

respectively. For Boolean expressions usually occur in conditionals and if these are supplied with two arguments a and b the former selects a and the latter b. See example 8.2.

The integers 0,1,2,3, ... can be expressed as

$$\lambda x.\lambda y.y$$
$$\lambda x.\lambda y.xy$$
$$\lambda x.\lambda y.x(xy)$$
$$\lambda x.\lambda y.x(x(xy))$$

and so on. The successor function, which produces a representation of $n+1$ given a representation of n, is just

$$\lambda x.\lambda y.\lambda z.y(xyz)$$

It will suit our purpose then to write λ-expressions which involve conditionals, equality, certain simple arithmetic operators and so on. We use the traditional mathematical symbols essentially to ease the burden of notation. But it should be understood that, if necessary, we could resort to strict λ-calculus and its substitution rule for justification. The strict foundation and basis of our mathematical objects resides in the rules of the λ-calculus.

Our previous discussion of the λ-notation (see subsection 3.3.3) highlighted a difficulty with respect to the recursive definitions of functions. The same problem exists in the λ-calculus. Recall that the λ-notation was intended to overcome the problem of having to specify the names of functions. In the λ-calculus it is tempting to write, with our new-found freedom of notation,

$$\lambda n. \text{ if } n = 0 \text{ then } 1 \text{ else } n \times f(n-1)$$

But this involves the free variable f which we are attempting to define. So let F represent

$$\lambda f. \ \lambda n. \text{ if } n = 0 \text{ then } 1 \text{ else } n \times f(n-1)$$

This is still not the factorial function since it is the curried version of a function of two parameters. But the factorial function g is such that

$$Fg = g$$

Turning the whole argument round, the factorial function g is a solution of the equation

$$Fx = x$$

We say that g is a *fixed point* of F since F applied to g produces just g. It is now convenient to introduce an operator which selects fixed points. The Y-operator does this and so we can write YF and thereby obtain the factorial function. The λ-expression

$$\lambda y. \ (\lambda x. y(xx)) \ (\lambda x. y(xx))$$

achieves the effect of the Y-operator. But note that this involves the application of a function to itself.

We conclude then with the remark that the Y-operator selects a fixed point which is just the required function. This hides many pitfalls. The equation defining the fixed point is an equation whose solution is a function. Just as equations whose solutions are numbers can have zero, one or many solutions, e.g.

$$x = x+1$$
$$x = 4$$
$$x = x^2-2x+2$$
$$x = x$$

so equations whose solutions are function can likewise have zero, one or many solutions. For this reason the Y-operator is sometimes referred to as the 'paradoxical combinator'. Is there a solution for Y to choose? If there are several solutions which solution does it select?

We shall return to consideration of these and similar questions in section 8.6.

8.3 Self-application and inconsistency

We have seen that the denotational semantics approach requires that we provide maps from syntactic domains into semantic domains. Thus integer numerals, for example, are mapped into the set of integers, and real numerals are mapped into the set of real numbers. The generalisation appears to be straightforward; structures and records are mapped into the Cartesian products of semantic domains, procedures of certain kinds are mapped into mathematical functions, etc.

The wisdom of the denotational approach would be called into serious question if it could be shown that the underlying mathematics was inconsistent, contradictory or ambiguous in some sense. A frequently cited instance of such a contradiction in mathematics is Russell's paradox. In its original form it is phrased in terms of sets. It is permissible to talk about sets of objects of any kind. In particular, it is permissible to talk about sets of sets and consequently we can talk about sets belonging to sets; we could even entertain the possibility of a set belonging to itself. The set S is then defined in the following way: x belongs to S if and only if x does not belong to x. We then ask the question: does S belong to itself? The definition of S provokes the response: S belongs to S if and only if S does not belong to S. This is a clear contradiction and is called Russell's paradox.

There are other formulations of the paradox. We look at one of the more popular renderings. In a town the barber shaves everyone who does not shave himself. Who shaves the barber? Yet another version is more suitable from the programming point of view. The adjective 'autological' can be applied to any objective that describes itself. Thus 'short' is autological because it is a short word; 'polysyllabic' is autological because again it is polysyllabic; and so on. An adjective which is not autological is said to be 'heterological'. Thus 'long' and 'monosyllabic' are both heterological. Russell's paradox then shows itself when the question is asked: is 'heterological' autological or is it heterological?

Suppose we now try to reproduce this situation in a programming language. Adjectives of the kind we have been discussing can be represented by functions which produce Boolean results. In particular, the adjective 'heterological' can be represented by a function h defined as follows (using an ALGOL 68 style of notation).

proc h = (**adjective** a) **bool** : ¬ $a(a)$

Suppose we now examine the procedure call $h(h)$, i.e. we try to reproduce the paradox. The call invokes another call ¬ $h(h)$; this again produces another call, and so on – the execution never terminates. The result is curious but satisfactory. Perhaps paradoxes cannot be reproduced in programming languages!

In all the examples given above the paradoxes were created by, what can be called, self-application. There are other situations in which self-application again occurs in programming. These can give rise to other situations which need close examination. To introduce one such case note the mode **d** with definition

mode d = proc (d) d

In ALGOL 68 this and other similar recursive mode declarations are all perfectly legitimate. But in mathematics there is a theorem due to Cantor which states that if D is a set consisting of at least two elements then the cardinality (i.e. a measure of the size) of the set of mappings from D to itself is strictly greater than the cardinality of D.

This observation raises the serious doubt of allowing the above mode declaration of **d** to be legitimate since its legality implies that $D \rightarrow D$ and D must have the same cardinality. In the usual mathematical situation this is just not so.

Similar apparent difficulties occur with many of the recursive mode declarations permitted in ALGOL 68 and in other languages. If procedures of the appropriate kind are mapped onto the usual mathematical functions, inconsistencies and contradictions may start to appear. Inconsistency, etc. is precisely what must be avoided if sensible meanings have to be given to syntactically correct constructs in programming languages.

Another difficulty arises from the nature of certain programming languages. In some cases procedures themselves can be passed to other procedures; this happens in ALGOL 60 and ALGOL 68, for example. In some languages it is possible to pass as parameters procedures of a very general kind; in ALGOL 60, for example, it is legal to write

integer procedure $f(n, g)$; **integer** n; **integer procedure** g; ...

The precise nature of the parameter g has not been specified and indeed a procedure of zero, one or more parameters could be passed across to f. The mathematical object which is equivalent to g is a very general kind of mapping. It immediately becomes possible – and the above example may even suggest it – to think of functions which take themselves as parameters. This in turn suggests the possibility of a version of Russell's paradox. In the λ-calculus consider, for example,

$$y = \lambda x. \text{ if } x(x) = 1 \text{ then } 2 \text{ else } 1$$

and look at $y(y)$.

Problems concerning self-application occur also in other spheres. If a programming language (perhaps even machine code) permits arbitrary commands or statements to be themselves stored and later accessed by program then self-application becomes a possibility and problems of inconsistency must be considered.

Until Scott tackled this self-application problem there was no mathematical theory of functions which could cope with these situations without itself leading to some kind of inconsistency.

The difficulties were resolved by mapping syntactic domains not into their obvious mathematical equivalents but into semantic domains of a more specialised nature. When these domains are defined in terms of themselves they are referred to as *reflexive domains* and this represents a special case of self-application. These new domains were introduced by Scott who was then able to show that inconsistency of the kind described above could not occur in his domains. Consequently they provide the natural sets and function spaces into which our programming language constructs should be mapped.

8.4 The idea of approximation

The idea behind Scott's mathematical work is the idea of approximation In its stark mathematical setting the idea lacks motivation. Consequently we begin with some observat ons which provide the necessary background.

In high-level programming languages the objects which are manipulated are in some sense approximations of their mathematical ideals. In the case of integers, characters, etc. the approximations are exact subject to constraints about ranges, and so on. But real numbers, for example, are not in general held accurately. Instead only approximations, e.g. to ten decimal digits, are held. In a similar kind of way complex numbers, arrays of reals, structures or records involving reals are all held as approximations.

Consider now what happens when a procedure to map real numbers into real numbers is programmed in some high-level programming language. This might evaluate square roots, *sin*, *cos* or *log*, for example. The procedure will, on being given an approximate parameter, produce an approximate result. In general, however, it will have the very desirable

220

property that given a better approximation to the parameter it will produce a better answer. Procedures of this kind therefore are equivalent to mathematical functions which possess a special property – they are *monotonic,* i.e. more accurate parameters produce more accurate results. But we can go further yet. It is to be hoped that as the approximation to the parameter comes closer and closer to the mathematically exact quantity the result will also come closer and closer to the mathematically correct result; indeed it should be possible to get as accurate an answer as required by supplying a sufficiently accurate parameter. Procedures with this extra property are equivalent to mathematical functions which are said to be *continuous.*

The idea of approximation is fundamental. So also are the concepts of monotonic and continuous functions, as described in vague terms above. As might be expected the denotational approach to semantics will result in procedures in programming languages being mapped onto these continuous functions.

We now approach these concepts from an abstract mathematical standpoint. But we keep in mind the ideas which motivate the work.

If x and y are two elements of the set D we write

$$x \sqsubseteq y$$

and say that x is an approximation to y or that y is consistent with or more accurate than x. $\sqsubseteq$ is called the *approximation relation* and will be assumed to be

· reflexive, i.e. for any $x \in D$ $x \sqsubseteq x$
· transitive, i.e. $x \sqsubseteq y$ and $y \sqsubseteq z$ imply that $x \sqsubseteq z$
· antisymmetric, i.e. $x \sqsubseteq y$ and $y \sqsubseteq x$ imply that $x = y$.

Intuitively these are reasonable properties to expect of an 'approximation relation'.

A relation with the properties described above is called a *partial ordering* and imposes on the set D a structure which makes it a partially ordered set. For the purposes of denotational semantics something slightly stronger is required.

Definition
A *complete lattice, D,* is a partially ordered set in which each subset X of D has both a least upper bound written $\sqcup X$, and a greatest lower bound, written $\sqcap X$. Both $\sqcup X$ and $\sqcap X$ are members of D.

Formally $y = \sqcup X$ has the following properties

(i) $x \sqsubseteq y$ for all $x \in X$
(ii) if $z \in D$ is such that

$$x \sqsubseteq z \text{ for all } x \in X$$
$$\text{then } y \sqsubseteq z.$$

In a similar way $s = \sqcap X$ is defined by

(i) $s \sqsubseteq x$ for all $x \in X$
(ii) if $t \in D$ has the property that
$$t \sqsubseteq x \text{ for all } x \in X$$
then $t \sqsubseteq s$.

There are two objects which merit special attention, the least upper bound of the empty set $\emptyset$ and the least upper bound of the entire set D. We write

$$\bot = \sqcup \emptyset \text{ and } \top = \sqcup D$$

$\bot$ is referred to as the *weakest* element or the *bottom* of D; we refer to $\top$ as the *strongest* or the *top* of D. We then have

$$\bot \sqsubseteq x \sqsubseteq \top \quad \text{for all } x \in D.$$

Since any element of D is an approximation to $\top$, $\top$ is sometimes referred to as the *overdetermined* or *inconsistent* element. In a similar way $\bot$ is sometimes called the *underdetermined* element of D.

Henceforth we shall use the word *domain* to refer to complete lattices whose partial ordering is the approximation relation $\sqsubseteq$. (There is now possible confusion between these domains and the domains on which functions are defined. In all cases the meaning will be clear from the context.) Within these domains it becomes possible to talk about the behaviour of better and better approximations. For if

$$X = \{ x_i : i = 0,1,2, \dots \}$$

is a *chain* of elements of D, i.e. if

$$x_0 \sqsubseteq x_1 \sqsubseteq x_2 \sqsubseteq \dots \sqsubseteq x_n \sqsubseteq \dots$$

then this set must have a least upper bound which is written as

$$\sqcup X \text{ or as } \bigsqcup_{n=0}^{\infty} x_n$$

This is called the *limit* of the sequence and is written $\lim_{n \to \infty} x_n$.

Sets such as the set X described above constitute special cases of a more general kind of set.

Definition
A set X is said to be *directed* if every finite subset of X has an upper

222

bound in X itself. These directed sets will become more relevant after the following discussion of functions.

The functions which shall be of interest in the present context should act reasonably with respect to approximations. Given that an argument y is more accurate than an argument x, $f(y)$ should be more accurate than $f(x)$. To be more precise if $f : D_0 \rightarrow D_1$ and $x, y \in D_0$ are such that $x \sqsubseteq y$ then one would expect to find that

$$f(x) \sqsubseteq f(y)$$

Functions which possess this property for all pairs $x, y \in D_0$ with the property that $x \sqsubseteq y$ are said to be *monotonic*.

It would seem reasonable at this stage to look for functions which are somewhat more restricted than mere monotonic functions. It would seem reasonable to look for functions which are in some sense continuous, i.e. small changes in the accuracy of the arguments do not result in gross changes in the accuracy of the function values. Following the mathematical definition of continuity leads to:

Definition
A function $f : D_0 \rightarrow D_1$ is said to be *continuous* if for every directed subset X of D_0

$$f(\sqcup X) = \sqcup \{f(x) : x \in D_0\}$$

These continuous functions will then be the functions of interest.

8.5 The semantic domains

We return now to the problem of describing the semantics of programming languages. In particular, what form do the various semantic domains take? Firstly there are primitive domains; for example

$$\{ \dots, -2, -1, 0, 1, 2, \dots \}^{\circ}$$
$$\{ \textbf{true}, \textbf{false} \}^{\circ}$$
$$\{ \text{``a''}, \text{``b''}, \dots \}^{\circ}$$

represent the domains of integers, Booleans and characters respectively. The $^{\circ}$ indicates that the basic sets are augmented by including $\bot$ and $\top$ where in each separate augmented set

$$\bot \sqsubseteq x \sqsubseteq \top \quad \text{for each } x \text{ in that set}$$

Because of their special nature $\bot$ and $\top$ will be referred to as the *improper* elements of a domain. The other elements are then the *proper* elements of the domain.

We now look at ways of constructing new or more complex domains from these primitive domains. Programming languages typically allow more complex data types to be constructed from basic data types to produce arrays, structures or records, lists, disjoint unions, procedures or functions, and so on. More complex domains will be constructed from primitive domains in similar ways.

Let $D_1, D_2, ..., D_n$ be disjoint domains. Then the sum or union

$$D = D_1 + D_2 + ... + D_n$$

represents the set consisting of the set-theoretic union of the proper elements of each D_i augmented with a special top $\top$ and bottom $\bot$. An approximation relation $\sqsubseteq$ is defined on D as follows. In the first place

$$\bot \sqsubseteq x \sqsubseteq \top \quad \text{for all } x \in D$$

Apart from this, two elements x, y of D can be compared under $\sqsubseteq$ only if both x and y belong to the same D_i and then $x \sqsubseteq y$ has the same meaning as $x \sqsubseteq_i y$ where $\sqsubseteq_i$ is the approximation relation of the domain D_i.

Again if $D_1, D_2, ..., D_n$ represent domains, which now need no longer be disjoint,

$$D_1 \times D_2 \times ... \times D_n$$

represents the set of n-tuples $\langle x_1, x_2, ..., x_n \rangle$ of elements where each $x_i \in D_i$. The ordering imposed on this set is defined as follows:

$$\langle x_1, x_2, ..., x_n \rangle \sqsubseteq \langle y_1, y_2, ..., y_n \rangle$$

only if, for each $i = 1, 2, ..., n$,

$$x_i \sqsubseteq_i y_i$$

where $\sqsubseteq_i$ represents the relation of the domain D_i.

The notation D^r is then used as a convenient abbreviation for $D \times D ... \times D$ (r terms) and represents the set of all lists of elements of D of length r. The set of all finite lists of elements of D, including the empty list **nil**, can then be represented by D^* where

$$D^* = \{\text{nil}\}^0 + D + D^2 + ... + D^n + ...$$

Finally we construct new domains from more primitive domains by looking at mappings of particular kinds. The notation

$$[D_1 \to D_2]$$

represents the set of all *continuous* functions from D_1 into D_2. On primitive domains, continuous functions conveniently turn out to be the monotonic functions. An approximation relation $\sqsubseteq$ can be imposed on these functions in a straightforward way. If f, $g \in [D_1 \rightarrow D_2]$ we write

$$f \sqsubseteq g$$

provided that

$$f(d) \sqsubseteq_2 g(d) \text{ for all } d \in D_1$$

Here $\sqsubseteq_2$ is the approximation relation associated with D_2. The bottom (top) elements of $[D_1 \rightarrow D_2]$ are the functions which map all elements of D_1 onto the bottom (top) element of D_2.

These then are the various ways of constructing new domains from more primitive domains. The methods employed correspond to the methods commonly available in programming languages.

In constructing sums or unions of domains we insisted that the component domains were disjoint. This restriction was imposed so that, given a proper element of the sum, it would be possible to discover from which component set that element originated. Consequently, given a domain D where

$$D = D_1 + D_2 + \dots D_n$$

we introduce some notation for the three operations of *inspection, projection* and *injection*:

(a) inspection : given $d \in D$ then

$$d \in D_i \quad = \quad \begin{cases} \textbf{true} \text{ if } d \text{ corresponds to some } d_i \in D_i \\ \textbf{false} \text{ otherwise} \end{cases}$$

(b) projection: given $d \in D$

$$d | D_i \quad = \quad \begin{cases} d_i \text{ if } d \text{ corresponds to } d_i \in D: \\ \bot \text{ otherwise} \end{cases}$$

(c) injection: given $d_i \in D_i$

$$d_i \text{ in } D = d \text{ where } d \in D \text{ and } d | D_i = d_i$$

In an obvious way these three operations can be extended to operate not just on finite sums but also on domains of the form D^*.

8.6 Application of Scott's work

As previously mentioned we map constructs in the programming language we wish to define onto their mathematical counterparts. Integers, Booleans, etc. are mapped onto the semantic domains discussed in the previous section. Functions, etc. are mapped onto the set of continuous functions as defined by the approximation relation and the superimposed lattice structure. Recursive data types and recursive functions will be mapped onto corresponding domains.

The problems of self-application reduce, in Scott's terminology, to problems involving domains. Given an equation involving domains can this be solved and, if so, how?

Suppose there is an equation of the form

$$f = F(f)$$

where $F \in [D \to D]$ and $f \in D$. It can be shown that there is a continuous function

$$Y : [D \to D] \to D$$

which has the property that

$$Y(F) = \lim_{i \to \infty} F^i (\bot)$$

and which is a solution of

$$f = F(f)$$

Moreover this solution is the least solution in the sense that if $g = F(g)$ then

$$Y(F) \sqsubseteq g$$

Y therefore selects the least fixed point of the equation.

This theorem then allows us to make remarks about the existence of fixed points and about the nature of the fixed points chosen by Y. Basically it provides information about the elements of domains where these elements are defined recursively using continuous functions. But the theory applies also to domains themselves where the domains are defined recursively.

To recall, the domains of Scott are built from simpler domains D, D_1, D_2 by allowing

Cartesian product	$D_1 \times D_2$
discriminated union	$D_1 + D_2$
continuous functions	$[D_1 \to D_2]$
n-tuples	D^n
finite lists	D^*

It can be shown that the spaces formed in these ways are themselves formed by continuous functions acting on the component domains.

Given these new domains then, the next stage is to look at domain equations of the kind already considered, e.g.

$$D = [D \to D]$$
$$D = A + [D \to B]$$

and so on where A and B are some suitable domains. As long as the domains are constructed from basic domains using only the methods described above, Scott's theory will indicate that appropriate solutions of these equations exist. But how can they be constructed? In the case of

$$D = [D \to D]$$

for example, the process that is undertaken involves defining a hierarchy of spaces $D_0, D_1, D_2, \ldots$ where

$$D_{n+1} = [D_n \to D_n]$$

Then suitably embed each D_n in D_{n+1} and take limits on both sides as $n \to \infty$.

The domains which result from these constructions can be shown to be mathematically consistent. They do not permit set-theoretic paradoxes or paradoxes of the kind described earlier, and they permit finite approximations. Fortunately the crucial continuity property means that no inconsistency can occur in the resulting domains. Fortunately also there are no unnatural restrictions on the way in which the domains can be constructed. Recursion in all its generality can be applied without fear of provoking inconsistency.

Returning now to the problem of specifying semantics using the denotational approach, the semantic or interpretation functions will map syntactic domains into Scott domains. Numerals representing integers are thus mapped into the mathematical set of integers augmented with the appropriate $\perp$ and $\top$, and so on. Recursively defined data types are mapped onto reflexive domains. Procedures of various kinds, even those defined recursively, are mapped onto appropriate continuous functions. No inconsistencies can occur.

8.7 Environments and stores

In describing the semantics of programming languages mappings will be used to map syntactic domains into domains of values. It is important to be clear about the nature of these domains of values. In particular, it is important to distinguish between the set of compile-time values represented by the idea of an environment and the run-time values represented by the idea of a store.

Two kinds of values in programming languages can be distinguished, denotable values and storable, or stored, values. The denotable values form a domain consisting of all those items which can be represented in a program by identifiers. In ALGOL 60, for example, identifiers can be used to represent integer variables, real variables, Boolean variables, arrays, procedures, functions, labels, switches and strings. The set of denotable values must also include **own** variables together with all items that can be passed as parameters to procedures. The set of denotable values will be represented by D. The relationship, i.e. mapping, between the set Id of identifiers and the set D is called an *environment* and is represented by ρ. Thus

$$\rho \in U = [Id \rightarrow D]$$

We shall write $\rho \llbracket I \rrbracket$ to indicate application of the environment ρ to the identifier I and this produces the appropriate denotable value, i.e. the object represented by the identifier I in the environment ρ.

One particular consequence of these remarks is that the domain D must contain as one of its component parts a set L of locations. Identifiers used as variables are mapped at compile-time onto locations within the computer; usually these locations are in one-to-one correspondence with the integers $\{ 0,1,2, ... \}$.

The environment ρ is quite static in nature. All the information it contains can be deduced from the text of the source program and so can be deduced by a compiler. It does not include such items as the values of expressions which are, in general, not known until run-time. These values, the values that can appear on the right of an assignment statement, are called the *stored* values of the programming language and are denoted by V. These are dynamic in nature and cannot be deduced at compile-time. In ALGOL 60 the stored values include the integers, reals and Booleans.

With these ideas we can now discuss a simple model of the store of a machine. The store can be represented by a function σ where

$$\sigma \in S = [L \rightarrow V]$$

Thus it maps locations into values.

There are two primitive operations that can be performed on stores. These correspond to the processes of inspecting and of updating the contents of particular locations. More precisely

· let L denote the set of locations; let $\alpha, \alpha' \in L$
· let V denote the storable values; let $\beta \in V$ and
· let $S = [L \rightarrow V]$ represent the store; let $\sigma, \sigma' \in S$

then

(a) *contents* has functionality, i.e. domain and codomain, given by $[L \rightarrow [S \rightarrow V]]$ and is defined by *contents* $(\alpha)\,(\sigma) = \sigma(\alpha)$
(b) *update* has functionality $[L \times V] \rightarrow [S \rightarrow S]$ and is defined by

$$update\ (\alpha,\beta)\ (\sigma) = \sigma'$$

where σ' is the same as σ except that at location α the value held is β, i.e.

$$contents\ (\alpha')\ (\sigma') = contents\ (\alpha')\ (\sigma)\ if\ \alpha \neq \alpha'$$

and

$$contents\ (\alpha)\ (\sigma') = \beta$$

With these ideas and with this notation we can now express the meaning of assignment:

$$\mathscr{C}\,[\![\,x := E\,]\!]\,\rho\sigma = update\ (\alpha,\beta)\ (\sigma)$$

where

$$\alpha = \mathscr{E}\,[\![\,x\,]\!]\,\rho\sigma \mid L$$

and

$$\beta = \mathscr{E}\,[\![\,E\,]\!]\,\rho\sigma \mid V$$

Note that the projection used in the expressions for α and β performs a kind of type or context-sensitive check.

In this simple exposition we have outlined a very straightforward representation of the store. In more complicated cases the store might be much more complex but must contain $[L \to V]$ as one of its components in some form. We mention just some of the possible alternatives:

(a) if the language permits dynamic allocation and deallocation of store then each location might be provided with a tag to record whether the location is currently active or inactive. Consequently if T denotes the tag we may have a storage model of the form

$$\sigma \in S = [L \to T \times V]$$

Certain primitive functions must be provided for allocating and deallocating locations

(b) for intermediate input and output it may be convenient to extend the store to include other components and, if so, appropriate input and output primitive operations are required

(c) if the language permits coercions, i.e. implicit mode or type changes, it will be necessary to extend the primitive concept of a store.

8.8 Continuations

Given two arbitrary commands or statements Γ_1 and Γ_2 a very naive approach to describing the semantics of the sequence

$$\Gamma_1 ; \Gamma_2$$

in terms of $\mathscr{C}[\![\Gamma_1]\!]\rho$ and $\mathscr{C}[\![\Gamma_2]\!]\rho$ is to say that, in general,

$$\mathscr{C}[\![\Gamma_1 ; \Gamma_2]\!]\rho = \mathscr{C}[\![\Gamma_2]\!]\rho \circ \mathscr{C}[\![\Gamma_1]\!]$$

The problem stems from the fact that Γ_1 might be a jump of some kind. In these circumstances Γ_2 will not, in general, be executed and the above would give an erroneous description of what happens. So some new mechanism must be introduced; this is just the idea of a *continuation*.

In describing semantics we have seen that we have to deal with both commands and expressions. Corresponding to these two sets of objects there will be command continuations and expression continuations. The former deal with jumps as described above, the latter deal with problems of having expressions which produce side-effects.

We have already seen that the value $\mathscr{C}[\![\Gamma]\!]$ of a command is a function which takes as parameter an environment ρ. We now revise this idea and arrange that it takes two parameters ρ and θ and write this in the form of a curried function $\mathscr{C}[\![\Gamma]\!]\rho\theta$. The extra parameter θ is the *command continuation*; it describes the state change that occurs as a result of executing the remainder of the program, i.e. the commands that would be executed if Γ terminated naturally. Thus given the program fragment

$$lab : \Gamma_1 ; \Gamma_2 ; \Gamma_3 ; \Gamma_4$$

and assuming that each of $\Gamma_1, \Gamma_2, \Gamma_3$ and Γ_4 does not cause a jump of any kind then the continuation of Γ_1 involves Γ_2, Γ_3 and Γ_4, the continuation of Γ_2 involves Γ_3 and Γ_4 and so on. Suppose now that Γ_3 is a jump command, e.g. **go to** *lab*. Under these circumstances the continuation of Γ_1 still involves Γ_2, Γ_3 and Γ_4, the continuation of Γ_2 involves Γ_3 and Γ_4 and the continuation of Γ_3 itself involves Γ_4. The last section of this statement seems curious but it implies that if Γ_3 is the jump defined above then $\mathscr{C}[\![\Gamma_3]\!]\rho\theta$ is independent of θ, i.e. independent of what happens if Γ_3 terminates normally. This indeed explains the use of the word 'continuation'.

With this new notation we can now look again at the meaning of $\mathscr{C}[\![\Gamma_1 ; \Gamma_2]\!]$.

$$\mathscr{C}[\![\Gamma_1 ; \Gamma_2]\!]\rho\theta = \mathscr{C}[\![\Gamma_1]\!]\rho \; \{ \mathscr{C}[\![\Gamma_2]\!]\rho\theta \}$$

In words, the effect of executing $\Gamma_1 ; \Gamma_2$ in the environment ρ and with the continuation θ is just the same as executing the command Γ_1 in the environment ρ and with continuation $\mathscr{C}[\![\Gamma_2]\!]\rho\theta$. Of course the functionality of the various items has now altered. In detail

230

$\theta \in C = [S \to S]$, the set of continuations
$\mathscr{C} \in [Cmd \to [U \to [C \to C]]]$

Consequently both θ and $\mathscr{C} [\![\Gamma_2]\!] \rho \theta$ are, as expected, of the same functionality, namely $C = [S \to S]$. Commands executed with respect to continuations therefore produce continuations which will be passed to the next command, and so on.

We now have the very desirable situation in which

· $\mathscr{C} [\![\Gamma]\!]$ describes the effect of a command in isolation
· $\mathscr{C} [\![\Gamma]\!] \rho$ describes the effect of Γ when executed in a particular environment, namely ρ
· $\mathscr{C} [\![\Gamma]\!] \rho \theta$ describes the effect of Γ executed in the environment ρ and in the context of the other commands, described by θ.

We have not yet given any consideration to certain important questions concerning continuations. What, for example, should be the nature of the initial continuation or what happens if a program fails to terminate?

The initial continuation is θ_0 where, if ρ_0 represents the initial environment consisting of standard identifiers etc., $\mathscr{C} [\![Prog]\!] \rho_0 \theta_0$ describes the effect of an entire program. In the simple case where a program itself is defined in isolation θ_0 could be taken to be the identity function. But if we wish to express the meaning of programs in the wider context of an operating system or whatever then the initial continuation can be taken to represent a jump returning control to the operating system.

If a piece of program fails to terminate, then the continuation for that piece of program is undefined. Consequently the corresponding θ will take the form of the undefined element of the appropriate domain, i.e. $\bot$.

Before ending the discussion of command continuations we should remark that, although we have regarded each θ as a mapping of the form $[S \to S]$ where S represents the machine state, this is not the only possibility. Indeed, it might seem more natural to describe the final outcome of a computation in terms which exclude irrelevant aspects of the machine state and include only a set of possible answers, A. It then becomes more natural to regard θ as a mapping of the form $[S \to A]$. The earlier discussion about command continuations is basically unaffected by this alteration.

Now we must look at the other kind of continuation, the expression continuation. We first note the essential difference between a command and an expression. Whenever a command is executed it produces a new state which is then passed to the next command. But when an expression is evaluated it produces not just a new state but also a value; what happens to the value depends on the context in which the expression occurs. The significance of this observation is that expression continuations inherit values and states; thus they are not of the form $[S \rightarrow S]$ or $[S \rightarrow A]$ but they must be of the form $[E \times S \rightarrow S]$ or $[E \times S \rightarrow A]$, where E is the domain of expression results. Curried, these produce functions of the form $[E \rightarrow [S \rightarrow S]]$ or $[E \rightarrow [S \rightarrow A]]$. In other respects the expression continuations are similar to command continuations.

Let

$$K = [E \rightarrow [S \rightarrow S]] = [E \rightarrow C]$$

The semantic function $\mathscr{E}$ for expressions then has functionality

$$Exp \rightarrow [U \rightarrow [K \rightarrow C]]$$

i.e.

$$\mathscr{E} \in [Exp \rightarrow [U \rightarrow [K \rightarrow C]]]$$

To illustrate typical definitions of $\mathscr{E}$, let κ be some arbitrary expression continuation, i.e. $\kappa \in K$.

$$\mathscr{E}[\![\textbf{true}]\!]\rho\kappa = \kappa(tt)$$

where tt is the truth value corresponding to **true**. Similar definitions of $\mathscr{E}$ can be given for **false** and other constants. For an identifier ξ

$$\mathscr{E}[\![\xi]\!]\rho\kappa = \kappa(\rho[\![\xi]\!])$$

i.e. the environment ρ is applied to ξ to obtain the value which the identifier denotes.

The ideas outlined here cover only some of the problems that arise in describing program semantics. But they can be extended to cope with any of the more complex aspects of semantics such as

- jumps out of blocks
- jumps from recursively nested calls
- jumps from partially evaluated expressions and back in again.

Note that these remarks are intended to indicate the power of the idea of a continuation, not to indicate approval of the use of these habits in programming.

8.9 Illustrations

To conclude this investigation into denotational semantics we shall look at the definition of some typical constructs in programming languages. We choose not to look at the definition of any particular programming language, because of the amount of detail that would be required. The interested reader can refer to, for example, Mosses (1974) for a complete definition of ALGOL 60 and to Tennent (1976) for a definition of GEDANKEN.

Any complete specification of a programming language using the denotational approach must supply an accurate mathematical specification of the following:

- the syntactic categories – this will include the numerals, truth values, identifiers and so on, together with the commands or statements of the language
- the syntax – a BNF definition or some such definition of the syntax; for the purpose of describing the semantics essentially only an abstract syntax is needed
- the value or semantic domains – these will be domains of the kind we have been considering and will include, for example, domains of integers, truth values, locations, answers, expression values, stored values, environments, continuations of various kinds, and machine states
- the functionality of the semantic functions – the domain and range or each function used in the definition of the semantics
- the definition of the semantic functions.

Moreover there will be certain standard or predefined values or functions whose existence will be assumed; the precise set of these and their nature and meaning should all be clearly defined.

In what follows we shall look at certain constructs in programming languages and show how the ideas of this chapter can be applied. In particular we shall look at identifiers, Booleans, substitution, sequencing, conditionals, while loops, jumps and simple procedure calls. It will suit our purpose to use a simple programming language and to describe its complete definition in terms of the requirements outlined above. Throughout we shall attempt to maintain the notation that has been used in previous sections of this discussion on denotational semantics.

Syntactic categories

$I \in Id$	Identifiers
$\Gamma \in Cmd$	Commands or statements
$E \in Exp$	Expressions
$\Phi \in Pri$	Some primitive commands
$\Pi \in Pre$	Some primitive predicates
$\Omega \in Ops$	Some binary operators
$N \in Nms$	Numerals (integers)
$\Psi \in Prog$	Programs

Semantic domains

$$\theta \in C = [S \to S] \qquad \text{Command continuations}$$
$$\delta \in D = T + N + C + G$$
$$+ L \qquad \text{Denotations}$$
$$E = D \qquad \text{Expression values}$$
$$G = [C \to C] \qquad \text{Procedures}$$
$$I \in Id \qquad \text{Identifiers}$$
$$\kappa \in K = [E \to C] \qquad \text{Expression continuations}$$
$$L \qquad \text{Locations}$$
$$N \qquad \text{Integers}$$
$$S \qquad \text{Machine states}$$
$$T \qquad \text{Truth values}$$
$$\rho \in U = [Id \to D] \qquad \text{Environments}$$
$$V = T + N + C + G \qquad \text{Storable values}$$

Syntax

$$\Psi ::= \Gamma$$
$$\Gamma ::= \Phi \mid$$
$$\quad\textbf{dummy} \mid$$
$$\quad \Gamma_1 ; \Gamma_2 \mid$$
$$\quad \textbf{let } I = E \textbf{ in } \Gamma \mid$$
$$\quad \textbf{if } E \textbf{ then } \Gamma_1 \textbf{ else } \Gamma_2 \mid$$
$$\quad \textbf{while } E \textbf{ do } \Gamma \mid$$
$$\quad \textbf{go to } E \mid$$
$$\quad E_1 := E_2 \mid$$
$$\quad \textbf{call } E$$
$$E ::= I \mid \sqcap \mid \textbf{true} \mid \textbf{false} \mid N \mid E_1 \ \Omega \ E_2 \mid$$
$$\quad \textbf{let } I = E_1 \textbf{ in } E_2 \mid$$
$$\quad \textbf{if } E_0 \textbf{ then } E_1 \textbf{ else } E_2$$
$$\Omega ::= + \mid - \mid \times \mid /$$

Semantic functions – functionality

$$\mathcal{O} : \quad Ops \to [E \times E] \to E$$
$$\mathcal{C} : \quad Cmd \to U \to C \to C$$
$$\mathcal{E} : \quad Exp \to U \to K \to C$$
$$\mathcal{M} : \quad Prog \to U \to C \to C$$

Note that $\mathcal{M}$ defines the meaning of a program. $\mathcal{M}$ has been given a rather crude functionality; a more ambitious or convenient definition might have been

$$Prog \to U \to In \to Out$$

where *In* and *Out* denote sets of input values and output values respectively.

234

The functions $\mathscr{R}$ and $\mathscr{L}$ are used below in evaluating expressions. $\mathscr{R}$ performs the evaluation one would expect on the right of an assignment, $\mathscr{L}$ performs the evaluation one would expect on the left. Note that in the latter case an address or variables would be expected, in the former a value. In fact we can write

$$\mathscr{L}[\![E]\!]\rho\kappa = \mathscr{E}[\![E]\!]\rho\{l\kappa\} \quad \text{and} \quad \mathscr{R}[\![E]\!] = \mathscr{E}[\![E]\!]\rho\{r\kappa\}$$

where l and r are functions which take continuations expecting certain values and produce a continuation expecting a general kind of value: l and r have functionality $[L \to C] \to [E \to C]$ and $[V \to C] \to [E \to C]$ respectively.

Semantic functions – their definition

$$\mathscr{M}[\![\Psi]\!]\rho_0\theta_0 = \mathscr{C}[\![\Psi]\!]\rho_0\theta_0$$
where ρ_0 and θ_0 denote the appropriate initial environment and initial continuation respectively

$\mathscr{C}[\![\Psi]\!]\rho =$ an appropriate element of $[C \to C]$ associated with Φ
$\mathscr{C}[\![\textbf{dummy}]\!]\rho =$ the identity mapping on C
$\mathscr{C}[\![\Gamma_1 ; \Gamma_2]\!]\rho = \mathscr{C}[\![\Gamma_1]\!]\rho \circ \mathscr{C}[\![\Gamma_2]\!]\rho$

$\mathscr{C}[\![\textbf{let } I = E \textbf{ in } \Gamma]\!]\rho\theta = \mathscr{E}[\![E]\!]\rho \{\lambda\delta. \mathscr{C}[\![\Gamma]\!](\rho[\delta/I])\theta\}$
Recall that $\rho[\delta/I]$ is the same environment as ρ updated with the information that I has the value δ

$\mathscr{C}[\![\textbf{if } E \textbf{ then } \Gamma_1 \textbf{ else } \Gamma_2]\!]\rho\theta =$
$\qquad \mathscr{R}[\![E]\!]\rho \{Cond(\mathscr{C}[\![\Gamma_1]\!]\rho\theta , \mathscr{C}[\![\Gamma_2]\!]\rho\theta)\}$
Cond is basically a function which when applied to $\mathscr{R}[\![E]\!]\rho$ will produce as result either $\mathscr{C}[\![\Gamma_1]\!]\rho\theta$ or $\mathscr{C}[\![\Gamma_2]\!]\rho\theta$ depending on the value of $\mathscr{R}[\![E]\!]\rho$

$\mathscr{C}[\![\textbf{while } E \textbf{ do } \Gamma]\!]\rho\theta =$
$\qquad Y(\lambda\theta'. \mathscr{R}[\![E]\!]\rho \{Cond(\mathscr{C}[\![\Gamma]\!]\rho\theta' ,\theta) \})$
Note that **while** E **do** Γ is equivalent to
$\qquad$ **if** E **then** $(\Gamma;$ **while** E **do** $\Gamma)$ **else dummy**;
this recursive definition leads to the above semantic rule

$\mathscr{C}[\![\textbf{go to } E]\!]\rho\theta = \mathscr{R}[\![E]\!]\rho \{Jump\}$
The right-hand side is independent of the continuation θ and *Jump* is a function defined by

$$Jump(\delta) = \text{if } \delta \in C \text{ then } (\xi|C) \text{ else } Wrong$$

$\mathscr{C}[\![E_1 :=E_2]\!]\rho\theta = update(\mathscr{L}[\![E_1]\!]\rho\theta , \mathscr{R}[\![E_2]\!]\rho\theta) \theta$
$\mathscr{C}[\![\textbf{call } E]\!]\rho\theta = \mathscr{E}[\![E]\!]\rho \{ \lambda\delta. \text{ if } \delta \in G \text{ then } (\delta|G)\theta \text{ else } Wrong\}$
$\mathscr{E}[\![I]\!]\rho\kappa = \kappa(\rho[\![I]\!])$

Appropriate evasive action must be taken if I is not a legal identifier

$\mathscr{E}[\![N]\!]\rho\kappa = \kappa(\mathscr{N}[\![N]\!] \text{ in } E)$ where

$\mathscr{N}$ is defined as in section 8.1

$\mathscr{E}[\![\textbf{true}]\!]\rho\kappa = \kappa(\text{true in } E)$
$\mathscr{E}[\![\textbf{false}]\!]\rho\kappa = \kappa(\text{false in } E)$
$\mathscr{E}[\![\textbf{if } E_0 \textbf{ then } E_1 \textbf{ else } E_2]\!]\rho\kappa =$

$\qquad \mathscr{R}[\![E_0]\!]\rho \ \{Cond(\ \mathscr{E}[\![E_1]\!]\rho\kappa\ ,\ \mathscr{E}[\![E_2]\!]\rho\kappa)\}$

$\mathscr{E}[\![\textbf{let } I = E_1 \textbf{ in } E_2]\!]\rho\kappa =$

$\qquad \mathscr{E}[\![E_1]\!]\rho \ \{\lambda\delta . \ \mathscr{E}[\![E_1]\!](\rho[\delta/I])\kappa\}$

$\mathcal{O}[\![+]\!]<\epsilon_1,\epsilon_2>\kappa = \nu \equiv N \rightarrow \kappa\ (\nu \text{ in } E), \textit{Wrong}$

where $\nu = (\epsilon_1 \mid N) + (\epsilon_2 \mid N)$
and + denotes the usual integer addition.

Other operators are defined in a similar manner.

Here only a relatively brief description of the use of the ideas of denotational semantics has been given. Little or no mention has been made of arrays or structures, input or output, procedure or function calls other than of a very simple kind (no parameter passing was discussed), parallel processing, coercions, coroutines and so on. The interested reader should refer to the more detailed literature for further reading material.

8.10 Language design

Much of the work associated with the study of denotational semantics has been concerned with an investigation into much of the mathematics or mathematical logic which underlies many aspects of programming. It is to be hoped that such a rigorous approach to the problem of accurately specifying semantics might highlight some sensible principles for the design of programming languages. At least two such principles emerge, the principle of *correspondence* and the principle of *abstraction*. The former is, in fact, one aspect of the principle of orthogonal design pioneered by the designers of ALGOL 68. The latter can be looked at in the same light (though strictly speaking ALGOL 68 does not adhere to it); certainly it constitutes one aspect of regularity.

In the earlier parts of this chapter we did not investigate the semantics of parameter passing. Nevertheless, the principle of correspondence can be explained and discussed. None of the detail of denotational semantics is necessary to understand it.

The principle of correspondence relates to the nature of declarations and of parameters of procedures. Both of these aspects of programming languages allow a programmer to introduce identifiers, to associate with them a type or mode and to use them in some special way (usually determined by the type or mode).

The various rules which govern the syntax of declarations of different kinds vary considerably from language to language and even within languages according to the nature of the declaration. The differences within one language are annoying, they tend to increase the size of both the syntax and semantic sections of a definition and they tend to result in irregularities which are highly undesirable. Well-designed languages therefore tend to have a common method for the declaration of objects of differing types.

The strong similarity between the semantics of declarations and parameters tends to suggest that these two aspects of a language should be designed jointly and be similar. This is the principle of correspondence. Such an approach to language design then has the highly desirable effect of removing irregularities and undesirable interactions from the language, uncovering peculiar aspects of the syntax and semantics, and so on.

Had the correspondence principle been adopted in the design and definition of ALGOL 60, for example, many of its irregularities would have disappeared (see chapter 3). ALGOL 68 on the other hand was much more regular in this respect. However, criticisms could be levelled at it on the grounds that there is no parameter mechanism associated with mode declarations or operator declarations; the possible declarations occurring in for clauses and in conformity clauses are also anomalous. The programming language PASCAL can be criticised much more severely than ALGOL 68 in its ability to satisfy the principle of correspondence.

Now let us turn to the principle of abstraction. In mathematical logic the term abstraction has various possible meanings. We select and highlight one of these. The term abstraction can be applied to

· the process of associating a set with a predicate; given a predicate such as $p(x)$, for example, the set would be just $\{x : p(x)\}$, i.e. the set of elements x satisfying the predicate $p(x)$

· the process of associating a function with an expression $f(x)$ in x; the function would be just $\lambda x.f(x)$ and the effect of applying this to the argument 4, for instance, would be equivalent to evaluating the expression for $x=4$.

In both cases there is an abstraction mechanism or facility for expressions – effectively the expression is used to define some meaningful object, the set or function introduced above. In what follows we shall use this interpretation of the term abstraction.

It has been shown that the mathematics which underlies denotational semantics provides the theoretical justification for the use of particular (recursive) modes or types. These are shown to be meaningful and the fact that the usual features of programming languages are continuous (in the sense of this chapter) means that no paradoxes, similar to Russell's paradox for set theory, can arise. These observations are fundamental to the principle of abstraction since there is then the implication that perfectly general modes (perhaps recursive) can be defined and manipulated without danger. In particular, abstraction can be permitted, i.e. a new mode or type can be introduced and defined in terms of other modes or types; no peculiar restrictions, etc. are necessary and, in fact, would be unnecessary irregularities. But it would be inappropriate to limit the discussion to just modes or types.

Abstraction in programming languages can be applied to any semantically meaningful set of objects from some syntactic class. Thus it can be applied to statements, expressions, types or values, declarations, and so on; but it would not be applied to, for example, terms and primaries – the latter would typically be used in defining the syntax of the semantically more prominent classes such as statements and expressions.

The principle of abstraction then dictates that it should be possible, in a well-designed programming language, to provide abstractions in the language for any semantically meaningful class of objects. To take some examples then, there should be abstractions for expressions (these would typically be function declarations in the programming language), for statements (these would typically be procedure declarations), for types or modes (these would be akin to the ALGOL 68 mode declaration), etc. This principle of design then suggests the following approach to language design: identify all the semantically meaningful categories and supply appropriate facilities for these including abstractions.

Again let us take ALGOL 68 and criticise it in the light of this principle of design. We choose ALGOL 68, not because it is badly designed but for quite the opposite reason – it has an orthogonal design and in its regularity etc. it is one of the better and more sophisticated languages in existence. Criticisms of other languages in the light of the principle of abstraction would be even more severe.

ALGOL 68 does not allow general mode declarations. Both

mode null = ref null

238

and

> **mode list = union (void, struct (int** *item,* **list** *rest***))**

are illegal. Mode declarations in ALGOL 68 are governed by restrictions
which ensure that

- (*a*) coercions change mode
- (*b*) the space requirements of all objects can be deduced by the
  compiler (arrays are represented by descriptors whose size is
  regulated by the number of dimensions in the array, not by
  the bounds on each dimension).

Above, (*a*) disqualifies the mode declaration of **null** since dereferencing
leaves the mode unaltered; (*b*) disqualifies the mode **list**. Yet both mode
declarations can be given sensible interpretations. The former is somewhat uninteresting but can be implemented as a location holding its
own address; the latter is equivalent to the BNF definition

> <list> ::= <empty> | <integer><list>

It could be argued then that more general modes could be allowed –
there are no theoretical (only practical) reasons for some of the limitations that exist. As mentioned earlier (in chapter 7) ALGOL 68 also
lacks a modules facility for capturing the concept of a data abstraction,
i.e. it is not possible to supply a mode and a set of operators for the
manipulation of objects of this mode without letting the user have full
access to the internal structure, etc. of the mode – it should be possible
to hide internal structure and even declarations themselves if necessary.

9
SOME CONCLUDING REMARKS

In this final chapter we shall summarise the contents of the previous chapters and add further remarks about alternative possibilities and alternative lines of development in the area of the formal definition of programming languages.

It is of interest to mention briefly the size of some of the documents which have been used in describing programming languages over the years:

ALGOL 60 (Revised)	17 pages
FORTRAN 66	35 pages
FORTRAN 77	about 200 pages
ALGOL 68 (Revised)	236 pages
PL/I Standard	about 400 pages
COBOL 1974	about 500 pages.

The trend is frightening!

9.1 Syntax

The first realistic attempts at formally defining aspects of programming languages were contained in the ALGOL 60 Report. The formal part of the Report was the syntax and this was more successful than the informal semantics sections. This experience led to attempts to put into the formal syntax more aspects of the definition of programming language. Consequently there was the trend that led through the ALGOL W definition to the definition of ALGOL 68. In the Revised ALGOL 68 Report the syntactic sections contained essentially those aspects of the language which one might expect to be checked by a compiler: thus all the context-sensitive aspects of the language are there. The result was, it is generally agreed, rather complex, though the ALGOL 68 authors would argue that their document was never intended for learners or for the majority of users. It was intended only for experts.

One aspect of the syntactic definition of ALGOL 68 was the inclusion under the one mechanism of various devices including both synthesised and inherited attributes. We have outlined a definition of PASCAL

240

which essentially abstracts from the ALGOL 68 definition mechanism and uses attributes in a more explicit fashion.

The other trend in the definition of syntax has been the recognition of a difference between concrete and abstract syntax. This started with some early work of McCarthy and was incorporated in the PL/I Standard. PL/I also showed another novel method of describing context-sensitivity, the idea of designator nodes in parse trees.

Abstract syntax has certain advantages over concrete syntax. In particular, it is independent of typographical features such as character sets and stropping conventions; it is independent of the manner of representation in the sense that $x + y$ could be represented as $+ x\ y$, $y + x$, $+ y\ x$, $x\ y +$ etc. including variations of these with brackets. The abstract syntax has further advantages in that it exhibits the essential syntactic structure of a program and is free of such considerations as operator precedence and implied bracketing. From the point of view of the interpreter, an abstract form is more easily managed than a concrete program.

We have looked at abstract syntax mainly from the standpoint of attempts at defining PL/I. In both the VDL and in the formalism used in the PL/I Standard a parser/translator transformed concrete programs to abstract programs. In a sense, therefore, concrete syntax was the starting point. But note that it is quite feasible to assume that the abstract syntax is the starting point and to provide in place of a parser, etc. a program which essentially maps abstract programs to concrete programs.

Syntax rules should not be chosen merely to define the set of legal strings of characters permitted in a language. In most of the formalisms we have studied syntax rules and descriptions of meaning have been closely interrelated. Consequently syntax rules, non-terminals, etc. can and should be chosen to aid the task of describing meaning.

The separation into abstract and concrete syntax is not the only possible division of aspects of the syntax. Both the Revised ALGOL 60 Report and the PL/I Standard (and indeed other definitions) highlighted the hierarchical nature of syntactic descriptions of programming languages. Another possible division is the separation into *inner* and *outer syntax* (see Wilkes, 1968). This was prompted by the observation that aspects of syntactic descriptions of programming languages tend to fall into two almost separate categories. The inner syntax is concerned with those parts of the language which are used to perform calculations; thus the nature of identifiers, the basic data types, the nature of predicates and even the basic statements of the language are all part of the inner syntax. The outer syntax, on the other hand, is concerned with the flow of control and the more global program structure. In the description of this, <identifier>, <basic type>, <predicate> and <basic statement> are all treated essentially as known terminals. Loops, conditionals, procedures and so on are all legitimately part of the outer syntax. From these two sets of syntax an *inner language* and an *outer language* emerge. It is possible to imagine one outer language with several possible inner languages and vice versa.

9.2 Semantics

The task of giving a precise specification of semantics has been more difficult than the task of specifying syntax. Informal approaches such as those adopted by ALGOL 60 and FORTRAN were not accurate or precise enough. Formal approaches, on the other hand, demand that meaning is described in some other language or formalism which is free from ambiguity, inaccuracy, and so on. In a sense, the problem of precise specification of meaning is transferred to this other language.

We have seen three formal approaches to the problem of specifying semantics. These are the operational approach, the denotational approach and the axiomatic approach. In the order specified these give decreasing amounts of detail about the meaning of a construct or piece of program and these can be regarded as different levels of abstraction of meaning.

The operational approach to defining semantics is based on the idea that semantics can be defined by a compiler or interpreter for that language. The compiler or interpreter selected as the model on which all other compilers or interpreters should be based has traditionally been idealised in various ways and it operated on some abstract machine. The semantic definition of a piece of program then takes the form of the sequence of actions and changes of the machine state performed by the abstract machine in executing or interpreting that piece of program.

This approach raises all kinds of problems. In the first place the abstract machine and its operations all have to be rigorously defined. In a sense, therefore, the problem of defining the semantics of a programming language whose programs must run on this machine is transferred to the problem of rigorously defining the abstract machine and its operations.

The operational approach tends to reflect the requirements that an implementor might have of a formal definition. It will tend to suggest implementation details, techniques, etc. yet the problem of proving that an actual implementation is indeed a true reflection of the given definition is usually difficult because the abstract machine is often quite unlike the real machine and its operations are quite different –

242

see for example the Vienna Definition Language. Moreover, implementors do not like to be too rigorously constrained by a language definition. They prefer to be given a certain amount of freedom to exercise their skills, to optimise, to improvise, to invent and so on.

Unfortunately operational definitions tend to contain a great deal of implementation detail which is not usually of interest to someone merely wishing to understand the meaning of some piece of program. As with any compiler or interpreter there are problems in deciding whether or not the desired effect has been properly described. There is usually no guarantee against the abstract program looping, against the presence of inconsistencies, against peculiar side-effects, etc. The fundamental problem with operational methods is overspecification.

Mention can be made of two of the main problem areas in operational semantics.

(a) A suitable storage model must be chosen; this should reflect such features of the language as equivalence in FORTRAN and overlays in PL/I. It is important that the various features of the language are correctly modelled and that neither extra flexibility nor extra constraints are introduced.

(b) Input/output must be treated properly. Usually files or datasets can be accessed by programs written in a variety of programming languages. Consequently any definition of the semantics of one programming language must assume that interference from other programs written in possibly other languages is a definite possibility.

One final comment on the operational approach derives from the effect achieved in tracing through a program. The tracer does not obtain an overall view of what his program does, he obtains instead the result of a particular calculation. In general, it is more helpful to know that if, for example, *n* is supplied as data then *factorial* (*n*) results than it is to know that if 4 is supplied then 24 results. Thus it is more helpful to know what function has been implemented than it is to know the value of the function for a particular input.

Just as the operational approach assumes that the abstract machine and its operations are all well-defined, so the denotational approach assumes that the mathematical objects and functions are consistent and could not lead to contradictions and paradoxes. The work of Scott is aimed at showing that inconsistencies, etc. cannot arise and cannot therefore cast doubt on the intended semantic meaning.

The mathematical ideas involved in giving a sound theoretical basis to the work on denotational semantics are quite sophisticated. Indeed they are so sophisticated and specialised that few language designers, compiler writers, users, etc. would have the knowledge necessary to understand a definition given in these mathematical terms.

Yet this argument, about the level of knowledge of the various users of a language definition has arisen repeatedly. In each case people familiar with a particular method of definition argue in its favour. The advocates of denotational semantics claim that their approach is free of the implementation detail of the operational approach and is more helpful than the axiomatic approach; they claim it contains just the correct amount of detail. Yet their claim is not wholly justified. In defining semantics using the denotational approach it was necessary to introduce the concepts of machine state, environment, store, stored values, continuations, and so on. Many of these are essentially implementation matters and are unnecessary for the understanding of meaning. Consequently some of the same overspecification problems which are associated with the operational approach are associated also with the denotational approach.

There remains the axiomatic approach to the task of specifying semantics. In this method there is no explicit concept of machine state. Yet implicitly it must exist since a machine state is nothing more than a collection of the relevant variables and their values together with other subsidiary information. The axiomatic method attempts to remove from consideration *all* irrelevant aspects of the machine state – this, of course, is the essence of abstraction. The method focuses attention only on the relevant aspects of a machine state and portrays these in the form of a predicate which describes the interrelationships between the various program variables. Program statements cause the machine state to change – in axiomatic terms they transform the predicates.

The very abstract nature of the axiomatic method means that it is of most interest to programmers and to theorists, people who tend to be uninterested in implementation details. Ideally it suits the program prover. But modern thinking about programming and about axioms has suggested that the construction and verification of (eventually highly reliable) programs should proceed hand-in-glove. The correctness proof will tend to suggest the use of certain programming constructs. For further reading, see Dijkstra (1976).

9.3 Other directions of progress

In the course of this work we have described only some of the attempts that have been made at giving satisfactory definitions of programming languages. At the time of writing (June, 1979) we would argue that we have described what seem to be the most significant but not the only efforts. Other approaches to language definition do exist but these have not been used in presenting (what have come to be regarded as) standard definitions of major programming languages. In what follows we shall mention some of the alternative directions of progress. We begin by mentioning briefly current work on the definition of the new programming language Ada.

Around 1975 the American Department of Defense was becoming increasingly concerned about the amount of money being spent annually on software. About six billion dollars were being spent each year and about 50% of this was devoted to testing and editing procedures of various kinds. Only about 20% was being spent on coding.

It was clearly in the interests of the Defense Department to select for their applications a single programming language which they could adopt as a kind of standard for their various applications. Their requirements were somewhat specialised but in rough terms they required a language for real-time applications whose design paid careful attention to efficiency in terms of time and space, reliability, maintainability, facilities for parallelism and exception handling and yet had a wide application area, was relatively easy to implement and relatively easy to learn.

A review of the then-existing languages concluded that no language was sufficiently well equipped to meet their needs. Accordingly the Department formed a very detailed list of its requirements. It circulated these for comment and then modified them in the light of the responses received from the European Community, NATO countries and civil and military agencies. Various design groups started work. Finally, around May 1979, the programming language Ada emerged as their choice.

At the time of writing a preliminary version of Ada has just been published. The language is heavily based on PASCAL, but has a wider range of applicability, allows parallelism, real-time applications and so on. In its final stages the language design was influenced by attempts to write a translator for the language and by attempts to provide a formal definition using denotational techniques. Comments on this preliminary version of Ada have been requested and it is hoped that a final version of the language will emerge in 1980. It is likely that this language will have a very strong influence on computing over the next few years.

To date, two documents concerned with Ada have been published: there was a *Preliminary Ada Reference Manual* which acted as a definition of the language; the other document, the *Rationale for the Design of the Ada Programming Language,* was more informal and explained the reasons for the various design decisions that had been taken. (See Ichbiah *et al.,* 1979.)

The reference manual makes use of a syntactic notation which is a simple extension of traditional BNF notation. Non-terminals appear as sequences of lower-case letters, possibly with embedded underscores: thus

object_declaration ::=
    identifier_list: [**constant**] type [:= expression];
  identifier_list ::= identifier { , identifier }

The square brackets [and] surrounded optional parts of rules and curly brackets { and } indicate that the enclosed part can appear zero or more times.

Another extension of BNF notation introduces the use of italicised words in syntactic rules. Thus

subprogram_call ::=
  *subprogram*_name
  [(parameter_association { , parameter_association })]

Here the italicised *subprogram* and the following underscore have no syntactic significance. The rule given above is equivalent to the same rule with *subprogram*_ removed. The prefix, as it was called, conveys information of a semantic nature to the reader.

The BNF notation is used also to provide information about the suggested or preferred method of paragraphing (i.e. laying out) of programs. The rule for the if_statement, for instance, appears in the form

if_statement ::=
  if condition **then**
    sequence_of_statements
  { **elsif** condition **then**
    sequence_of_statements }
  [**else**
    sequence_of_statements]
  end if;

indicating that, whatever combination of **if, elsif, else** and **end if** appears in a program, these words should be on separate lines and indented by the same amount.

The meaning of the syntactically legal strings of characters is given in an informal manner using English prose. The previously mentioned use of italicised words also provides information of a semantic nature. But no other new techniques are used in describing the meaning of syntactically legal programs.

Let us now turn to a discussion of other current and continuing work. The languages FORTRAN and COBOL seem to be in a continual state of evolution, development and improvement. Sub-committees are continually working towards improving both the languages and their methods of definition. In the case of PL/I much effort is being directed towards defining sublanguages which are subsets of and consistent with the 1976 PL/I Standard. The complete definition of BASIC still requires the presence of standard enhancement modules to accompany Minimal BASIC. Attempts are being made to produce a PASCAL Standard.

Now we look at alternative directions in which language definition has progressed. In 1966 the programming language EULER and its method of definition attempted to extend the earlier work on ALGOL 60. Attempts to bring out the relationship between the syntactic structure and meaning were stressed. Basically the definition was interpreter-oriented and related very closely to the syntax of the language.

The syntax of EULER was chosen with a particular parsing strategy in mind (simple precedence). Consequently it was rather unnatural since extra non-terminals had to be included just to ensure that the parsing strategy would perform satisfactorily. On the other hand, this approach meant that a parser could be given as part of the formal definition and this was combined with a process for translating source text into Polish notation. This was then interpreted. In essence, then, a processor for the language could be automatically generated from the formal definition. The result was a definition heavily oriented towards the needs of the implementor.

Two-level grammars are, as we have seen, a very powerful mechanism. Affix grammars are similar to van Wigngaarden grammars but have more desirable properties from a compiler writer's point of view. In the first place, the parsing problem is solvable. But further, most of the parsing strategies and techniques for manipulating context-free grammars are applicable in a modified form to affix grammars.

Another formalism for language definition makes use of production systems. Underlying these production systems are the productions of a context-free grammar. But associated with each such production is a predicate which expresses the context-sensitive rules and restrictions. The predicates, unlike ALGOL 68 predicates, are expressed in terms of previously defined functions. These functions when applied to a particular production must be supplied with an environment ρ; at any point in a program this is just a list of all variables which are in scope at that point and their attributes.

To illustrate, the following defines an assignment statement in a simple language.

ASGT STM $<ref := exp ;> $ & LEGAL $<*:\rho>$
$\leftarrow$type$_1$ = *DECLARED TYPE* $(ref\!: \rho)$ &
   type$_2$ = *DECLARED TYPE* $(exp\!: \rho)$ &
   CONVERTIBLE $<$type$_2$: type$_1>$

Notes on

> ASGT STM : the context-free syntax of an assignment statement takes the form
>
> $$ref := exp;$$
>
> LEGAL : for this to be legal within environment ρ, certain conditions must be satisfied; these follow the backward arrow $\leftarrow$
>
> type$_1$: look up environment ρ and find the type associated with the variable *ref*; similarly for type$_2$
>
> CONVERTIBLE : check that type$_2$ can be converted to type$_1$

Advocates of the production systems technique argue with some justification that their approach has the following advantages:

> • the underlying context-free grammar is clearly visible
> • the context-sensitive and the context-free requirements have been separated

Another direction in which progress has been made is towards dynamic syntax. The basic idea behind this trend is illustrated by looking at identifiers. From the context-free grammar describing a language, rules such as

> $<$simple variable$>$ ::= $<$identifier$>$

where

> $<$identifier$>$ ::= $<$letter$>$ | $<$identifier$>$ $<$letter$>$
> | $<$identifier$>$ $<$digit$>$

can be noted. Declarations within a program are then viewed as phrases of the language which cause new productions of the grammar to be created at compile-time. Thus in a simple language

> **var** x,y,z

would cause the new syntax rule

> $<$simple variable$>$ ::= $x|y|z$

to be formed.

In this way occurrences of identifiers used in expressions are then legal or illegal according to whether there is or is not an appropriate production at the time compilation is taking place.

Of course these ideas have to be extended considerably. But this can be done by distinguishing between identifiers of differing types. Even such complexities as block structure or mutual recursion can be accommodated. Moreover, the relevant ideas can all be suitably formalised. (Somewhat similar to the idea of dynamic syntax is the notion of a grammar form. Again productions are created at compile-time and these are used in the parsing phase of compilation.)

These two notions of dynamic syntax and grammar forms have certain advantages. From a compiler writers' point of view the phase of compilation which causes productions to be created can be imagined to exist between the lexical analysis phase and the parsing phase. Consequently the complete grammar is available immediately prior to the parsing phase. It will be context-free and all the usual techniques apply.

It should be noted that these approaches are both reminiscent to some extent of the axiomatic method. In that approach declarations have the effect of introducing identifiers and associating an appropriate set of axioms with them. In dynamic syntax the declarations essentially cause identifiers to be put in tables together with their mode. This is a more concrete realisation of essentially the same action.

Many of the more recent developments in language definition have arisen from combining several of the basic ideas from earlier methods. This can be seen to some extent in the work we have already done : there is a clear relationship between the ALGOL 68 definition and the use of attribute grammars; in defining semantics using the van Wijngaarden formalism the execute and evaluate functions mirrored the $\mathscr{C}$ and $\mathscr{E}$ functions of the denotational approach, and so on. Following the development of the VDL, workers at the IBM Vienna Laboratories have produced a Vienna Development Method. This is basically a denotational approach to the problem of language definition based on the VDL.

The reader is referred to the references at the end of the book and, in particular, to the references in the 'further reading' section for more detailed information.

9.4 Final remarks

To conclude we merely remark that none of the existing attempts at defining usable programming languages can be regarded as perfect. Indeed, all of them have faults of some kind – errors in the definition, inadequacies, inconsistencies and/or obscurities: no widely accepted methods free from some criticism yet exist for defining either the syntax or the semantics of programming languages.

It is likely that as programming languages develop, so also will the methods used to define them. For, traditionally, progress in one direction has been linked to progress in the other direction.

The questions given below are intended to stimulate thought and discussion and to provide possible exercises for classwork. Many of the questions have no simple or unique answer and are likely to require further reading of various language definitions. Moreover, the reader is invited to produce, for each question given below, two other similar questions which should also be answered.

The order in which the questions appear below corresponds only vaguely to the progression through the various chapters. Many of the questions and answers require knowledge which straddles several chapters.

1. Discuss the advantages of brevity in language definition.
2. Discuss the advantages of formality in language definition.
3. In what ways was the FORTRAN 1966 Standard successful as a language definition? In what senses was the FORTRAN 1977 Standard (a) an improvement, (b) a step backwards?
4. In what ways was the Revised ALGOL 60 Report successful as a language definition? Comment on the suitability of the Modified ALGOL 60 Report.
5. Discuss the advantages and disadvantages of defining the syntax of a programming language using an LR(k)-grammar.
6. Design a grammar which itself defines the structure of a BNF definition of the syntax of a programming language. Adopt conventions (to be clearly stated) which ensure that there is as little confusion as possible between the language and the metalanguage.
7. Discuss the relevance of theoretical results in grammar theory to the definition of programming languages.
8. What are the advantages and disadvantages of definition by substitution?
9. Explain why the use of BNF notation (as used in the Revised ALGOL 60 Report) tended to encourage the design of a more regular language than FORTRAN.
10. Discuss the advantages and disadvantages of describing the semantics of a programming language in terms of itself (as in the case of LISP).

11. Compare and contrast the methods of definition adopted in the COBOL and BASIC Standards.
12. What contribution did the FORTRAN 66 Standard and the Revised ALGOL 60 Report make to language definition?
13. There have been two different Standards for both FORTRAN and COBOL. Compare the attitudes adopted by the language designers in producing the revised Standards.
14. What attitude should be adopted by a set of people defining a programming language which has existed for several years?
15. In the original PASCAL Report the semantics of the repeat clause was defined recursively using definition by substitution. What is the benefit, if any, of using recursion?
16. It was stated earlier that a method of language definition should encourage the discovery of unnecessary restrictions and irregularities in the syntax or semantics and unexpected interactions. Give examples of each of these from languages with which you are familiar.
17. What role have errors and machine limitations played in language definitions?
18. Compare and contrast different approaches to the question of conforming to a Standard in the context of language definition.
19. Compare and contrast the VDL and the Hursley approach (as typified by the PL/I Standard) to language definition.
20. Discuss the design of FORTRAN (both 66 and 77) from the point of view of

   · the principle of correspondence
   · the principle of abstraction
   · orthogonality.

21. Discuss the

   · Revised ALGOL 60 Report
   · Modified ALGOL 60 Report

   from the point of view of orthogonality of design.
22. To what extent should implementation be a consideration in language design and definition?
23. Discuss the merits of the operational approach to language definition from the point of view of the compiler-writer.
24. How were context-sensitive restrictions inserted in the definition of FORTRAN, ALGOL 60, the VDL and the PL/I Standard? Comment on the relative merits of the different methods.
25. Describe the relationship between inner and outer syntax and orthogonality.

26. Write a program in PASCAL to find the highest common factor of two positive integers. Provide informal and formal proofs of the partial correctness of the program.

27. It has been suggested that the definition of ALGOL W is a half-way house between the definitions of ALGOL 60 and ALGOL 68. In the text the syntax has been examined. Discuss the observation from the point of view of the semantics.

28. Discuss the relative merits of the differing approaches to the production of hierarchical syntactic specifications as contained in

   · the Revised ALGOL 60 Report
   · the PL/I Standard approach
   · the use of inner and outer syntax.

29. Give semantic valuation functions for real numerals as they appear in, for example, Revised ALGOL 60.

30. What are the

   · advantages of the operational approach
   · disadvantages of the axiomatic approach

to language definition?

31. What faults in the Revised ALGOL 60 Report would have been removed if the designers of that language had adhered to the principle of correspondence?

32. Given

$$y = \lambda x. \textbf{ if } x(x) = 1 \textbf{ then } 2 \textbf{ else } 1 \textbf{ fi}$$

consider $y(y)$. In programming this does not lead to a contradiction. Explain.

33. Discuss the lessons in language design that have been obtained from

   · an axiomatic approach
   · a denotational approach
   · an operational approach

to language definition.

34. To what extent do different methods of language definition provide conflicting messages for the language designer?

35. 'The designers of most programming languages gave very little thought to the question: "how should a program be designed?"' Discuss this. How, if at all, does this impinge on language definition?

REFERENCES

Due to the nature of this work it has been unavoidable that reference should have been made to numerous articles and reports. To help the reader in finding the primary sources and to encourage further reading these references have been arranged by topic; within each topic they are arranged alphabetically. The division by topic is as follows:

1. General references
2. Theoretical references
3. FORTRAN
4. ALGOL 60
5. LISP
6. ALGOL W
7. COBOL
8. BASIC
9. PL/I
10. PASCAL
11. Attribute grammars
12. Axiomatic method and program verification
13. ALGOL 68 and two-level grammars
14. Denotational semantics
15. Further reading

1. General References

Lee, J.A.N. (1977). Considerations for future programming language standards activities. *Communications of ACM,* **20, 11,** 788–94.
Marcotty, M., Ledgard, H.F. & Bochmann, G.V. (1976). A sampler of formal definitions. *ACM Computing Surveys,* **8, 2,** 191–276.
Steel, T.B. (ed.) (1966). *Formal Language Description Languages.* Amsterdam: North Holland.

2. Theoretical References

Aho, A.V. & Johnston, S.C. (1974). LR parsing. *ACM Computing Surveys,* **6, 2,** 99–124.
Aho, A.V. & Ullman, J.D. (1972). *The Theory of Parsing, Translation and Compiling.* Englewood Cliffs, New Jersey : Prentice-Hall.
Foster, J.M. (1968). A syntax improving device. *The Computer Journal,* **11, 1,** 31–4.
Foster, J.M. (1970). *Automatic Syntactic Analysis.* New York : Macdonald/Elsevier.

Griffiths, M. (1974). *LL*(1) grammars and analysers. In *Compiler Construction,* Lecture Notes in Computer Science, no. 21, ed. F.L. Bauer and J. Eickel, pp. 57–84. Berlin : Springer-Verlag.

Hopcroft, J.E. & Ullman, J.D. (1969). *Formal Languages and their Relation to Automata.* Massachusetts : Addison-Wesley.

Horning, J.J. (1974). *LR* grammars and analysers. In *Compiler Construction,* Lecture Notes in Computer Science, no. 21, ed. F.L. Bauer and J. Eickel, pp. 85–108. Berlin : Springer-Verlag.

Lewis, P.M., Rosenkrantz, D.J. & Stearns, R.E. (1976). *Compiler Design Theory.* Massachusetts : Addison-Wesley.

Salomaa, A. (1973). *Formal Languages.* ACM Monograph Series. New York : Academic Press.

3. FORTRAN

Backus, J. (1978). The history of FORTRAN I, II and III. *ACM SIGPLAN Notices,* **13, 8,** 165–80.

Basic FORTRAN (1966). *USA Standard Basic FORTRAN,* USAS X3.10–1966. New York: USA Standards Institute.

Brainerd, W. (ed.) (1978). FORTRAN 77. *Communications of ACM,* **21, 10,** 806–20.

Day, A.C., Clarke, P.A. & Hill, D. (1976). The Proposed New Standard for FORTRAN – a critical examination. *The Computer Journal,* **19, 3,** 268–71.

FORTRAN (1966). *USA Standard FORTRAN,* USAS X3.9–1966. New York: USA Standards Institute.

FORTRAN (1969). Clarification of FORTRAN Standards – Initial Progress. *Communications of ACM,* **12, 5,** 289–94

FORTRAN (1971). Clarification of FORTRAN Standards – Second Report. *Communications of ACM,* **14, 10,** 628–42.

FORTRAN (1978). *ANSI FORTRAN,* X3.9–1978. New York: American National Standards Institute.

Heising, W.P. (1964). History and summary of FORTRAN standardisation development for ASA. *Communications of ACM,* **7, 10,** 590.

Larmouth, J. (1973). Serious FORTRAN. *Software – Practice and Experience,* **3, 2,** 87–107.

Wooley, J.D. (1977). FORTRAN: A comparison of the New Proposed Language (1976) to the Old Standard (1966). *ACM SIGPLAN Notices,* **12, 7,** 112–25.

4. ALGOL 60

Chaplin, R.I., Crosbie, R.E. & Hay, J.L. (1973). A graphical representation of Backus–Naur form. *The Computer Journal,* **16, 1,** 28–9.

De Morgan, R.M., Hill, I.D. & Wichmann, B.A. (1976). A supplement to the ALGOL 60 Revised Report. *The Computer Journal,* **19, 3,** 276–88.

De Morgan, R.M., Hill, I.D. & Wichmann, B.A. (1978). Modified ALGOL 60 and the step–until element. *The Computer Journal,* **21, 3,** 282.

De Morgan, R.M., Hill, I.D. & Wichmann, B.A. (1976). Modified Report on the algorithmic language ALGOL 60. *The Computer Journal,* **19, 4,** 364–79.

Herriot, J.G. (1969). An ambiguity in the description of ALGOL 60. *Communications of ACM,* **12, 10,** 581.

Hill, I.D. (1972). Wouldn't it be nice if we could write computer programs in ordinary English – or would it? *The Computer Bulletin,* **16, 6,** 306–12.

Knuth, D.E. (1967). The remaining trouble spots in ALGOL 60. *Communications of ACM,* **10, 10,** 611–18.

Naur, P. (ed.) (1963). Revised Report on the algorithmic language ALGOL 60. *Communications of ACM,* **6, 1,** 1–17.

Naur, P. (1978). The European side of the last phase of the development of ALGOL. *ACM SIGPLAN Notices,* **13, 8,** 15–44.

Perlis, A. (1978). The American side of the development of ALGOL. *ACM SIGPLAN Notices,* **13, 8,** 3–14.

Taylor, W., Turner, L. & Waychoff, R. (1961). A syntactical chart of ALGOL 60. *Communications of ACM,* **4, 9,** 393.

Wichmann, B.A. (1973). ALGOL 60: *Compilation and assessment*. New York: Academic Press.
Wirth, N. (1977). What can we do about the unnecessary diversity of notation for syntactic definitions? *Communications of ACM*, **20, 11**, 822-3.

5. LISP

McCarthy, J. (1963*a*). Towards a mathematical science of computation. In *Information Processing*, Proceedings of IFIP Congress 1962 (Munich), pp. 21-8. Amsterdam: North Holland.
McCarthy, J. (1963*b*). A basis for a mathematical science of computation. In *Formal Programming Languages*, ed. P. Braffort & D. Hirschberg, pp. 33-70. Amsterdam: North Holland.
McCarthy, J. (1969). *The LISP 1.5 Programming Manual*. Cambridge, Massachusetts: The MIT Press.
McCarthy, J. (1978). History of LISP. *ACM SIGPLAN Notices*, **13, 8**, 217-23.
Sandewall, E. (1978). Programming in the Interactive Environment: The LISP Experience. *ACM Computing Surveys*, **10, 1**, 35-71.

6. ALGOL W

Bauer, H., Becker, S., Graham, S. & Satterthwaite, E. (1968). *ALGOL W Language Description*, Computer Science Department, Stanford University, California.
Eve, J. (1972). *ALGOL W Programming Manual*, University of Newcastle upon Tyne, England.
Wirth, N. & Hoare, C.A.R. (1966). A contribution to the development of ALGOL. *Communications of ACM*, **9, 6**, 413-31.

7. COBOL

COBOL (1968). *USA Standard COBOL*, X3.23-1968. New York: American National Standards Institute.
COBOL (1974). *USA Standard COBOL*, X3.23-1974. New York: American National Standards Institute.
Jackson, M.A. (1977). COBOL. In *Software Engineering*, ed. R.H. Perrott, pp. 47-58. London: Academic Press.
Sammet, J.E. (1978). The early history of COBOL. *ACM SIGPLAN Notices*, **13, 8**, 121-61.
Triance, J.M. (1976). The significance of the 1974 COBOL standard. *The Computer Journal*, **19, 4**, 295-300.

8. BASIC

BASIC (1978). *USA Standard Minimal BASIC*, X3.60-1978. New York: American National Standards Institute.
Kurtz, T.C. (1978). BASIC. *ACM SIGPLAN Notices*, **13, 8**, 103-18.

9. PL/I

Abrahams, P.W. (1976). The definition of the PL/I standard. In *Proceedings of Fourth International Conference on the Design and Implementation of Algorithmic Languages* ed. R.B.K. Dewar, pp. 99-123. New York University.
Elgot, C.C. & Robinson, A. (1964). Random-access stored-program machines: an approach to programming languages. *Journal of ACM*, **11, 4**, 365-99.
Landin, P.J. (1965*a*). Correspondence between ALGOL 60 and Church's lambda notation, Part 1. *Communications of ACM*, **8, 2**, 89-101.
Landin, P.J. (1965*b*). Correspondence between ALGOL 60 and Church's lambda notation, Part 2. *Communications of ACM*, **8, 3**, 158-65.
Lucas, P., Lauer, P. & Stigleitner, H. (1968). *Method and Notation for the Formal Definition of Programming Languages*. Technical Report 25.087, IBM Laboratories, Vienna, Austria.
Lucas, P. & Walk, K. (1969). On the formal description of PL/I. *Annual Review in Automatic Programming*, **6, 3**, 105-82.
McCarthy, J. (1965). A formal description of a subset of ALGOL. In *Formal Languages Description Languages*, ed. T.B. Steel, Jr., pp. 1-12. Amsterdam: North Holland.
Marcotty, M. & Sayward, F.G. (1977). The definition mechanism for standard PL/I. *IEEE*

Transactions on Software Engineering, SE-3, 6, 416–50.

Neuhold, E.J. (1971). The formal description of programming languages. *IBM Systems Journal*, 10, 2, 86–112.

PL/I (1976). *American National Standards Programming Language PL/I*, ANSI X3.53–1976. New York: American National Standards Institute.

Radin, G. (1978). The early history of PL/I. *ACM SIGPLAN Notices*, 13, 8, 227–41.

Walk, K., Alber, K., Fleck, M., Goldmann, H., Lauer, P., Moser, E., Olivia, P., Stigleitner, H. & Zeisel, G. (1969). *Abstract Syntax and Interpretation of PL/I*. Technical Report 25.098, IBM Laboratories, Vienna, Austria.

Wegner, P. (1972). The Vienna definition language. *ACM Computing Surveys*, 4, 1, 5–63.

10. PASCAL

Addyman, A.M., Brewer, R., Burnett-Hill, D.G., De Morgan, R.M., Findlay, W., Jackson, M.I., Joslin, D.A., Rees, M.J., Watt, D.A., Welsh, J. & Wichmann, B.A. (1979). A draft description of Pascal. *Software – Practice and Experience*, 9, 5, 381–424.

Donahue, J.E. (1976). *Complementary definitions of programming language semantics*, Lecture Notes in Computer Science, no. 42. Berlin: Springer-Verlag.

Hoare, C.A.R. & Wirth, N. (1973). An axiomatic definition of the programming language PASCAL. *Acta Informatica*, 2, 335–55.

Jensen, K. & Wirth, N. (1975). *PASCAL: User Manual and Report*. Berlin: Springer-Verlag.

Tanenbaum, A.S. (1978). A comparison of PASCAL and ALGOL 68. *The Computer Journal*, 21, 4, 316–23.

Watt, D.A. (1979). An extended attribute grammar for PASCAL. *ACM SIGPLAN Notices*, 14, 2, 60–74.

Wirth, N. (1971). The programming language PASCAL. *Acta Informatica*, 1, 35–63.

11. Attribute grammars

Bochmann, G.V. (1976). Semantic evaluation from left to right. *Communications of ACM*, 19, 2, 55–62.

Knuth, D.E. (1968). Semantics of context-free languages. *Mathematical Systems Theory*, 2, 127–45. (Correction in 5 (1971), 95.)

Stearns, R.E. & Lewis, P.M. II (1969). Property grammars and table machines. *Information and Control*, 14, 6, 524–49.

Watt, D.A. & Madsen, O.L. (1979). *Extended attribute grammars*, report 10, Computer Science Department, University of Glasgow, Scotland.

12. Axiomatic method and program verification

Alagic, S. & Arbib, M.A. (1978). *The Design of Well-Structured and Correct Programs*. Berlin: Springer-Verlag.

Anderson, R.B. (1979). *Proving Programs Correct*. New York: John Wiley & Sons, Inc.

Ashcroft, E.A., Clint, M. & Hoare, C.A.R. (1976). Remarks on 'Program proving: jumps and functions' by M. Clint and C.A.R. Hoare. *Acta Informatica*, 6, 317–18.

Clint, M. & Hoare, C.A.R. (1972). Program proving: jumps and functions, *Acta Informatica*, 1, 214–24.

Dijkstra, E.W. (1975). Guarded commands, non-determinancy and a calculus for the derivation of programs. *Communications of ACM*, 18, 8, 453–7.

Dijkstra, E.W. (1976). *A Discipline of Programming*. Englewood Cliffs, New Jersey : Prentice-Hall.

Knuth, D.E. (1974). Structured programming with go to statements. *ACM Computing Surveys*, 6, 4, 261–301.

Lampson, B.W., Horning, J.J., London, R.L., Mitchell, J.G. & Popek, G.L. (1977). Report on the programming language EUCLID. *ACM SIGPLAN Notices*, 12, 2, 1–79.

Liskov, B., Snyder, A. & Atkinson, R. (1977). Abstraction mechanism in CLU. *Communications of ACM*, 20, 8, 564–76.

London, R.L., Guttag, J.V., Horning, J.J., Lampson, B.W., Mitchell, J.G. & Popek, G.L. (1978). Proof rules for the programming language EUCLID. *Acta Informatica*, 10, 1–26.

258

Manna, Z. (1974). *Mathematical Theory of Computation.* New York: McGraw-Hill Book Company.
Manna, Z. & Pneuli, A. (1974). Axiomatic approach to total correctness of programs. *Acta Informatica,* 3, 243–63.
Shaw, M., Wulf, W.A. & London, R.L. (1977). Abstraction and verification in Alphard: defining and specifying iteration and generators. *Communications of ACM,* 20, 8, 553–64.
Wirth, N. (1973). *Systematic Programming: An Introduction.* Englewood Cliffs, New Jersey: Prentice-Hall.
Wirth, N. (1974). On the composition of well-structured programs. *ACM Computing Surveys,* 6, 4, 247–59.
Wulf, W.A. (1977). Languages and structured programs. In *Current Trends in Programming Methodology,* vol. 1, ed. R.T. Yeh, pp. 33–60. Englewood Cliffs, New Jersey: Prentice-Hall.
Yeh, R.T. (ed.) (1977). *Current Trends in Programming Methodology,* vol. 1, *Software Specification and Design.* Englewood Cliffs, New Jersey: Prentice-Hall.
Yeh, R.T. (ed.) (1977). *Current Trends in Programming Methodology,* vol. 2, *Program Validation.* Englewood Cliffs, New Jersey: Prentice-Hall.

13. ALGOL 68 and two-level grammars

Cleaveland, J.C. & Uzgalis, R.C. (1977). *Grammars for Programming Languages.* Elsevier Computer Science Library (Programming Language Series, vol. 4). Amsterdam: Elsevier.
Hansen, W.J. & Boom, H. (1976). Report on the standard hardware representation for ALGOL 68. *Algol Bulletin,* no. 40, 24–43.
Koster, C.H.A. (1974). Two level grammars. In *Compiler Construction,* ed. F.L. Bauer & J. Eickel, pp. 146–56. Berlin : Springer-Verlag.
Lindsey, C.H. & Boom, H. (1978). A modules and separate compilation facility for ALGOL 68. *Algol Bulletin,* no. 43, 19–53.
Lindsey, C.H. & van der Meulen, S.G. (1977). *Informal Introduction to ALGOL 68 (Revised).* Amsterdam: North Holland.
McGettrick, A.D. (1978a). *ALGOL 68 – A First and Second Course.* Cambridge, England: Cambridge University Press.
McGettrick, A.D. (1978b). An introduction to the formal definition of ALGOL 68. *Annual Review in Automatic Programming,* 9, 1–84.
Paillard, J.-P. & Simonet, M. (1977). Attribute-like W-grammars. In *Proceedings of 5th Annual III Conference on the implementation and design of algorithmic languages,* ed. J. André & J.-P. Banatre, pp. 13–24. Rocquencourt : IRIA.
Simonet, M. (1977). An attribute description of a subset of ALGOL 68. *Proceedings of the Strathclyde ALGOL 68 Conference. ACM SIGPLAN Notices,* 12, 6, 129–37.
Sintzoff, M. (1967). Existence of a van Wijngaarden syntax for every recursively enumerable set. *Annales de la Societé Scientifique de Bruxelles,* 81, 115–18.
van Wijngaarden, A. (1965). *Orthogonal Design and Description of a Formal Language.* MR 76, Mathematical Centre, Amsterdam.
van Wijngaarden, A. (ed.), Mailloux, B.J., Peck, J.E.L. & Koster, C.H.A. (1969). Report on the algorithmic language ALGOL 68. *Numerische Mathematik,* 14, 79–218.
van Wijngaarden, A., Mailloux, B.J., Peck, J.E.L., Koster, C.H.A., Sintzoff, M., Lindsey, C.H., Meertens, L.G.L.T. & Fisker, R.G. (eds.) (1975). Revised report on the algorithmic language ALGOL 68. *Acta Informatica,* 5, 1–236.
Watt, J.M., Peck, J.E.L. & Sintzoff, M. (1974). ALGOL 68 Syntax Chart. *Algol Bulletin,* no. 37, 68.

14. Denotational semantics

Hoare, C.A.R. & Allison, D.C.S. (1972). Incomputability. *ACM Computing Surveys,* 4, 3, 169–78.
Milne, R. & Strachey, C. (1976). *A Theory of Programming Language Semantics.* London: Chapman & Hall; New York: John Wiley & Sons, Inc.

Mosses, P.D. (1974). *The Mathematical Semantics of ALGOL 60 (and Commentary on this)*. PRG-12, Oxford University Computing Laboratory, England.

Scott, D. (1970*a*). *Outline of a Mathematical Theory of Computation*. PRG-2, Oxford University Computing Laboratory, England.

Scott, D. (1970*b*). *The Lattice of Flow Diagrams*. PRG-3, Oxford University Computing Laboratory, England.

Scott, D. (1971). *Continuous Lattices*. PRG-7, Oxford University Computing Laboratory, England.

Scott, D. (1976). Data Types as Lattices. *SIAM Journal of Computing*, **5**, 522–87.

Scott, D. & Strachey, C. (1971). *Towards a Mathematical Semantics for Computer Languages*. PRG-6, Oxford University Computing Laboratory, England.

Stoy, J.E. (1977). *Denotational Semantics: The Scott–Strachey Approach to Programming Language Theory*. Cambridge, Massachusetts: The MIT Press.

Strachey, C. (1973). *The Varieties of Programming Languages*. PRG-10, Oxford University Computing Laboratory, England.

Strachey, C. & Wadsworth, C. (1974). *Continuations*. PRG-11, Oxford University Computing Laboratory, England.

Tennent, R.D. (1976). The denotational semantics of programming languages. *Communications of ACM*, **19**, 8, 437–53.

Tennent, R.D. (1977). Language design methods based on semantic principles. *Acta Informatica*, **8**, 97–112.

15. Further reading

Bjørner, D. & Jones, C.B. (eds.) (1978). *The Vienna Development Method: The Meta-language*. Lecture Notes in Computer Science, no. 61. Berlin: Springer-Verlag.

Ginsburg, S. & Rounds, E.M. (1978). Dynamic syntax specification using grammar forms. *IEEE Transactions on Software Engineering*, SE-4, 1, 44–55.

Hanford, K.V. & Jones, C.B. (1971). *Dynamic syntax : a Concept for the Definition of the Syntax of Programming Languages*. IBM Technical Report TR 12.090.

Ichbiah, J.D., Barnes, J.G.P., Heliard, J.C., Krieg-Brueckner, B., Roubine, O. & Wichmann, B.A. (1979). *Preliminary Ada Reference Manual* and *Rationale for the Design of the Ada Programming Language*. *ACM SIGPLAN Notices*, **14**, **6**.

Koster, C.H.A. (1971). Affix grammars. In *ALGOL 68 Implementation*, ed. J.E.L. Peck, pp. 95–110. Amsterdam: North Holland.

Koster, C.H.A. (1974). Using the CDL compiler-compiler. In *Compiler Construction*, ed. F.L. Bauer & J. Eickel, pp. 366–426. Berlin: Springer-Verlag.

Ledgard, H.F. (1974). Production systems: or can we do better than BNF? *Communications of ACM*, **17**, **2**, 94–102.

Ledgard, H.F. (1977). Production systems: a notation for defining syntax and translation. *IEEE Transactions on Software Engineering*, SE-3, **2**, 105–24.

Rustin, R. (ed.) (1972). *Formal Semantics of Programming Languages* (Courant Computer Science Symposium, New York, 1970). Englewood Cliffs, New Jersey: Prentice-Hall.

Wilkes, M.V. (1968). The outer and inner syntax of a programming language. *The Computer Journal*, **11**, 260–3.

Wirth, N. & Weber, H. (1966). EULER: a generalisation of ALGOL and its formal definition: Part I. *Communications of ACM*, **9**, **1**, 13–23.

Wirth, N. & Weber, H. (1966). EULER: a generalisation of ALGOL and its formal definition: Part II. *Communications of ACM*, **9**, **2**, 89–99.

SUBJECT INDEX

abstraction 213, 252
abstract machine 98–9, 123–6, 242–3
abstract program/syntax/form/tree 59, 96,
    99–109, 112, 118, 121–31, 233, 241,
    258
accept state 24–5
accuracy (of numbers) 2, 4, 41
action 22, 146, 152, 204
ADA 245, 260
affix grammar 247, 260
ALGOL 60 (Revised) 4, 30, 42–61, 69–72,
    95, 138, 175–8, 183, 219, 227–8, 233,
    237, 240–2, 247, 251–7, 260
ALGOL 68 5, 15, 50, 53, 71–2, 127, 147,
    156, 175–209, 219, 236–41, 249, 253,
    255, 258–60
ALGOL W 5, 71–83, 178, 183–4, 201, 240,
    253, 255, 257
aliasing 173
alphabet 8
alternative 186
ambiguity 18–19, 28–9, 44–5, 54, 59–60,
    71, 157, 177, 189–90, 197, 212, 218,
    242, 256
ANSI (American National Standards
    Institute) 31, 38, 84, 92, 97–8,
    256–8
antecedent 166–7
a posteriori mode 194
applicability clause 2
application 212–19, 228
apply 68
approximation (relation) 220–7
a priori mode 194
ASA (American Standards Association) 31
assertion 160–5
assignment statement/assignation 32, 76,
    93–4, 104, 108–9, 112, 118, 123,
    155–6, 165, 169, 192–4, 197–200,
    229, 235
assignment axiom/rule 166
association list 68
atoms/atomic symbols 61–4
attribute 76, 80, 96, 105, 123, 125, 139–60,
    183, 198–9, 205, 240, 247

inherited 141–60, 183, 198, 205, 240
    synthesized 140–60, 183, 205, 240
attribute directory 125, 130
attribute grammar 139, 142–53, 249, 255,
    258
attribute occurrence 144–8
attribute translation grammar 146, 152
axiom 166–9, 174
axiomatic approach/semantics 159–74, 206,
    242, 244, 249, 253, 255, 258–9

back substitution 162–5
backtracking 20, 23, 26
Backus–Naur Form, *see* BNF
BASIC 5, 71, 91–4, 247, 252, 255, 257
block activation 124–9
BNF (Backus–Naur Form) 42–53, 57, 59, 66,
    69, 87–8, 93, 99, 100, 112, 139, 153,
    183–4, 210, 233, 239, 246, 251, 260
bottom element 222–4
bound/bound variable 65, 212–14

𝒞 211–12, 230–1, 234–6
car 63–6
cardinality 219
case statement 169, 203
cdr 63–6
chain 222
characteristic condition 115
characteristic set 115
Chomsky hierarchy 11–12, 191
Church–Rosser 216
circularity 147–9
clauses 87–9
CLU 258
COBOL 5, 71, 83–91, 240, 246, 252, 255,
    257
CODASYL 84
codomain 210, 212
coercion 183, 192–6, 229, 239
command 211–12, 229–33
command continuation 230–4
comments/commentary 57
compiler/compilation 3, 4, 14–15, 19, 30,
    43–4, 53–4, 57, 59, 69–71, 86–91, 97,

263

267